Between a Rock and a White Blaze

Searching for Significance on the Appalachian Trail

Julie Urbanski

Between a Rock and a White Blaze: Searching for Significance on the Appalachian Trail

Self-published by Julie Urbanski
Images and editing provided by Matt and Julie Urbanski
www.urbyville.com
First Edition

ISBN: 1480230413
ISBN-13: 978-1480230415

To my mom, my first best friend. Because of you, I have no fashion sense, I can't cook a meal beyond spaghetti, and I still have no idea what shade of lipstick to choose; and yet, I know how to endure.

CONTENTS

To live is to suffer, to survive is to find some meaning in the suffering.
- Friedrich Nietzsche

PROLOGUE

It is 10:00 p.m., our third night on the Appalachian Trail, and I'm too scared to move or even breathe.

Gusts of wind roll down from the mountaintop above us, gathering momentum and speed as they reach the curve of the mountain and spread out across the flat ground, exactly where we are camped. It sounds like a train pulling into a station as the wind travels down the mountain and violently shakes our tent, the poles almost buckling. The full strength of the storm is upon us as the deafening claps of thunder and blinding strikes of lightning are in unison. Rain is falling down in such quantity, and with such force, that it has splattered each side of the tent with a six-inch wall of mud.

I fear the rain fly will be ripped off at any moment, leaving us exposed to the downpour. I want to film the entire storm for proof of such an intense event, but I take no chances in moving to reach for the camera. Instead, I close my eyes and bury my head in my sleeping bag, hoping to block it out, but the booming thunder and fluorescent light still find me.

I look over at Matt and see his profile with each lightning strike. He too is frozen in shock and amazement in being in the presence of such a pure, untamed form of nature.

All I can think is, "What have I gotten myself into?"

1 BUYING OUR FREEDOM

The Appalachian Trail was never on my radar. That is, until 2:00 a.m. on February 6, 2011.

On February 5, at 6:00 a.m., a starting gun fired loudly into the clear, dark sky to begin the Rocky Raccoon 100 Mile Trail Run in Huntsville, Texas. It was nineteen degrees that morning, an unseasonably cold temperature for Texas, even in February. There was frost on the ground and threats of snow to the upcoming Super Bowl game just a few hours away in Dallas. I, my husband Matt, and his brother Jeff, all toed the line of the race, each of us unsure what the next twenty-four hours would bring. For all three of us, it was our first attempt at running one hundred miles in one shot, and while each of us thought we were capable of finishing the event, anything could happen over the course of the race. Nothing was a sure thing.

Now, I know you might be thinking, "Wait, I thought this book was about the Appalachian Trail. Why am I reading about a running race?"

Rest assured, this book is certainly about the Appalachian Trail (AT). In order to tell the story of the AT, I must first tell how the idea of thru-hiking ever came to be, especially considering the fact that I was living across the country and working for an investment firm just six weeks prior to starting my AT journey. Everyone starts their AT thru-hike for a different reason, and our story starts with a trail race in Texas.

The one hundred mile course was a twenty-mile loop that was to be repeated five times, with every twenty miles leading us back to the start/finish area, where the temptation to quit grew stronger and stronger every loop. I started the first loop with Matt, both of us glad to start running so we could warm up and let our nerves calm down over the beginning miles. We began the race in the darkness with several hundred people and all the runners quickly formed a single-track line along the trail, headlamps bobbing one after another. With the sunrise, we welcomed the company of Jeff, who had unknowingly been only a hundred meters behind us, and Matt soon left Jeff and I to run together while he chased a faster time.

Lap two started out as the most physically comfortable lap for me. I finally thawed out, my legs found their rhythm, and I had the company of Jeff and two other runners. Unfortunately, Matt's excitement early in the race caught up to him just thirty miles into the race, and we passed him while he walked through unexpected knee pain. He was hobbling at a pace that barely qualified as a walk, and I suspected he was done for. It was oddly exciting to see him hurting, and I thought, "Maybe we can quit together if I end up hurting too."

Over the course of that second lap, I grew uncomfortable with Jeff's pace and the mental doubts started to creep in. The logical part of my brain knew that I had only trained for a December marathon over the last few months and had no business attempting one hundred miles on such ill-equipped training. The passionate part of me thought that if I just kept putting one foot in front of the other, I could accomplish any distance. I let Jeff go before we reached forty miles and hoped to recover with a slower pace.

My wheels officially fell off on lap three, when passion collided with logic about fifty miles into the race. I felt increasingly intense pain in my hip flexors and had difficulty lifting my legs, ailments which my weak core muscles were all too familiar with. In the past, I had succeeded in barely lifting my feet off the ground in smooth road races, but not in a trail race that involved technical footing full of rocks, roots, and hills.

Parts of the course had out-and-back sections that allowed us to see the runners ahead of us, and in the last few miles of my third lap, as I ran/walked the race course alone, I saw Jeff on his way out for his fourth lap. I gave him the look that said, "I'm not so sure about this Jeff." He knew that look of doubt and wished me luck, probably knowing that I was on the verge of quitting.

Upon reaching the aid station at sixty miles, I decided to quit the race. I had already mentally written my explanation story for quitting during those last few miles into the aid station. My training was inadequate, my hip flexors were in bad shape, and I wasn't prepared for the mental side of such a long race. At that moment, I was proud to have accomplished sixty miles with a severe lack of training. Looking back at the event, I allowed myself to quit with surprising ease. The excuses had multiplied over the course of the miles and it wasn't that hard to give in to them. I later realized that I was defeated before I had even begun because I told myself that it was ok to quit before the race had started. It was the first time I used that race strategy and it's the only race I've ever quit since I started running in 1997.

I had also expected, or dare I say hoped, that Matt would quit with me. If he quit, I would feel less ashamed about my failure. With that comforting thought in mind, I pulled the timing band off my ankle, turned it in to the timing director, changed out of my sweaty race clothes, and awaited Matt's arrival into the aid station.

Forty-five minutes later, Matt ran into the aid station, appearing refreshed and excited. It was 6:45 p.m., dusk was settling into a clear sky, and with the descent of the sun came cooler temperatures once again. Matt told me that he felt so restored that he had hopes of catching Jeff. Because of that, he was focused on getting in and out of the aid station with minimal time wasted.

I had expected him to arrive just as defeated as I had been, sympathetic of my decision to quit, and open-armed with a shoulder for me to cry on. Instead, he barely acknowledged that I had quit, much less showed surprise, and asked me to get him a few items out of his gear bag. Despite my efforts to suggest that he take into account the cool evening, he left the aid station for the next twenty-mile loop dressed in shorts, a singlet, and arm sleeves. He was motivated to catch Jeff and didn't want to waste another moment listening to my advice for his next loop. I watched him run away from the aid station, disappearing after a right turn one hundred meters down the trail, and I wondered what state he would be in with twenty more miles on his mind and body.

Then I played the waiting game that many race spectators have played for hours on a race course. I set my watch for an optimistic time to expect Matt and sat on the side of the trail in a lawn chair. For hours I kept my eyes on the well-worn path that faded into the darkness that the aid station lights could not reach. With every hour that passed and every runner that came into the aid station that wasn't Matt, I lost hope for his chances of finishing. Jeff completed eighty miles around 10:00 p.m. Just twenty miles stood between him and the finish and he had a runner by his side that was ready to finish the last lap with him. Before Jeff left the aid station, he delivered the news that he'd seen Matt on the trail, but that he didn't look good. My fading hope turned into growing worry; the air had cooled from nearly seventy degrees in the daytime to low twenties at night. Sadness overcame me as I thought of Matt running alone in the dark with nothing but a dull headlamp to guide him and a mere tank top to warm him. I knew that if he was reduced to a walk, his body temperature would plummet. There was nothing I could do but wait and hope for the best. I partially blamed myself for allowing him to leave the aid station with such little clothing.

Soon it was 1:00 a.m. and I had watched runners sprinkle into the finish line for hours. The darkness surrounded the runners as they approached the aid station and they looked like planes coming in for a landing as their headlamps guided them single-file into the finish. I watched that landing pad with such vigilance that my neck stiffened from the lack of movement; I didn't want to miss a thing. I perked up when I saw a runner come into the light of the aid station at a crawling pace, heavily favoring one leg over the other, slightly hunched over, wearing red shorts and a green long-sleeve shirt. It was Matt, and he looked like each step could be his last if someone didn't support him. He had managed to pick up extra clothing from other runners along the way, but not before his body temperature dropped so much that his legs froze up, hindering his movement and breaking his stride beyond repair.

I quickly wrapped blankets around him and sat him next to a portable heater under the aid station tent, worried not so much about him finishing the race, but about him simply living past it. He looked out-of-sorts and could barely find words to tell me how to take care of him. After throwing up in a garbage bag next to him, while the other runners around the heater watched with concern in their eyes, he was finally able to have a conversation with me. To my surprise, he didn't want to talk about the race. It was as if he had quit it long ago, miles back on the trail, and had already moved on to thinking about life to come Monday morning, when we went back to work.

"Julie, I want us to quit our jobs," he resolutely stated.

At the time, we were living in Vancouver, Washington, both of us working at the same investment firm, logging fifty to sixty-hour work weeks. In our spare time we focused all our energy on running, and beyond those two priorities of work and running, nothing else mattered unless it was the weekend.

There at the race course, I tried to hide my shock at his conclusion and spoke logically while I kneeled at his feet and held his ice-cold hands between my palms.

"Well, we can talk about that later. Let's just get you warm and we'll see what we think in the morning."

I knew all too well that my most drastic thoughts have come after sundown, as if a different mindset comes out with the darkness, and I thought Matt had fallen prey to that phenomenon during the race. I also knew that the next morning, after sleeping on it and once again greeting the sun, I've thought to myself, "How did I think that was a good decision?" I assumed the same would apply to Matt once he rested and put distance between himself and the race.

Still, he insisted that we quit our jobs and do something different. He hadn't even taken off his timing chip yet and he was already thinking well into the future. Matt explained that he was broken in so many ways, from working so hard and running so much, that he needed to renew himself before he completely lost his passion for life. I saw conviction in his eyes as he said it and I knew that he was serious, even as he sat hunched over with a plastic bag of puke next to him. I took my mind off the subject and refused to talk about it as I continued to warm him up by changing his clothes, wrapping him in blankets, and awaiting the arrival of Jeff so that we could leave the race course and put the failed run behind us.

Three of us started the race but only one of us left the course with the belt buckle that has become the coveted finisher's medal of one hundred miles races. Jeff finished the race in just over twenty and a half hours, unable to fully enjoy his accomplishment because I had quit after sixty miles and Matt had quit after eighty. The main take-away from the race for Matt and me, besides injured legs and defeated egos, was the question, "What are we going to do now?"

The brains behind the compensation structure at the investment firm where we worked knew exactly what they were doing. They took the concept of the golden handcuffs and applied it so well to our jobs that there really never was a good time to quit. In addition to my competitive salary, my job's bonus structure was built such that every three months, I was eligible for a bonus that was based on my performance. Three months in the corporate world, where every day was filled with meetings, deadlines, projects, and emails, passed by in the blink of an eye. It felt like I was always just receiving the last bonus or awaiting the next one. Matt's bonus structure paid every six months, so not as often, but with a possibility for more money each time. Then there was Christmas, which meant the possibility for a Santa visit if the firm did well and if we performed just as well in our roles.

We were hooked into the pay structure and every time we talked about quitting, the bonus got in the way because it was continuously on the horizon. For three years we played the corporate game without seriously thinking about quitting, and only about stockpiling what we termed the Freedom Fund. It represented our get-out-of-dodge money that could buy our freedom for a finite amount of time and give us a break from the suits and ties, the legally compliant correspondence, and the office politics. We played our roles to the best of our abilities, but we felt like Clark Kent underneath, superhero outfit donned for the random chance to fly away and save our souls, or at least our zest for life that drained with each passing day under fluorescent lights and watered-down coffee.

While co-workers bought flat-screen TVs with their bonuses, ours went straight into savings, and while others purchased homes, we lived with friends and paid $375 in rent on two investment firm salaries. We shared one car, I walked to work, and we refused to trade in antiquated flip-phones for smart phones. The phones couldn't even text because we were too cheap to pay for it. Every single expense was tracked in a spreadsheet and every month showed money flowing in with very little money trickling out. We lived what most would call boring lives, but we didn't care what others thought because we knew we'd soon be trading dress slacks for jeans and morning alarms for natural circadian rhythms. We had a group of friends that liked cheap entertainment just as much as us, so we spent our weekends playing board games, running long runs, and eating potluck meals. Bowling a few frames was considered splurging. Our focus on the goal of saving as much money as possible to buy our freedom never wavered, and we benefited greatly from that dedication.

By the time we ran the one hundred mile race, we had managed to squirrel away enough money in cash to allow us the freedom from work for at least a year. While we were ready to turn in our resignation letters the day after the race in early February, each of us still felt that tug of the upcoming bonuses in April and June. It was the trump card that the investment firm held on us and we weren't sure if we were ready to fold our cards and leave the playing table just yet.

Part of me knew the decision to quit our jobs was already made before the discussion even began. Though we still gave a full effort to our jobs, both of us had been hanging on by a string of motivation to enter the office each day. We looked forward to each ensuing weekend more and more, and we let the Sunday afternoon depression creep in and clench our chests so tightly that we no longer took full breaths in order to face the new work week. At that point, it was a matter of coming up with a good exit story for our managers and for the rest of the firm.

Within forty-eight hours of quitting our one hundred mile race in Texas, we were back in our offices in Washington, handing in our resignation letters to our bosses with the reasoning that we were taking time off to adventure around the world. We weren't entirely sure what that adventure would be, but the idea of a cross-country bicycle trip was the most appealing at the time. Our managers were both disappointed to hear that we wanted to leave the firm, but found our reasons to be admirable and socially cool. We left the firm without burning any bridges and with an interesting plan for our post-office freedom.

By the end of February, we had worked our three-week notices and trained new employees in our places, after which we cut the cord of the life we knew in Vancouver, Washington. Anything that didn't fit in our car was given away to friends or Goodwill, and we drove straight to Findlay, Ohio, where we planned on storing our belongings in Matt's parents' basement while we traveled on a tandem bicycle around the country.

Looking back, it's no surprise to me now what happened next, but the reality that awaited us was demoralizing at the time. After we arrived in Ohio and passed the first few days visiting family and catching up, we started to put our plan into action. We contacted bike shops, looked at gear online, and realized just how expensive the trip would be once we took into account the cost of a bike, gear to hold our stuff on the bike, maps, clothing, and bike maintenance tools. We were also told from the local bike shop that it would take several weeks to receive a tandem bike from a bike shop near Portland, Oregon. Oh, the irony that we would wait for weeks on a bike that we lived just twenty minutes away from a few weeks prior.

We considered the possibility of single bikes, but that equation still left us spending thousands of dollars that we weren't ready to part with in one swipe of the credit card. We had just spent years building up our savings and our goal was to drain the money as slowly as possible. A bike trip seemed less ideal with each price tag that was added to the pile, and the idea soon crumbled out of existence.

We had never seriously ridden bikes and had delayed the research until we were home in Ohio, so our lack of knowledge in prices and lack of logistics preparation left a gaping hole in our plans. Suddenly, we were in a pickle. The life we had just built up over the last few years was gone, as were our friends that we left behind in Vancouver, a thirty-seven hour drive away. We needed something to do with our freedom, we wanted to spend as little money as possible, taking into consideration the bills that never ended, like college tuition and health insurance, and we needed a solution quickly, as our patience with living at home with parents was sure to dwindle.

Our answer to the failed bike trip was to make a life list.

In order to prevent any biases, Matt and I each sat in separate rooms and wrote out adventures that we wanted to complete in our lifetimes. Whatever overlapped would be considered as fair game for our first adventure as purposefully unemployed individuals. In the midst of my list-making, I took a deep breath and wrote on two separate lines, among other ideas, "Hike the Appalachian Trail (AT)," and "Hike the Continental Divide Trail (CDT)."

Matt's second cousin Tim, who also lived in Findlay, was planning to start his AT thru-hike in just a few weeks, so it had been on my mind since we ate lunch with him and shared our advice about backpacking. We also had a friend in Vancouver that was soon starting his Pacific Crest Trail thru-hike in April. The fact that those two had an adventure planned for themselves weighed on me. I was jealous that they had a goal to work towards, an adventure that promised to be difficult yet fulfilling, and I wanted something like it. While I wasn't completely sure I wanted to thru-hike the AT, I wanted the benefits that came with it, and so it made the list just as easily as organic farming and living in Central America. Yet, it stood out from the other ideas because of the challenge that it represented.

Once we regrouped, I saw that Matt had also written down the CDT, but not the AT, because he had already hiked it in 2000, before we met. He was surprised to see the AT on my list, but after seeing the CDT on both of our lists, he suggested it as a qualifier for the final round of adventure choices. When he mentioned the CDT as a prospect, I selfishly shot down the idea and said, "I don't want you to complete your triple crown before I do." He only needed to hike the CDT to complete all three major long-distance hikes in the country, while I needed the CDT *and* the AT. That left the AT up for grabs as the top finalist and ultimate winner.

As we sat there on the bed in his parent's guest bedroom, notebook and pen in hand, I couldn't believe the twists that our fate had taken, from working for an investment firm in Washington in February, to discussing an Appalachian Trail thru-hike in March.

We looked ahead at the calendar, giving ourselves a few weeks to prepare for the hike, and set a start date of Saturday, April 2.

2 GETTING THE RUST OFF

Matt and I thru-hiked the Pacific Crest Trail (PCT) in 2007, a journey of over 2600 miles from Mexico to Canada through California, Oregon and Washington. It was my first experience in long-distance backpacking. It was hard and to be honest, I had a very difficult time getting used to the lifestyle and was unhappy for much of the time.

My unhappiness stemmed from my lack of knowledge in backpacking, my expectations for the hike, and my actual pack weight. The most hiking I had done up to that point was a week-long trip that covered fifty miles. While the trip had its unpleasant moments, I still found enjoyment in walking outside for a string of days with my life on my back. Yet, that short trip was not enough to prepare me for the physical and mental challenges of a thru-hike, of walking and living outside for months at a time. That was the first strike against the start of my PCT hike.

Next were my expectations and the ultimate reasons that lead to my trail name of Stopwatch. I started the trail with the mindset that the goal was to get from point A to point B as quickly as possible, just like a running race. I timed the miles for the first few days of the hike, thinking the purpose was to hike them as fast as possible. As you can imagine, my obsession with the watch got me in trouble on the trail, where terrain and elevation changes made it difficult to keep a consistent pace. In order to keep my sanity and find enjoyment in the trail, I had to give up the control that I was so accustomed to having in my running life. It took time for me to realize that the only time expectations of my hike were those set by me, and that the process of walking from Mexico to Canada was much more enjoyable if I ignored the finish and paid attention to all the events in between the two end points.

Lastly, my pack weight at the start of the PCT was simply laughable. My base weight, with no food or water in it, was twenty-five pounds. I started with a paperback copy of *Anna Karenina*, a towel, and a long sleeve shirt in addition to my jacket and down sleeping bag, on a trail that starts with seven hundred miles of hot desert. With so few water sources throughout Southern California, we often carried six to eight pounds of water. Add in three to five days of food and my pack was averaging about forty pounds, which was almost a third of my body weight. I often look back at pictures and say, "I can hardly see myself under that huge pack!"

Such a heavy pack made for slow, difficult miles and I held a lot of unnecessary resentment towards the climbs because of how much harder they were under the weight of my belongings. Luckily, things improved. I became better accustomed to the trail life and learned how to deal with the challenges that the trail presented; admittedly, it took me most of the trail to accomplish that. I also gave up my watch, literally, as I carried it deep in my pack for half the hike until I was mature enough to wear it without worrying so much about the timing of the miles. I also shed pack weight. By the time we made it to Washington, my pack was twenty-five pounds with all the food and water included.

I learned a lot about myself on the PCT. It took much more self-honestly than I ever imagined it would and by the end of the hike, I cried tears of gratitude for such an enlightening experience that had changed me forever. I viewed myself in a different light, along with my relationship with Matt, and I finished the hike with plans of taking my new-found outlook back to the real world where I once again had to face a job, bills and responsibilities. I was ready to take on the world.

That world was the corporate world, and in short, it crushed me.

After finishing the PCT in the fall of 2007, Matt and I were ready for the challenge of working corporate jobs. I had just turned twenty-six, he twenty-seven, and having never stayed at a corporate job for more than a year and a half, we were ready to commit to a company for at least three years. Three years represented a respectable amount of time for us to give to one firm and we knew we would need at least that much time to build up our savings. While we both thrived in our roles at the investment firm, I took it as my excuse for becoming the person that started the Appalachian Trail.

I don't know how people can work in the corporate world for decades of their lives. I worked just three years in it and became a person that even today I don't recognize. I was cold-hearted, cut and dry, boring, and stressed. I lost all passion for creativity, spontaneity, and risk-taking. Every move was calculated to figure out how it affected my two-part life of work and running, and if the plans didn't enhance work or running, I took no part in them.

I had such little fun and even fewer friends.

At the investment firm, there were two women that worked near me that were referred to, behind their backs of course, as the Ice Queens. I came to admire that quality; I loved that they could be cold, logical, and objective in dealing with others, and I confused others' reactions of fear for respect. Though I started out as one who would bend the rules because I could see the personal side of the story, I gravitated more and more towards being a cold person. I thought being callous was seen as a good thing. I now know that people prefer working with a nice person that still gets the job done over an insensitive person that makes the job more unpleasant than it has to be.

My daily work routine included waking up at 4:45 a.m. to head to the office for ten hours where I worked my fourth entry-level job since graduating from college in 2003. Throughout college, I had pictured myself climbing the corporate ladder at a Fortune 500 company, yet there I was, eight years out of college, and I hadn't even made it past the associate level. Matt, just one year older than me, was making double my salary, nearly triple with bonuses included, and was in a management position. He walked through the office with an energetic stride, he made eye contact with others as he walked past their desks, and they nodded back in approval of his status at the firm. Colleagues, myself included, recognized the charisma inside him that exuded the confidence that said, "I can do anything you throw at me."

I, on the other hand, felt like the dowdy wife that walked alongside him while others looked to him first, then to me, and asked themselves, "How in the world did he end up with her?" I held my head down as I hurriedly walked through the building, only because I wanted to get from the kitchen or bathroom to my seat as quickly as possible, and I avoided conversations with others that sat in my path. I didn't start out that way at the office, but after years of doubting my abilities to excel beyond entry-level positions, I felt inferior to those surrounding me and it was an easy persona to uphold.

At one point, I had thought of myself as creative, with a special spark that would one day light fire to show the world that I was better than an office job. However, time and dwindling energy pushed those thoughts to the deep crevices of my mind, never to surface again unless strongly provoked. My aha moment never came, or at least I never recognized it, and I was simply going through the motions of the life we had built in Washington. My spirits, which were on such a high after finishing the PCT, had sputtered out over the years.

Looking back, I do not blame it on the job or even the environment of a corporate office. I blame it on me for taking the easy road in the choice to be a good person. I chose to be a person without much regard for good beyond that of basic civility. I chose to be selfish, to do the bare minimum towards my relationships with my family and friends, and I disliked the person I had become, especially given that I entered the corporate world with so much fire in my belly and hope for personal growth.

Even though running was an outlet for Matt and me, we also took that aspect of our lives to the extreme. We trained at least six, sometimes seven days a week, logging fifty to sixty miles a week in my case and upwards of eighty to one hundred miles a week for Matt. We ran with a core group of runners and we met them every day, without fail, at the same running trail or track, for easy runs, long runs, and workouts. Our hard work at running paid off in personal records across all distances from the mile to the marathon, but by the time we quit our jobs, we were running on fumes. I hadn't done a workout in four months because of touchy hamstrings and a lack of motivation, and Matt was barely running due to knee and foot pain. Our running careers served us well while we were working, but we were ready to set aside our identities as runners for the time being while we hiked the trail and healed the pieces of us that had been broken from pushing ourselves so hard at the office and on the track.

By the spring of 2011, I was twenty-nine years old, and being on the brink of thirty instilled in me a fear of aging. Though I was plain-Jane when it came to makeup and appearances, I looked in the mirror with fervor like never before, looking for new wrinkles, strange facial hairs, or any sign that I was getting older. I should have focused on how to simply look my best, but I felt helpless as I sat back and watched age take over. I let new thoughts run through my mind all the time, such as, "I'm already stressed, aged, and overworked…and I don't even have kids yet!" I didn't know where the sudden fear of age came, but I obsessed about the subject. I also wondered, as I observed Matt's sister and brother-in-law raise two young boys, "What's going to happen when I'm actually stressed with kids?"

As for actually having kids, that was another beast I was not ready to tackle. One of the mysteries in my life is the answer to when I stopped liking children. At a recent gynecologist exam, in the questionnaire section about how many children I planned to have, I wrote zero to one, and reluctantly wrote down even one.

Thus began my predicament at the start of the trail with reaching the age of thirty and disliking the idea of being around children, including giving birth to them and raising them. I thought the motherly instinct would have kicked in by then, but it had yet to show up. According to everyone around me, my clock was certainly ticking and hiking the AT was not on the traditional path to motherhood. "No, really," they said, "you should really think about having kids right now, because once you're in your thirties…" The conversations usually end there when I assured them I knew my clock was in fact ticking, and that I knew the risks based on my age, and to not worry, we had a plan to have children. I didn't have the guts to admit that I didn't like children and that my clock could tick-tock away if it would like to, and that I would be happy with a yellow lab if life ended up handing me a bum clock to begin with.

Lastly and most importantly, Matt and I were newlyweds heading into the trail. We had technically been together for eight years and had made it through the PCT thru-hike as a dating couple, but marriage still changed things. To me, it meant that the rope of our relationship that we had wound so tightly together would be that much harder to unravel if it was termed a divorce rather than a break-up. We were only married for a year upon starting the hike, so I had my doubts about our marriage being put through such a test, and we hadn't even begun the hard part of dealing with weather, hunger, or mood swings. I was fearful of the challenges that a thru-hike would bring to a young marriage.

Four years after the PCT, after we had quit our jobs and once again entered the land of freedom, the idea of a thru-hike grew on me. I felt ready to go back for seconds. I had digested enough of the PCT to look back on it with grateful eyes rather than resentful ones, and I was hungry for another hike. I welcomed the challenge with open arms, knowing I would soon have many moments where I would question my decisions for hiking. But, I pushed aside those doubts before starting and reminded myself that a different, better person came out on the other end of the PCT, so I looked forward to seeing how much different or how much better of a person I could be after a second thru-hike. At least experience was on my side and I applied much of what I learned about long-distance hiking to the upcoming AT hike.

I also had to accept the person I was when I started the Appalachian Trail. I had a cold heart, a ticking clock, and doubts in my union with Matt. It was not a person I had wanted or expected to become and because I was so far from the person I thought I would be by age thirty, I didn't even know where to direct myself. Yet, going into the trail I was optimistic and I felt grateful for the freedom that the Appalachian Trail provided. I would soon have hours each day to contemplate life and my choices going forward, and hours to plan what kind of life I wanted to lead after the trail.

The rust was thick, yet ready to come off, and I was ready to chisel away every layer that had built up over the years since the PCT. I didn't know how thick that rust was or how long it would take before I could benefit from all the AT had to offer, but I knew inside that I wanted to walk away from the self that I had created. I looked forward to improving my mental attitude towards the AT as compared to the PCT, which held many of my lowest moments. My challenge for myself was to see how happy I could be and to see how much I could enjoy each moment in the present without moaning over the past decisions that got me to that point. Could I actually enjoy the experience without looking towards the finish and without pining for the future moments when I could satisfy my needs for creature comforts?

I believed I was ready for my second thru-hike, for the challenges that the AT provided from Georgia to Maine, and most of all, for the personal tests of my happiness, my marriage, and my sanity. Only the act of putting one foot in front of the other would reveal the realities of my expectations for the hike.

3 GOING BACK FOR SECONDS

"Why in the world would you want to repeat *this*?"

It was a question that other hikers posed often to Matt during our first week on the AT. Those first few days, just like any new routine, were tough to get used to for a lot of people, myself included. The idea of going through the motions of an AT thru-hike twice in a lifetime was well outside the scope of normal.

"Well, I'm a totally different person now than I was eleven years ago, and the trail is totally different the second time," he often answered.

Well before I had ever met Matt, he had already made the journey from Georgia to Maine as a nineteen-year-old. In the spring of 2000, during his freshman year at the Naval Academy, he decided he would drop out of school at the end of the semester. He didn't know what he wanted to do, other than *not* be in the Navy, and that spring he heard of something called the Appalachian Trail, where people backpacked nearly 2,200 miles over the course of several consecutive months. It immediately struck a chord within him.

The trail sounded fascinating to him and he soon found a thru-hiker's blog online that sparked excitement for life outside of the Navy. As he read the blog, he said to himself, "Holy crap, this is awesome!"

His only experience backpacking up until then had been a three-day trip to the Grand Canyon with his dad when he was thirteen. That trip had left an imprint on him, yet he didn't recognize the pattern of it until he heard about the Appalachian Trail and promptly decided to do it.

It has always perplexed me how Matt ever ended up at the Naval Academy in the first place. While he can abide by the often strict and sometimes silly rules that are part of nearly all institutions, he is a very individualistic person that rarely likes to be told what to do. Mostly, he never likes to be told he is wrong. The only explanation I can come up with, and that Matt agrees with, is that he was driven by the challenges of getting into the school and completing an esteemed education. Also, the fact that he had to interview with a panel of people and get the seal of approval of a Congressman made it seem like it was the most elite club he could ever try and enter. He wanted in and gave every effort to make it happen.

It was in the winter of his first year at the Naval Academy when the elite club had lost its luster. He realized he could pass any test of strength, will, patience, or academic ability that they threw at him, and he no longer saw a purpose in his actions. He began to question the motives and methods of the institution, but he could never voice those questions, for fear of punishment or anger at the inability to change the system's momentum. The club that he had wanted to enter so badly turned out to be at odds with the kind of life he pictured himself leading in the future. He wanted out and saw his first steps towards a different life taking place on the Appalachian Trail.

He still believes that dropping out of the school was one of the best decisions he's ever made.

That could be because he hiked the AT immediately after leaving school. Another friend that attended the Naval Academy with Matt had also been thinking about leaving and heard about Matt's plans to hike the AT. Matt can still remember the moment of seeing Dan, a tall, skinny sophomore with a guarded demeanor, show up outside his dorm room. Dan told Matt he too was leaving the Naval Academy and asked if he could join Matt on the AT hike. Dan was a fellow member of the cross country and track teams with Matt, so they already had a common bond, and Matt appreciated the witty underside of Dan's otherwise shy encasing. Matt was ecstatic that someone wanted to join him on such an adventure and welcomed Dan's company, never knowing that the ball that was put in motion at that point would affect the rest of his life.

Before we started hiking the Appalachian Trail, everything about it was different from the first time Matt hiked it in 2000. To begin with, our start dates were two months apart. In 2000, he didn't finish his school year until June, so he started walking northbound in mid-June. It was already mid-summer by the time he started, so he remembered two things about the hike: hot days and a green tunnel of heavily leafed trees lining the trail. This time around, we had a planned start date of April 2. I read other hikers' online journals before we left and shivered while I read about frosty mornings and snow-covered ground. The trees lining the neighborhood streets in Ohio also warned us that plenty of time still needed to pass before the leaves would be fully grown on the trees, even if Georgia was located further south.

Because Matt and Dan started so late, they missed the crowds of hikers that typically started from March through April and they were pulling up the rear of thru-hikers. The towns were swarmed by the yearly crop of thru-hikers long before they arrived, and by the time they made it to towns, people mistook them for section hikers. People were so shocked to hear that Matt and Dan were northbound thru-hikers that they quickly warned them of the possibility of not finishing before winter. It was an aspect that Matt and Dan disliked about the hike, hearing other people tell them they couldn't do something, especially since that was the environment they had just left. They continuously promised themselves to stay focused in order to finish the trail.

Just looking back at the photos of Matt's 2000 hike displays what else was incredibly different about it. His metal, external frame backpack sticks high above his head in every picture, and his cotton, thrift-store t-shirt and cargo shorts would make even the novice gear-junkie wince at the heavy clothing and lack of breathability. Foot minimalists would certainly balk at his mid-cut hiking boots that probably weighed two pounds each. He knew very little about gear or hiking and simply used what was in his closet or his parents' basement. Yet, each picture shows a smile on Matt's young, energetic, idealistic face, and a light in his eyes says that he has found something that gives his life purpose and meaning.

In addition to backpacks, sleeping bags, clothing and shoes, the gear list of small essentials drastically changed from one hike to the next. At the time, the year 2000 seemed so advanced, but reflecting back on Matt's hike shows that technology has come a long way. For the 2011 hike, in order to update our online journal, we carried a small laptop and a new Android smart phone, complete with internet, texting, and tethering capability. Way back in the dark ages of 2000, Matt used a pay phone to call his parents' 1-800 number that had been set up for Matt to call home for free from any pay phone. The thought never crossed his mind to keep a blog, carry a phone that could create a wireless network, or bring a laptop that could upload stories and pictures to a website. In 2000, that sentence alone would have barely been decipherable, especially when talking about thru-hiking gear.

Taking out the external factors that affected one hike to the next, the difference in the two hikes boiled down to the fact that Matt was a completely different person eleven years later. He was no longer the nineteen-year-old with obligations that stretched only so far as himself, and instead was a thirty-year-old with a wife and a retirement fund. Rather than worry about what school he would attend next in order to finish his degree, he was worried about what stocks to pick in our portfolio and what health insurance to choose that best weighed our risks for the price we paid. Forget flirting with other young female hikers on the trail the second time around, in the case that there *were* any in a seemingly male-majority environment. He knew every evening that I would be curling up in the sleeping bag next to him.

Most importantly, he had to think of the feelings and emotions of a person outside of himself, which was me. The ups and downs of the trail had been hard enough the first time around and this time he had another person's safety, well-being, and happiness to take into account besides his own. I was no longer the girlfriend of the PCT, who he could break up with at the end of the trail in case it didn't work out, and I wasn't the friend that he hiked the AT with the first time, who he could stick with for the most part, but still make separate decisions from in case of disagreement. I was his other half, who equaled every stride of his own, who had a history of mental lapses in times of difficulty on a long-distance hike, and who counted on him for companionship each day.

The Matt that showed up to Springer Mountain, the southern terminus of the AT, on April 2, 2011, may have resembled the Matt that crossed the same path in June of 2000, but nearly everything about him had changed, including his lifestyle and perspectives. He carried a little more weight on his 5'7" frame than eleven years prior and was sporting his curly brown hair over the military academy buzz cut from before, but the sparkle in his brown eyes and proud smile were still the same. The two constants since the last hike were his trail name and his route. He would still be Optimist and the route would still follow the white blazes painted on the trees. Optimist was a name he wore proudly and a name which almost forced him to have a positive outlook on life and the trail. While he would be Optimist to all the hikers, he would still be Matt to me. You'll notice that throughout this book, he is addressed as Matt rather than Optimist because that's how I spoke to him on the trail.

The white blazes were like old friends that Matt needed to catch up with as he pieced together memories of the past. Before the hike began, Matt's memories of the trail were completely jumbled, with some of them crystal clear and others so foggy that only the feeling of a place could be conjured up. By the time he stepped foot on the trail for the second time, he was ready and excited to reignite his old memories, to shed a few extra pounds, and to experience the trail as a married man with completely different priorities.

4 IT'S ALL COMING BACK TO ME

To say that I was excited to start hiking the AT would be an understatement. Nearly two months passed between the day we put in our resignations and the moment we started walking, and we spent three weeks of that time telling people we were going to attempt the thru-hike. In that time, we visited more family and friends than we had over the last few years of living in Vancouver, and I was worn out from three years' worth of get-togethers being crammed into just a few weeks.

To top off the time we spent visiting family and friends before the trail, Matt signed us up to stay a week with his sister, Emily, and her two young boys in their home in South Carolina, while her husband went out of town for work. The boys were at the young, energetic, slightly destructive ages of three and five years old. The week was then capped off with a six-hour car drive to the start of the trail and a night of camping with the boys on the eve of our AT hike in Amicalola Falls State Park in Georgia. Matt and I were used to being around other people's kids for maybe one to two days at a time, so by the end of the week, we were tired and snippy with each other. We actually looked forward to the AT because it represented a much easier, less sleep-deprived lifestyle than that of raising children.

Perhaps it was best that our trail was prefaced with a week surrounded by children, because it made the AT that much more appealing. It could have been thirty-five degrees and raining for that first week on the trail, and I would have still been appreciative for the relief that the woods offered from a week with children. That being said, I still have the utmost respect for people who raise children; they are exhausting little creatures that take a lot of time and attention. Parenthood is a job I have been hesitant to sign up for, for good reason, and that week of being around kids was a good reminder of how much work it takes to raise them.

Before we started hiking, we ate breakfast with Matt's sister and her two boys at the Lodge at Amicalola Falls, and I sucked down as much coffee as I could stand, knowing it would only be in town that I'd be able to satisfy the caffeine habit I'd picked up while in the corporate world. I also stuffed myself before heading out for those first miles. I ate an English muffin with cream cheese and jelly, and forced down a bowl of cereal and a side of lukewarm scrambled eggs. I was upset about the three pounds of weight I had gained in the month since we quit our jobs, but I also knew the task at hand would soon burn it all off. The last month's reasoning, with every extra piece of cake or cookie that crossed my lips, had been, "I'll burn it off on the hike." Matt took the excuse of the hike to the extreme and carried eleven extra pounds at the start.

We said our goodbyes to Emily and her boys where the road crossed the Approach Trail one mile in, and it felt strange to have family members there to see us literally walk off into the woods. The reality of the adventure we were embarking on finally set in, as did the past moments leading up to it. I had mixed emotions of nerves and excitement, scared that my mind and body weren't ready for such a feat, yet happy to be free from the normal world. I wanted my bubble to include Matt and myself, even though I knew that hoping to shut out other people would only make them push harder to open the door. The week that we had spent with Emily and her family leading up to the trail flooded back to me and I felt guilty that my aversion to children was probably too apparent. It was one of the first moments when I realized what kind of person I had become over the last few years, and I hoped that the next time I saw them I would be much more enjoyable to be around.

Despite a chilly evening on the eve of our start, our first official day was sunny with just a few clouds in the sky. The winds were gusty around us and made for cold patches in the shade. With the morning sun, I immediately realized that I had forgotten sunglasses and thanked myself for remembering to pack a hat. In regards to packing, we felt that we had finally wised up and packed lightly, a big improvement from our PCT hike. We were confident that lighter packs would help increase the enjoyment of a long-distance hike, as compared to the past hike where our happiness was weighed down by overstuffed packs. Excluding water and food, my pack weighed thirteen pounds while Matt's was sixteen. Since the PCT, we picked up lighter backpacks, carried less clothing, and we paid much more attention to the little things in our packs that added up to so much unnecessary weight on the PCT hike. Our base weights weren't worthy of ultralight status because we still carried unnecessary luxury items, but we made huge strides towards lighter packs in comparison to the PCT.

The only new items that we purchased for the trail were Granite Gear

Vapor Trail backpacks, which were at least two pounds lighter than our previous packs. Other than the packs, we used the same REI Sub Kilo two-pound sleeping bags, one-pound Thermarest sleeping pads, a one-pound MSR Whisperlite stove, and a five-pound REI Half Dome tent. We didn't want to spend the money to upgrade to lighter gear, so the trail started out as a cheap adventure as compared to buying thousand dollar bikes to ride across the country.

Among the items we packed, the heaviest luxury item was a small laptop, which weighed about three pounds. We had decided to keep a website to document our travels, through stories and pictures, and justified the weight of the laptop with the ability to keep family and friends updated throughout the trail. While I was glad we had a way to stay in touch with people, I was most excited about the food we packed. One highlight of hiking the PCT was to eat every off-limits food I could find and still lose weight. I looked forward to eating the bag of M&Ms that I knew were sitting snugly in my food bag, along with the homemade trail mix of nuts, chocolate, and dried fruit. My anticipation of the trail food surprised me. It had taken me years to finally eat nuts and granola again since eating pounds of them on a daily basis on the PCT.

The first seven miles leading up to Springer Mountain, the official southern terminus of the AT, passed quickly, and I wanted to be nowhere else but on the AT. Matt and I both felt like we had cut the cords of stress, obligations, and to-do lists that had defined our lives in Vancouver. We were outside on a beautiful spring day, with nothing to do but cover miles at any pace we chose. Physically, we were fearful of blisters and the common rubbing points that occurred with wearing full packs, but we felt strong and able-bodied. Mentally, I felt surer about the decision to hike the AT than nearly every decision I had made since finishing the PCT in 2007. I was tired of hating the person I was and I finally felt like I was enjoying my own company again, out there on the trail.

I felt at home.

Part of thru-hiking that fascinated me was that our own engines were responsible for carrying us such distances, and anyone who has ever experienced that feeling of looking back on the horizon and saying, "I just walked that entire distance today," knows the sense of pride and achievement that comes with it. I wanted that feeling again and I could sense that I was close to it.

Once we made it to Springer and took our official starting pictures next to the well-worn plaques that so many others before us have touched with the hope of making it to Mt. Katahdin, the northern terminus, we started the descent down from Springer. From there, it felt like the real adventure began. The trail made for fairly easy walking, with dead leaves covering much of the trail, and new leaves barely sprouting on the trees around us.

The scenery was surprisingly brown to both of us, since all Matt remembered from hiking through the deep of summer was the green tunnel effect of the trail. I had only known his photos, and in my first impression of the trail, I said to Matt, "It's a lot less green than I imagined."

I also realized that I hadn't packed sunscreen and I made a mental note to pick it up as soon as possible. My fair skin hadn't seen the light of day for many months of living in rainy Washington. There was still a cool breeze in the air, but the sun brought the temperature up into the high sixties. Since it was a Saturday, there were a lot of people out on the trail, starting the thru-hike themselves or hiking in order to meet the year's batch of new hikers.

Everyone we met asked us, "Are you thru-hiking?"

It became a funny question to answer, at least for the first few days. Our response was often, "Well, we're trying!" At that point, we were *attempting* a thru-hike, but it felt awfully strange to call ourselves AT thru-hikers, when we knew what it would take to earn that title. The last thing we wanted to do was jinx our hike by claiming to be something we weren't.

That first day was also strange because we were semi-seasoned thru-hikers, though we felt as green as the next person. We already had trail names and we introduced ourselves as such, which made people aware of the fact that we weren't as completely new to hiking as most of the people surrounding us were. It became almost painful to admit that we'd already hiked the PCT because we didn't want to be seen as any sort of experts or seem like we held ourselves in a higher regard than those just starting out. It became less of an issue as time went on, as people picked up their own rhythms and trail names, but it made for mixed feelings at the start of the trail.

Almost twelve miles after Springer Mountain, with dusk approaching, we decided on our first night's campsite at Cooper Gap, which sat alongside a forest service road. It was already home to ten other hikers and we were happy to be with a group for the evening.

It was a beautiful evening that was cold enough to need our sleeping bags but warm enough to be comfortable, and we lovingly took over our roles that we had practiced so well for over one hundred days on the PCT. Matt cooked dinner while I set up the tent, and he started a fire while I gathered wood. It felt like the most natural state our relationship had been in for months, and already I felt the fresh, raw aspects of the trail life scrubbing away the layers of my own self that I was trying so hard to shed. We talked for some time with two other hikers as the fire died down and went to sleep satisfied with the day's mileage and excited for the days to come.

We awoke the next day to sore legs, backs, and hips, but felt the same anticipation in starting the day's miles as we did the day before. It was another chilly, clear morning, and we began to pride ourselves on picking such a great start date, for the weather seemed to comply perfectly with our plan to avoid spring showers. Rather than pick a mile marker to reach for the day, we simply started walking and planned to go until we felt like stopping. It was an effort to move away from the data book-driven days that we knew on the PCT, and we wanted to give our legs and feet a chance to warm up before taking on big miles. Our brand of hiking typically involved hiking from sunrise to sunset, and we enjoyed the satisfaction and sense of accomplishment that came with covering a lot of ground. It wasn't everyone's style, but that is a great characteristic of thru-hiking, that it allows for all different speeds, methods and quirks.

The second day, a Sunday, was just as crowded as the first, and we felt unexpectedly suffocated. Matt's observation was, "I guess I don't remember all these people because I was months behind them the first time around."

We shouldn't have been as surprised as we were, as we'd seen the starting journal at Amicalola Falls that told of thirty to fifty thru-hikers starting each day in late March and early April. It was difficult to translate that amount of people to daily hiking and by the time we experienced the numbers first-hand, the woods felt downright cramped. I had to take special care in peeing off the side of the trail for fear that someone would walk right by me as I did my business.

As we walked over numerous mini ascents and descents that second day, I fell into the rhythm of living outside easier than I had expected. The defining aspects of the trail life came back just as strongly as they had been when I left the PCT four years ago. My hips and shoulders ached under the weight of my pack and I looked forward to every moment that I could release myself from its grip, no matter how short the moment. I began to fear the uphill climbs for the potential pain that they represented, and I didn't dare take my eyes off my feet for more than a second with such a high likelihood of falling over a root or rock. Performing camp duties like getting water, setting up and taking down the tent, and packing up for the day, were on autopilot after just a couple of times. It felt good to my mind and body to go through motions that were so warmly familiar.

I also knew I had remained my Stopwatch self because I was already thinking about the miles going forward. Though I had to shed that pressure of timing the miles in order to survive the PCT, I was still a data-driven hiker who paid attention to our pace and mileage with the purpose of covering the miles to the best of our abilities. I was still Stopwatch, no matter how much I tried to escape that part of my personality.

And yet, there were parts of the AT that I had to get used to, like following the white blazes painted on the trees rather than typical PCT emblems or rock cairns, all of which I depended on greatly to show me the correct route. People bear-bagged their food starting on the first night and much of the talk among the hikers was the debate about what to do to protect our food. We slept with our food in our tent for the entire PCT, minus the bear canister required areas, and only once thought we heard a bear rustling near our campsite. Lastly, we were a lot closer to civilization than I had originally imagined. There were several remote sections on the PCT where we saw very few people, yet on the second day of the AT, we passed through Woody Gap, just eight miles into our day, where we were greeted with tables of food, drinks, and other trail assortments provided by trail angels that made trail magic into an efficient, reliable machine right there in the parking lot. I wondered what the rest of the trail's community was like if just a road crossing could produce this kind of high-quality trail magic.

I also wanted to suggest that they pack up and set up shop a few hundred miles up the trail, when I would *really* need it, rather than just twenty miles in, when I could still smell the lingering detergent on my clothing. Not that those thoughts kept me away from the cookies. I eagerly ate several baked goods as I stood in front of the assortment of food, and most importantly, I lathered a trail angel's sunscreen on my singed arms, neck, and face. The lack of leaves proved to be the most difficult aspect for me on those first two days.

The miles went quickly that day and we reached the climb up Blood Mountain in the early afternoon. The terrain changed from smooth trail to unstable rocks as we gained elevation and the pace slowed, but the hope that a good view awaited us drove us forward. Once we reached the Blood Mountain shelter at the top, I was tired from the climb and I sat down on the first flat spot that caught my eye. The views through the bare trees were good enough for me, but Matt wanted to see the panoramic views at the very top of the mountain, which required a small amount of rock climbing. I let him go up with the camera while I sat at the bottom, next to the shelter.

As I sat there with my eyes closed and my head tilted back, I heard Matt call my name over the edge.

"Julie, you've got to come up here. You won't believe what's at the top."

I reluctantly complied, but immediately understood the excitement in Matt's request for me to join him when I reached the top and saw his second cousin, Tim, aka Curmudgeon, sitting atop Blood Mountain, taking in the scenery while talking to his mom on his cell phone. He looked surprised to see us and it was touching to see that even a fifty-nine-year-old man still called his mom from the trail to check in.

Curmudgeon had started two days before us and was on his fourth day of hiking. He shared his stories from his first few days while we walked together on the rocky descent from Blood Mountain to Neels Gap, our first resupply point. He moved slower than us, being nearly double our age, but we were glad for the company and tickled to hear his first impressions of the trail. We also couldn't help but notice how much bigger his pack was compared to ours, and we had the exact same packs. His pack even sported a tumor, as he called it, which sat high above his head and pulled on the pack, causing it to lean to one side. We kept quiet about the tumor but both assumed he needed a serious lesson in not only packing lighter, but also packing smarter.

Once in Neels Gap, we split up with Curmudgeon so we could each take care of our resupply needs. We told him that rather than shower, we planned on buying food and hiking about a mile up the trail, hoping he would follow. His response, full of four days of exhaustion that only a newbie thru-hiker could relate to, was, "I have *got* to have a shower. I'm not leaving this place without one."

It was a funny moment for us, because we hadn't meant to suggest that he skip a shower, and his vulnerability and honest desperation were such a rare sight that it was almost tragically comical to see a man nearly lose his cool over his desire for a shower. We didn't tell him how entertaining the moment had been, as we knew exactly how he felt. We would also be at that point only too soon. Before leaving, we softly suggested to Curmudgeon that he allow the employees of the outdoor store to perform a pack shakedown to make sure he was only carrying what was necessary. He agreed to do so and as we left the store, we saw him looking at new sleeping bags while the rest of his pack contents were splayed out across the store's floor.

After a steep climb out of Neels Gap, my pack slightly heavier with a few more food items and a small bottle of sunscreen, we set up for the evening at Bull Gap. Curmudgeon showed up at camp about an hour after us, having left the store six pounds lighter and several hundred dollars poorer. He also left the store with more knowledge of how to actually pack a pack, and his tumor had shrunk dramatically by the time he joined us that evening. Aside from the lighter, more comfortable pack, he was noticeably cleaner and happier from his first shower. We talked with Curmudgeon until sundown and the evening's supply of stories was already in surplus after just thirty-one miles into the trail. Knowing we had such a long walk ahead of us, I looked forward to hearing Curmudgeon's future stories.

Lying in the tent that night, Matt and I repeated to each other, "Thank goodness we went to the top of Blood Mountain, or we could have missed Curmudgeon altogether." Matt never said it, but it hurt to know that I didn't want to go to the top. Had it been my choice, we would have skipped the extra steps that led us to Curmudgeon. We would have missed an incredibly important moment and the experiences that followed. It was a sign to me that so far, I was failing in improving the self that I created over the last few years. But, it felt like the tiniest spark of progress had been lit because I could at least recognize the shortcoming in order to make better decisions in the future.

As I fell asleep that night, I remained thankful for Matt's desire to experience it all, whether it counted as mileage in the guidebook or not, and I wondered what else I had nearly missed out on over the last several years of being with him. He had become my best friend in that time and I promised myself that I would return that best friendship by improving my attitude and my actions over the next 2000 miles.

5 LIVING THE DREAM

Our second cousin, Tim, or Curmudgeon, as he self-named himself before the hike began, spent much of his life never giving a thought to hiking the Appalachian Trail. People he met along the way, including myself, were quick to ask him, "Is this something you've wanted to do your entire life?"

He honestly answered in his matter-of-fact fashion, "No."

While it would make for a great story to say that Curmudgeon spent weekends hiking in his youth, that he yearned for months of freedom while he raised a family and made a career in the construction business, and that he finally found that freedom as an empty nester, he would never lead on that he was anything but the fifty-nine-year-old Curmudgeon that showed up to hike the AT for a late-life challenge.

It was in his fifties that he started to hear random murmurings about the accomplishments other people experienced while backpacking the PCT and AT. He literally lived two houses away from Matt's family in the small town of Findlay, Ohio, while Matt hiked the AT in 2000 and while we hiked the PCT in 2007. During that time, Curmudgeon joined Matt's dad for early morning runs and eagerly listened to all the adventures we were having while walking through the mountains. The thought of hiking grew on him for several years and he kept it in the back of his mind in case the timing ever seemed right.

To have thru-hiked a trail, a person knows that the timing will never be perfect, which is why so many people never make the leap to try it. For years after hearing about our 2007 PCT thru-hike, Curmudgeon kept busy at life with a wife, four grown children, three grandchildren, and full-time work. About a year before he started the hike, in the spring of 2010, when most people get the general itch to be outside after a long winter indoors, especially after Ohio winters, Curmudgeon began researching the AT on the internet. Like he'd done for the past few years, he printed off the information and stored it away in a desk drawer, telling himself that if the timing were ever right, it was an adventure he wanted to try.

A few months later, his wife Sharon discovered the papers and asked him if it was truly something he wanted to do. To that, he answered an unwavering, "Yes."

Curmudgeon is a quiet, reserved man, who will never complain no matter how much discomfort he is in, who will rarely say that he wants something in life that could be seen as a completely selfish act, and who will keep his nose to the grindstone for however long a job might take, even if it means driving himself to exhaustion. It is amazing to me to look back and see that he honestly answered yes to his wife. It showed how much he really wanted to attempt the hike.

Sharon must have also known how much he wanted to do it because she knew him better than anyone. She told him that she supported his decision to hike, and that she would help him achieve his dream. Then she asked him just one question.

"So how long will it take, like three or four weeks?" she asked innocently.

"No, like four to six months," Curmudgeon said reluctantly as he watched the expression on her face change from excitement to shock. In their thirty-four years of marriage, they had not been apart for more than a week at a time.

Nevertheless, Sharon didn't back down from her support, though she still openly called him crazy, to which he was in agreement. Curmudgeon was walking on the AT nine months later, living out his late-in-life dream. He left behind Sharon to work her full-time job as a business owner of a reality company, to pay the bills that never ceased, and to spend time with their children and grandchildren. Curmudgeon knew he would miss her greatly, but he felt that the timing and point in his life were right for a thru-hike.

Part of the impetus that led Curmudgeon to hike the AT, in addition to hearing about others' accomplishments and passion for hiking over the past few years, was that he was facing the inevitable: aging. He was fifty-nine years old and as he looked around at his relatives, for his deceased father was one of eleven children, eight of them men, he observed that the life expectancy of the men didn't reach far past eighty years of age. The math left him nearly three-quarters through his life, with the last quarter approaching quickly, and he didn't want to find himself unable to take on such a challenge later in life when the window of opportunity was even smaller. Once he realized that the AT would offer him the satisfaction of completing a challenge that so few people do or even attempt to do, at a time in his life when a thru-hike was very possible, he made every effort to make it happen.

In terms of age and life circumstances, Curmudgeon was certainly not alone on the trail, especially at the start. It seemed that the majority of people thru-hiking could often be categorized into two ends of the age spectrum, the first group being those young enough to hike because they were free from obligations like family and mortgage payments. The second group included those old enough to have grown children, to have established careers that could either be paused or ended, and to have savings that allowed for the expenses of such an adventure. Matt and I were actually the odd men out. Most of our friends, people in their late twenties and early thirties, were starting families and establishing careers, unable to spend time or money on a thru-hike.

There were a lot of people on the AT who were living out a life dream, working against time and aging bodies. Sometimes the older people who started the trail had a long way to go before their hiking legs grew in, and I often wondered, especially on the hard, technical sections of trail, "How in the world are they doing this?"

Even if their bodies didn't oblige as easily as their younger counterparts, the older hikers seemed to carry an extra piece of gear as compared to younger hikers: determination. They walked with a committed drive that spoke of different purposes and priorities as compared to younger hikers, all of which I believe increased their likelihood of success. Most older people that we met on the trail measured their effort in hours rather than miles, because time allowed them to whittle down the miles without focusing solely on speed.

Fortunately for Curmudgeon, he was already in fairly good shape from running a few times a week and from working a physical job. He also timed it such that his last job as a project manager ended in late March. In order to prepare himself as well as possible, he compiled books, maps, and gear, and read other hikers' online journals. Even so, he still doubted his possibilities of finishing, knowing what a small percentage of people were able to do so each year (the numbers hover around twenty-five percent) and knowing that both physical and mental challenges awaited him.

Just a few weeks before the hike, Curmudgeon started an online journal, and the reality of the hike seemed to hit him then, along with the reality of being away from his wife for so long. Gratitude poured from his journal post as he acknowledged that the hike truly was possible because of Sharon's support and willingness to stay behind and keep the machine of their lives in motion. Other than their children and grandchildren, he called her indulgence of his Appalachian Fantasy, as he phrased it, the greatest gift she had ever given him.

Curmudgeon started his hike on March 31, two days before us. He hiked his first few days with a friend from Georgia who was instrumental in helping him plan for the hike. The plan was to ease into the hike with short days in order to prevent any blisters or unnecessary back and leg pain from starting out with too many miles under a heavy pack.

Unfortunately for Curmudgeon, but natural to the time of year, his first day atop Springer Mountain was cold and damp. Like the thousands of thru-hike attempts before him, he was already asking himself the unavoidable question, "Why am I doing this?"

Yet, the rain didn't deter the excitement he felt in starting a new adventure and he hoped for the best. The idea of even getting to Maine seemed overwhelming to him in his first few days, so he took his mind off the thought, not allowing himself to see much past the next day's hike. He knew that Matt and I would be out there soon, joining him on the long walk north, and he hoped that our paths would cross so that he'd be around familiar faces.

After camping with us at Bull Gap on our second evening, Curmudgeon started earlier than us the next morning while we were still packing up camp and eating breakfast. Less than a few miles into the hike, we were hiking downhill when I saw Curmudgeon hiking the opposite way towards us.

"What in the world is he doing?" I whispered back to Matt as I led the way.

"Have you seen a blaze?" Curmudgeon asked, out of breath from speed-walking up the hill.

"Well, not for a while, but I'm pretty sure we're on the trail," I answered.

I hadn't been paying attention to the blazes for some time, but I also knew we hadn't passed any side trails that morning. We weren't going to turn around and go back uphill where Curmudgeon was headed, so we assured him that we were still on the trail and that he should keep moving forward. The fear of being off-trail was unsettling and I was nervous for some time, because there really was a stretch with very few blazes, but I refused to go backwards on an uphill just to double-check the blazes. We also hadn't seen any *other* colored blazes that indicated a side trail, so I wasn't worried enough to turn around.

At that point, I thought Curmudgeon should have been renamed BP, or Blaze Paranoia, because it was going to be a long, hard trail if he turned around and went south every time there was a section with sparse blazes on the trees.

In thinking about his name, I had no idea why he had named himself Curmudgeon. Perhaps he was a Curmudgeon on the inside, but outwardly to those around him, he was a soft-spoken man who wanted his sleep and shower more than any other creature comfort, but who'd never complain if he didn't get either of them. He went so far as to label all his gear, including his guidebook, with thick, black sharpie letters written as CURMUDGEON. At first it seemed as sweetly innocent as a kid excited to start the new school year, but after we had spent some time in the shelters, when other hikers came in for the day and unpacked their food, clothing, and sleeping systems all over the shelter floors and picnic tables, I quickly saw the intelligence in Curmudgeon's foresight of labeling all his gear.

We spent most of our third day's morning hiking with Curmudgeon and stopped for lunch with him after ten miles at the Low Gap Shelter. Though it had been a chilly morning, the afternoon was warming up and we enjoyed eating lunch at the sun-soaked picnic table outside of the shelter. There were already five other hikers at the shelter, a few of them eating lunch and a couple of them already done for the day.

We left Curmudgeon at the shelter that day, knowing it was unlikely that we would see him again for the rest of the hike. He planned to stop at the next shelter, seven miles away, and we wanted to walk at least ten more miles. We said our goodbyes, took our picture together, and wished each other luck. We all kept online journals, so we knew we'd get updates on each other's hike from the internet or through the family grapevine when we called home. It was hard to leave him, but it would have been wrong for any of us to go a pace we weren't comfortable with. We also wanted him to create his own personal brand of hiking that wasn't heavily influenced by our own.

As we walked away from the shelter, Matt and I talked about Curmudgeon's odds of finishing. I knew how much he had given up and left behind at home to fulfill his dream, so I assumed it would take a lot to derail his hike. I also knew what an incredible support system he had of family and friends. As Matt and I talked about all the new adventures Curmudgeon was having, I found myself more excited to hear how his hike panned out than I was to see how ours went. I wanted to skip to the end and read the last chapter of his hike, but all I could do was move forward and let time work its magic, and Curmudgeon did the same, with quite a few surprises yet to come.

Julie Urbanski

6 REALITY SETS IN

Starting out on the AT was like starting a new job.

I was learning new things every day, I was excited to get up in the morning and hit the trail because I was stimulated with new experiences each day, I met new people who were all on their best behavior in order to make a good first impression, and most of all, I promised myself that I was going to do the job correctly from the beginning, with complete dedication and commitment to any task at hand. I approached each day with a new supply of both energy and excitement.

Also like a new job, I went through the processes of learning my way around the office, in terms of the inevitable cons that came with the pros, and learning my place in the ranks. The thru-hiker lifestyle has downsides that are worth overcoming in order to appreciate the upsides, so I wasn't surprised when some of those downsides became apparent over the next few days. What did surprise me, or maybe what I simply needed a refresher on since the PCT, was that my place in the pecking order on the trail was actually quite low. Mother Nature called the shots. I could assert my skills all I wanted and carry all the gear that assured me I was worthy of living outside, but when it came to who was in the power position, all the gear in the world was no match for her. Things weren't *that* drastic, but for the first time on the AT, Mother Nature made her presence known at 10:00 p.m. on our third evening on the trail. She was the boss and I did not dare argue that fact.

We hiked a half mile past Unicoi Gap to reach our campsite around 6:00 p.m., and despite a sunny, beautiful day with warm temperatures, we heard warnings all day of thunderstorms rolling in for the evening. With most hikers able to check the weather on their phones, it was easy to get a forecast and even easier for the news to spread up and down the trail with how many of us were out there. We didn't want to believe it, but we continuously kept our eyes and ears on the increasing clouds and wind, paying attention to any sign of dangerous weather. We first set up the tent in case we needed to make an escape into its shelter and then washed our clothes in a stream nearby. Just as we hung up our clothes to dry, the raindrops started to fall. The fact that my clothes weren't going to dry was more upsetting to me than the prospect of rain, and we hurried into the tent with our wet clothes, hoping a shower would simply pass over.

Luckily it did, and I jokingly said to Matt, "Is that it? That's what everyone's been warning us about all day?"

Unfortunately, the weather heard me belittle its first performance.

That night, the real storm arrived. Our campsite was thirty feet off the trail, situated on an uphill climb out of Unicoi Gap and up to Rocky Mountain. The wind and rain combined to bring the wrath of the storm right past our campsite as it swept down the mountain, surrounding us with loud claps of thunder and blinding bolts of lightning. Our tent hadn't been tested in an intense thunderstorm or even in mild rain, and we watched the four sides of the crisscrossed tent poles nearly snap under the thrusts of wind that threatened to rip the rain fly off the tent. In order to cut pack weight, we didn't carry tent stakes with us, and I hoped that my shoddy rock piles on the corners of the tent would outlast the storm.

I closed my eyes in order to shut out the storm and fall asleep, but my efforts were pointless. The lighting hit so frequently and for so long each time that it seemed like someone had turned on the lights right above my eyes. Even with my head buried in my sleeping bag, I could still hear the whipping and flapping of the tent walls as the wind tried to tear them apart. I thought about taking a video of the storm, but I was so frozen in my sleeping bag, afraid of any movement that might jeopardize our dry enclosure, that I could barely find the courage to swallow, much less the guts to rummage through my pack for the camera.

Matt and I never said a word to each other as the storms passed over us, well into the late evening. We lay silently in the tent, shocked by the intensity of the storms and the fact that it was only our third day on the trail. We didn't have a drop of rain until the sixty-fifth day on the PCT. Think about that. We went two months without precipitation and there we were on our third day on the AT, already so far out of our comfort zone because of an aspect of the AT that we hadn't prepared for. Matt didn't even carry a rain jacket and my four-year-old rain jacket was no longer the barrier to the rain that it once was. I carried rain pants on the PCT, only to wear them a few times, and I chalked them up as unnecessary gear for the AT. As the precipitation came down around us that night, I questioned the clothing choices in my pack and how they applied to the AT, wondering if we had made too many decisions based on the PCT's weather.

At some point, we fell asleep that night and the thunderstorms abated, but I don't remember it. I remember that one moment I was terrified and the next moment I woke up in a daze from the damage that the storms had done to our nerves. At least our tent and the rock piles outlasted the weather. The trail held an eerie silence that followed the storms and I packed up on that fourth morning as if in a dream.

As we gathered ourselves that morning, we discovered another victim to the storms' intensity. Our food bags that we'd hung in a tree were completely soaked from swinging in the rain all night. A couple of plastic bags had been punctured and Goldfish crackers had turned into orange mush. The other tricky aspect was how to pack so many wet items, like the tent and our food bags. We only carried one dry sack for the computer and phone and relied solely on our four-year-old pack covers to keep our gear dry. Rather than pack the wet items inside our dry packs and risk every piece of gear getting wet, such as our extra clothing and sleeping bags, our packs turned inside out as we attached all the wet items to the outside with the hope that they would somehow dry throughout the day.

I spent that morning humbly accepting the fact that we should have done a little more research on the weather patterns of Georgia during early April. I asked Matt over and over again on that fourth day, "Don't you remember any of this rain?"

Matt was just as shocked as I was to receive rain so early on in the hike, as it was a relatively uncommon aspect during his first hike. We had relied on Matt's memory of Georgia in June, only to realize too late that two months made a big difference in weather.

The weather that day was frosty and windy. Not only were we shell-shocked from the storms, but we were also unmotivated. Reality had arrived. The real challenges of the trail showed up to join us and we had to convince ourselves to keep walking despite the mist coming down around us and the wind chilling us to the core. I felt heavy and sluggish for the first half of the day and the wind never let up. It was the kind of wind that disrupted our thoughts, threw us off balance, and stifled the conversation between the two of us.

I said to Matt on our first break that morning, "If this wind is normal, then I'm not sure how long I'll last out here."

We later found out that it wasn't normal, and that there was a wind advisory in place those first few days on the trail. At least we had *some* sense of what was normal weather for Georgia in April.

I was in a funk all morning until Matt told me a story that lifted me out of it as we made our way past the Deep Gap Shelter, thirteen miles into our day. As we peered down the side trail that led to the shelter, Matt's memory of his first few days on the trail in 2000 came back to him with absolute clarity, all from the familiar motion of peering down a side trail.

He recalled the third day of hiking with Dan and their curiosity in the shelters. They had no idea what purpose the shelters had, nor did they think they were available for hikers to use, so they camped in a tent for their first two evenings. It wasn't until they were around another hiker, as they passed a side trail to a shelter, when they finally asked, "What's with the buildings in the woods?"

I can only imagine the shock on the other hiker's face after hearing such an innocent, trail-naïve question. On the other hand, what a shock for Matt and Dan to learn that those buildings that they'd been too scared to venture into were shelters, placed there for their benefit and spanning the entire length of the trail.

It still makes me smile when I think of it. The shelter life seemed like such an innate piece of knowledge about the AT, but apparently I had taken it for granted as a piece of preparation that I already had without ever knowing it.

Talking about the shelters brought back other memories of Matt's steep learning curve on his first AT hike, like that of trail names. Again, they didn't start around a pack of people, so they introduced themselves to other hikers as they would in normal society, as Matt and Dan. Several days in, someone asked them what their trail names were, and their response of puzzled looks begged for an explanation. They finally learned why people wrote strange names in the journals in the shelters, and they were quick to participate in being named.

They didn't have much to go on, or at least they weren't feeling very creative at the time, because they looked down at each other's shirts and saw that Matt's blue thrift-store t-shirt said "Optimist" in white lettering, while Dan's white thrift-store t-shirt said "Animal" in black felt lettering. Thus, they were given trail names, easily yet fittingly.

The same hiker that explained the shelters to Matt and Animal also gave them a lesson in bear-bagging. So far, it had been a nightly competition between the two of them to see who could throw a rock the highest in a tree in order to hang a bear bag.

Matt still laughs each time he recounts competing with Animal with every ounce of effort he had left in the day, never knowing that hanging the bear bag in the notch between a branch and the tree trunk, no matter how high they could throw it, wouldn't deter any bear from getting their food. It was an enlightening moment to find out that the only protection their food had from bears up until that day had been the sheer lack of a bear's presence in their food's vicinity.

We went to sleep that fourth night near the Plumorchard Gap Shelter, and I had a smile on my face as I pictured Matt and Animal's first night sleeping in a shelter, after they had discovered the purpose of those strange buildings in the woods. It didn't take much for the emotional roller coaster of the trail to change course, because though I had started at a low point that morning, I felt rejuvenated by the end of the day.

The next day brought us to the Georgia-North Carolina border. It was hard to believe we had already completed one state, considering it took us seventy-three days to complete our first state on the PCT. I liked the idea of checking off more states more frequently and thought, "I could get used to this."

When looking back upon a day in the past, memory works in a strange way. I can look at that day of crossing the Georgia border and my memory is frozen on the few pictures we took that day. I can see Matt posing for a picture with the border sign, his face still carrying the extra weight he'd gained over the past month and his skin showing traces of stubble after a few days without shaving. I can't remember much else of that day except the circumstances surrounding that picture, with the leafless trees, the early morning sun burning off the fog through the tree limbs, and my anticipation for the rest of the states' borders. I was already excited for the next border so I could look back and see how far I'd come in terms of mileage and more importantly, in terms of personal change.

That evening, we camped at Betty Creek Gap under a low canopy of branches that encapsulated our tent site, just under ninety-six miles into the trail. We shared our campsite with several other hikers, including a few from Michigan and Ohio. It was comforting to share the clear, warm evening with others over a fire, especially those who were close to our roots, and we felt refreshed again. Matt was enjoying the hike and the feeling of getting stronger each day. Despite the fact that it was his second time on the AT, nearly everything was a new experience for him.

The next morning I got my second taste of the characteristics that defined the AT. In addition to the presence of precipitation, I learned that the AT often goes straight up in order to gain elevation, rather than using switchbacks, the common choice of the PCT. Our morning started with a climb up Albert Mountain, and it was the hands-on-the-knees, heavy-breathing kind of climbing. Though it was short, I was out of breath once we reached the top. The difficulty of the climb seemed like a mean joke to me, like someone was filming my struggle, but Matt assured me, "I definitely remember this about the AT. It just takes us up and over the mountains."

That piece of the AT reality pie left a sour taste in my mouth and I kept silent of how fearful I was of future climbs, especially if I thought a tiny one was difficult. Instead, we took snapshots at the top of the fire tower as we recovered from the climb and took in the panoramic views of the mountains. It wasn't the full-foliage shot I was expecting at the top, but the sun was out, a downhill awaited us, and we saw patches of green starting to fill in the hillsides.

Later that morning, Matt and I fulfilled a dream that we had four years ago on the PCT. We caught Troll.

While hiking the PCT, we were very cognizant of which hikers were ahead of us and by how many days, so that by the time we caught up to them, they were legends in our minds because we had been reading their journal entries for so long.

To us, Troll was a legend. He and his son Oblivious hiked the PCT the same year as us and we spent over two months following them. It wasn't until southern Oregon, when we were within a day of catching them, that we unknowingly passed them while they spent time in town. Once we passed them, our pace never slackened and we never took a day off, so they never caught back up with us. They simply saw two new names ahead of them in the journals: Optimist and Stopwatch. Disappointingly, after months of literally being within miles of each other, we never met them.

Fast forward to our sixth day on the Appalachian Trail, and as we made our way downhill into Rock Gap at mile marker 103.9, we saw the unmistakable branding that Troll had made for himself as a hiker. He hiked in a kilt. As soon as we saw him, we knew it was the hiker that we had chased for nearly 2,000 miles on the PCT.

In unison, Matt and I quickly asked him, "Are you Troll?"

"Yeeees," he answered slowly.

I struck my hiking poles into the ground and we threw down our packs in exaltation.

"Troll," Matt said as he stuck out his hand for a handshake, "we've been following you since 2007 on the PCT. We're Optimist and Stopwatch, and you have no idea how happy we are to finally meet you."

Our names clicked in his mind after he paused for a moment and thought back to the PCT. We sat there and chatted with him about the trail and at the same time, we met another influential person in the hiking community. Gordon Smith was an elderly man, dressed in a Michigan Wolverines sweatshirt, the yellow emblem standing out brightly from the navy background, and he wore navy pants and Velcro sandals strapped over saggy, calf-length socks. He didn't look healthy enough to be hiking or even driving the huge white van he stood next to, the sides of it decorated with stickers from each of the various scenic trails in the US. But, he looked happy. After we settled down from our excitement of meeting Troll, Gordon was quick to approach us.

"Root beer? Gatorade? Can I get you a chair?"

He moved slowly to and from the van, and his hands shook as he handed us Gatorades. We accepted the cold drinks as an awareness crept in regarding the state of his health and his unselfish dedication towards hikers.

While we were used to trail angels parking along the trail, giving out drinks and food, there was something different about him and we were intrigued to hear him talk.

"What's your story," Matt asked, "because it seems like you have an interesting one?"

Gordon told us that he was living to support hikers because he could no longer hike himself and because of the history he and his sister had with long-distance hiking. In 1982, he started hiking the AT with his blind, diabetic sister and eighty-year-old mother. They met a thru-hiker and immediately fell in love with the concept. After that, he and his sister hiked much of the US trail systems together, even after she went on dialysis.

After his sister passed away a few years ago, Gordon had back surgery and was in a nursing home. He said that after awhile, he thought of the hiking community and the drive people displayed on the trail. That thought motivated him to get moving again. He said that people in nursing homes were waiting to die and that he wasn't ready to do that just yet. Shortly after that realization, he bought a van and began helping hikers while living out of the van. He had been doing it ever since and left no doubt as to what he cared about when he told us, "I'm enjoying the hell out of life and I'm not ready to quit yet."

It was an incredible moment to be in the presence of someone who had seen so much in life and who could articulate his thoughts and feelings so well and so powerfully. Gordon was an impressive example of the trail community. I was thankful that Matt had asked such a simple, open-ended question, and I think Gordon was happy to answer. I doubted many hikers had ever paused to ask him about his life.

It's rare in the real world that people open up that quickly and honestly about their lives after meeting each other for less than a minute, and yet it was commonplace in a setting such as the AT. The trail has a way of stripping away dishonesty and it creates a safe haven for people to open up without fear of being judged. I loved those aspects of the trail as we listened to Gordon's story and walked away with a unique glimpse into his life.

After meeting Troll and Gordon, we pushed through the rest of the day with the goal of reaching the Nantahala Outdoor Center (NOC) by the next afternoon. We made it to the Wayah Bald Shelter that evening, our furthest day yet of twenty-three miles.

The late afternoon was just as beautiful as the evening before and the night of thunderstorms was well behind us and nearly forgotten. We camped close to the trail, out of sight-distance from the shelter, in order to make a quick escape in the morning towards town. There was plenty of daylight left as we cooked dinner, along with plenty of food, and since we knew we would reach town the next day, we celebrated and allowed ourselves to eat extra rations of food. It was pointless to carry the weight of the extra food the next day and it was the pre-town celebration that we took part in whenever possible.

The next morning, we were so overcome with the excitement of town that we never checked for a white blaze. It was still dark when we started walking with our headlamps and after fifteen minutes of ducking under tree branches, pushing through spider webs, and stopping to question which direction the trail headed, I had the dreaded, uneasy feeling of being lost. I felt sick to my stomach and we looked around in the trees for a sign of not only the white blaze, but any blaze. Once we found the trail again, my heart fell and I closed my eyes in disappointment after seeing a blue blaze. We had gone on a side trail for the last mile and had to head back and start our day over, a half hour later and two miles shorter than where we could have been.

Looking back, it was nothing in the scope of time or mileage that we would spend on the AT, but at the time, it dampened our spirits to waste our time and energy, especially since it was a town day. Both of us were to blame and we were frustrated with ourselves for missing a detail as simple as checking for the first white blaze to lead the way. We learned the hard way that hurrying into town wouldn't help and could even hinder our progress if we failed to check our first steps to make sure we were pointed in the right direction.

After finding the trail, we arrived at the NOC by early afternoon on our seventh day and took the opportunity to lounge in town for several hours. In addition to buying food for the next few days, we visited the River's End Restaurant, where we ate cornbread, salads, fresh vegetables, and sundaes. Because the afternoon went by at a crawling pace, we felt rejuvenated after dinner to keep hiking rather than stay in town overnight. Eight miles and 3300 feet of elevation gain faced us as we left town, so we split up the climb and hiked just two miles that evening. The combination of an uphill, newly acquired food, and full stomachs made for slow miles.

The next morning's climb was the hardest yet with six more miles and 2500 feet of elevation gain, and I was in need of a break by the time we made it to the top of Cheoah Bald. It was a beautiful morning, despite a chill in the air atop the bald. Aside from the rain, the other unexpected discomforts I dealt with were the sun blisters forming on my hands. Due to the lack of leaves on the trees and the fact that my hiking poles kept my hands exposed to the sun, my hands were red, swollen, and splotchy with blisters. I was frustrated that sunscreen wasn't enough to remedy the blisters and I already looked forward to the next town in order to find a solution.

Later that day, after calculating the miles until the next town and after assessing the hunger we felt the day after town, we realized that we had not bought enough food. Though we had trouble finishing our daily allotments of food for the first week, the hiker hunger kicked in that eighth day. The calories from our Pop-Tarts and Chex Mix weren't adding up to the energy we were expending. We later found out we weren't alone in this predicament, as the hiker hunger hit Curmudgeon around the same time. He dropped fifteen pounds soon after starting and his weight loss leveled off once he carried more food, ate every two hours, and kept trail mix in his pockets for accessible snacks.

Like many troubling moments on the trail, we asked and the trail answered. Within a mile of our destination shelter for the night, we were strolling downhill when the trail opened up to a road. We saw a car parked with its trunk open, a cooler inside of it, water jugs sitting on the ground, and four guys standing next to the car. Two of them were young and couldn't have been much over eighteen, and two of them appeared to be in their early forties.

After introducing ourselves, we found out that the two younger ones were thru-hiking and the two older ones had thru-hiked nearly twenty years ago, both of which were friends of one of the younger thru-hiker's dads. The two younger hikers had left NOC the day before, and based on the first story they told us about their crazy night of partying in NOC, we took the hint that the two older guys were out there to make sure the kids were having fun, just not *too* much fun.

After talking with them for a few minutes, I mentioned that we also just left NOC and unfortunately didn't pack enough food. I admit it was a bit of a selfish plug for Matt and me, because I hoped they might have some extra food to spare in their trunk. Even if they knew I was fishing for an offering of food, they didn't let on. Within minutes of mentioning food they gave us packets of oatmeal and a jar of peanut butter and jelly to help us get to the next town.

That night we stayed with them and four other hikers near the Cable Gap Shelter, and I was glad to have the company. We fell asleep on our eighth evening looking forward to the section that would begin the next day in the Great Smoky Mountains National Park. As I lay in the tent, I looked back at the last few days leading up to the Smokies. So many unique, challenging, and entertaining events had already come together for the beginning of our AT adventure. The downsides of the thru-hiker lifestyle had also shown up, including weather, challenging ascents, and hunger, but I knew that circumstances could change in an instant. I promised myself to not get stuck in a difficult moment, for I might miss a better one passing me by.

Julie Urbanski

7 SERIOUS IN THE SMOKIES

Though I had hiked almost 3000 miles at that point, including the PCT and the beginning of the AT, I couldn't claim to be an outdoorsy person. Sure, I have spent time outdoors, ok *lots* of time outdoors, and I have a deep appreciation for long-distance trails because of the opportunities for personal growth, but I rarely get excited about outdoorsy things, like wildlife and flowers. The fact that I don't stop and smell the roses, mainly because I just don't find them that interesting, has plagued me since my first few days on the PCT. Why am I not a nature lover?

The answer to that question could possibly be found in the Smokies. Not because of what happened to me in the Smokies this time around, but because of what happened the first time. Yes, the first time, a faint memory from my childhood that has subtly affected me ever since.

When I was eight years old, my family took a trip from Cincinnati, Ohio, to Gatlinburg, Tennessee. My parents, my sister, and I spent Halloween weekend with another family that also had two daughters. One of the events we planned was an out-and-back day hike. Heck, we might have even been on the AT.

Near the top of the climb, our group reached a flat spot and took a snack break. All the women, six of us total, sat down in the dirt or on a log while the two dads stood there, hands on their hips as they waited for us to get back up. Instead, the women staged a protest and refused to hike to the top of the mountain. The female majority vote overruled and my dad and his friend left us sitting there while they hiked to the top and back. I remember thinking, "Why are they making us do this? Did we do something wrong?"

Looking back, I see what a strange vacation choice that was for my family. Since I was born, our yearly summer vacation had been a two-week stay in a condo in Hilton Head Island, South Carolina. It never occurred to me that families spent their free time anywhere else but the beach. I grew up thinking the outdoors encompassed our back yard, the creek between our yard and our neighbor's, and the network of backyard trails that led to my grade school friends' houses. We didn't have mountains and the extent of my exposure to wildlife included deer and squirrels.

When our family attempted one vacation out of our comfort zone that ended in six unhappy females, I imagine our dad's false hope of breeding outdoorsy children was squelched right there off the side of the trail near Gatlinburg. That was our first and last effort at an outdoorsy vacation and from them on, we never went anywhere else for vacation but Hilton Head Island. That was my first impression of the Smokies and apparently such a bad one that I didn't go back for twenty years.

Our ninth morning started out chilly and cloudy as we climbed the hill after the Cable Gap Shelter. I anticipated the Smokies because they symbolized a fresh, new section of trail. After eating a late breakfast of ramen noodles near the Fontana Dam Shelter, while the sun broke through the clouds, we made our way along the road, past the Dam Visitor Center and towards the official park entrance. As we walked towards the entrance that morning, Matt described exactly what the entrance sign looked like, the flash of a memory still vivid in his mind so many years later. He could picture him and Animal standing next to a large brown sign, eager to be making headway on their hike.

To our surprise, the entrance location had changed since 2000, as well as the signage, and the disappointment in Matt's voice was palpable.

"It's gone. The sign is gone. They moved the entrance. It looks nothing like what I remember."

I wasn't sure at the time why it had been so important for him to see that sign again and match his memory with the real thing. I realize now that he was trying to piece together memories that had been so jumbled over time, and the unexpected change in the sign temporarily displaced the past hike in his mind.

We didn't have long to lament the loss of the sign because the Smokies welcomed us with an uphill climb of 2000 feet over three miles. The longer we hiked, the higher the temperatures rose. Several hikers on their way down the mountain updated us on the current temperature of eighty degrees. It was the hottest day yet on the trail and we were noticeably thirstier than normal. We had taken for granted that we hadn't yet worried about the reliability of clean, well-flowing water, and we were suddenly in a bit of a bind. The rising temperatures essentially turned off the water valve for the springs and by the time we were near the top of the climb, the one spring we passed had slowed to a trickle. We filled up as best we could in one of the few pools of water and felt that familiar PCT moment of, "Oh crap. We don't have enough water." The PCT was defined by many twenty-plus mile sections of waterless trail and up until that point, the AT already had many more water sources than the PCT.

The next reliable water source was in ten miles and since we both only carried one thirty-two ounce plastic bottle, we rationed our water until then. It was an element that we weren't prepared for, as if the entrance to the park had taken us into another climate zone, where the temperatures rose and the water supply fell. It also made for a tough afternoon of hiking and by the time we took a break at the Mollies Ridge Shelter at 4:00 p.m., eighteen miles into the day, I was desperate for the opportunity to rest.

The shelter sat about three-quarters up a thousand foot climb, and we reached it just after we crested a small hill. I stretched out on the grass, ate a Luna Bar, and chugged the rest of my water. Sitting outside of the shelter were three women who were hiking for a few days in the park.

Matt quickly struck up a conversation with them about their hike, but they seemed more interested in hearing about our thru-hike.

"Don't you just love it out here?" they asked me.

"Well…sort of," I answered hesitantly.

It had been a tough morning of climbing, especially given the lack of water, and we still had around five more miles to hike for the day. I also knew I was in it for the long haul of a multi-month hike. To top it off, there wasn't a privy at the shelter and I had to face a latrine ridden with flies and toilet paper scattered about on the ground. I was in a bit of a grumpy mood and therefore wasn't in a great position to be giving my opinion on thru-hiking.

With each ensuing question that I answered, I saw the disappointment settle into the women's expressions. I didn't hold back on the aspects that made thru-hiking difficult, and while I didn't say I disliked it, I was clear about how difficult it was even though there were also many moments that I loved about it. I wanted to give honest answers about how I felt, and the excitement about thru-hiking that they had expected to pour from me didn't come out. In the past, I had always been careful about how sparkly of a picture I painted thru-hiking to be, and I did the same as I talked to the women. They wanted Van Gogh and I gave them paint-by-number. It was incredibly unsexy in every way.

"Well, why do you do this?" they asked me.

"For the challenge," I said. "I love the mental and physical challenges, and I know I'll come out a different person at the other end. But I also know I'll have to go through a lot of crappy moments to get there."

The conversation didn't go much further and it bothered me for the rest of the day. Why couldn't I just give them the overflowing joy that they wanted? Why did I feel the need to bring up both the highs and lows of thru-hiking? I couldn't quite grasp an answer to these questions and I left the shelter feeling incredibly misunderstood. I felt mistaken for a grouchy, negative sourpuss who only complained about the hike. It was a shocking irony because I was enjoying the overall experience more than I had expected, and yet I left feeling judged as the pessimist that I was running away from.

I was glad to move on to the next shelter and we finished the day at a crowded Spence Field Shelter. We arrived just before 7:00 p.m. and the shelter was almost full with ten men inside. We claimed our shelter space with our sleeping pads on the top floor, where there were already three hikers lying down. I contemplated changing in my sleeping bag with the men sitting right next to me, but opted for the open-air change behind the shelter while Matt cooked dinner. While the shelters offered a roof and a chance to be social, they lacked any form of privacy.

We hiked twenty-three miles that day and it felt further based on how tired and thirsty we were by the end. After the unsettling meeting with the women earlier that day, it was oddly comforting to be surrounded by men in the shelter that night. Not one person asked me about how much I was enjoying the hike thus far, no one balked when I admitted that I often bitched about uphill climbs until they were over, and there was a sense of respect for our mileage. Most importantly, I felt accepted.

While I still had to take my pack off to pee and had to be more careful about changing my clothes, I felt that I was on an equal playing field with the men because I could hang with the best of them, whether that meant hiking big miles, consuming large quantities of food, or even discussing the finer details of poop, which came up surprisingly often. They had all been out there for days and weeks so far, and knew the same terrain that I had just covered. I was happy to be in the circle of fellow thru-hikers that night.

We awoke the next morning with new energy. Our mileage options were limited by the park rules of staying in or around shelters, and our best option was a shelter twenty-seven miles away. The upcoming rolling terrain threatened to slow our pace and therefore decrease our chances of making it to the further shelter, so we were quick to get moving. The day was just as beautiful as the one before, with the sun shining behind a few puffy clouds. We looked forward to reaching Clingmans Dome, a popular landmark along the AT, as well as the highest point, and though I feared the uphill climb, the relatively easy footing made for a quick pace.

Once at the top, I sat just below the tower while Matt climbed to the top of it for a better view. It was a clear day with panoramic shots of the surrounding mountains and he didn't want to miss the chance to see the best views from atop the tower. I have a lot of regrets in my life and looking back, I regret not going to the top of that tower. I told myself that I didn't care about the views, that I could always come back in my car, and that I was only out there for the hiking part. The honest part of me knew I was being lazy and caving in to being tired, just like I did in the corporate world. It was the kind of laziness that came with not recognizing that something amazing was in front of me, and that someone who loved me was asking me to share in that amazement.

It wasn't that extreme of a feeling while I sat at the bottom of the tower, looking up to see Matt call my name over the edge to come join him, but as I sat there, I knew I was making the lazy choice that I'll never be able to undo. I may never go back to that spot or get that beautiful of a day again, and I certainly won't ever be that same person again. I look back on the Julie that made that choice and I'm angry with her. I want to shake her and wake her up to see her surroundings, but as I've found when dealing with the choices of other people, it's often ourselves that are the most difficult to convince of what is the best choice to make. I was disappointed in my choices as I walked away from the tower that day. I was wasting my opportunities to change on the Appalachian Trail.

Later that day, we took a break at the parking lot at Newfound Gap, where many hikers were getting on and off the trail for a break in Gatlinburg. We sat and talked with Gordon Smith again while he waited around to give hikers a ride into Gatlinburg.

As we sat on the curb of the parking lot, a sudden gust of wind kicked up the dead leaves around us and I felt a sense of urgency to get moving. The weather felt ominous, like it was bringing more than just wind our way, and we quickly packed up as dark clouds started rolling in. We still had three more miles to the shelter and about a thousand feet of elevation to gain, on legs that had already hiked twenty-four miles. We both hoped for room at the shelter so we wouldn't have to withstand another storm in our tent. Though the tent had performed valiantly in the first storm, we didn't feel the need to test it again.

Once we arrived at the Icewater Spring Shelter, we were disappointed to see that we weren't the only ones worried about the weather. The two-level shelter was beyond its twelve-person capacity, with at least fifteen hikers on the floorboards and several more sleeping on the ground in front of the shelter, still under the roof's overhang. Most hikers were awaiting the storm as they burrowed in their sleeping bags.

Three other tents had already taken the best spots within the vicinity of the shelter, so we had to accept the only windswept, slightly down-sloping, patch of ground that remained. While Matt cooked dinner in the shelter, I set up the tent with our gear inside of it to weigh it down so the increasingly strong winds wouldn't blow it away.

After dinner, we huddled in the tent for the night and hoped for the best. We were just ten days into the trail and already hoping our tent walls would hold out for the second time. The frequency of storms was unsettling to me, as was the fact that it was the second Monday on the trail that we were experiencing such inclement weather. I saw a pattern and I didn't like it. I thought I had left the corporate world and its unpopular Mondays behind me, but the day still held a negative connotation in my mind.

That night was as sleepless as the last storm-ridden night. I was sure our tent fly would be ripped off at any moment, whisked away into the sky like so many scenes of roofs being torn off in tornadoes. Matt and I lay in the tent the same as before, frozen in our sleeping bags, unable to take our eyes off the rain fly above our heads, too scared to move.

We welcomed the daylight the next morning and awoke to a tent still intact, with only our nerves frayed once again. Though the storms had ended, the wind hadn't died down and it was still raining. To make matters worse, the temperature hovered around forty degrees, and though we'd been sweating in eighty degree heat just two days prior, not able to drink enough water, at that moment we were freezing in our summer clothes and surrounded by so much water that thirst was the last concern on our minds. I wore a rain jacket, a long and a short-sleeve shirt, and hiking pants, while Matt wore running shorts and a long and short-sleeve shirt. We both had gloves on, but they would only stay dry in the lightest of mist, and it was pouring outside.

As we ate a warm bowl of ramen noodles for breakfast, we looked at the guidebook's upcoming shelter options. Most importantly, we looked at the elevation for the day and saw that the first seventeen miles were well above 5000 feet, with several spots above 6000 feet. That might not sound high to west coast hikers, but it was some of the highest elevation on the entire trail. It didn't take much for the temperatures to drop into the thirties at that high of elevation, even in the summer.

According to the guidebook, the shelter twenty miles away sat just under 4800 feet. It was still too high and too cold. We simply weren't prepared for temperatures that low, especially when coupled with rain. We knew we needed to be lower.

Twenty-seven miles away was the Davenport Gap Shelter, which sat just under 2600 feet. We decided to remain open to stopping at either shelter, but were mentally prepared to hike the full twenty-seven miles. Our motto for the day was simply, "Get me down from here."

The longer we hiked that day, the further the weather deteriorated. With the steady rain and a lack of soil on the trail, the trail became a small stream over the rock-laden trail, and our clothing was completely soaked through, including my rain jacket. I gave up on puddle jumping and saved time and energy by simply trudging through the wet trail, soaking my shoes and socks and numbing my feet. Above 6000 feet, the rain turned to snow and I practically skied across the inch accumulation with my hiking poles.

We stopped in a shelter for lunch after thirteen miles and both had trouble finding the coordination to do simple tasks like unclip our belt buckles. We were in bad shape and the weather wasn't letting up. I had a few pieces of dry clothing in my pack, but I was reserving them for sleeping that night. Other than that, I had my sleeping bag, which I prayed was staying dry in my pack. I didn't have much faith in my pack cover to keep everything in my pack completely dry; it had a tendency to accumulate water in the bottom of it.

As we sat there cold and wet in the shelter, we contemplated whether to push on or dry out in the shelter. It seemed too early in the day to stop at 1:00 p.m., so we decided to hurry through lunch and continue walking. Though I didn't want to leave the safety of the shelter, I couldn't warm up just by sitting there in my wet clothes. We still had four miles before the elevation showed any signs of lowering much below 5000 feet. We practically ran those miles.

At the same time, we were incredibly careful with the rocky, slick terrain, because one misstep could have meant a twisted ankle or worse. We had complete focus as we hammered through the afternoon miles. If there were any views to see, we didn't see them because we were either too busy focusing on our feet or because it was so cloudy and rainy that there wasn't much to see anyway.

Two hours after lunch, we made it to the Cosby Knob Shelter, twenty miles into our day and already full of hikers. Since we had been prepared to move on, the decision to keep walking was easy and painless. Before leaving, I needed the help of a dry hiker to open my Luna Bar wrapper. My hands had lost all dexterity and it was my only chance to eat a snack for the rest of the day. We had seven more miles to go, during which we repeated to each other, "Just get down. Just get down."

By mid-afternoon, with just a few miles to go and still 2000 feet of elevation to lose, I desperately needed to pee. It was the first time I had to pee since we started walking. I only drank sixteen ounces of water for the day because I was so cold and almost felt that my body was consuming water by osmosis through my surroundings. Matt confessed that he couldn't stop to wait for me because he was fearful of hypothermia. He was colder than I realized and so I pushed on, contemplating peeing in my pants to warm up my legs, knowing the rain would probably wash my pants. Instead, I looked forward to an uphill climb and the moment I felt life creep into my frozen hands after a short ascent, I quickly pulled off the side of the trail, dropped my pack, and struggled to unclip my belt buckle. Matt watched me with fear in his eyes for his own safety, and I told him to keep moving. He didn't want to risk us being alone, so he waited for me to relieve myself. Buttoning my pants took so much effort that it brought tears to my eyes.

In the last mile of the hike, the rain slowed to a mist, the temperatures warmed up significantly, and we finally breathed relief as we saw the walls of the shelter off the side of the trail. We arrived at the Davenport Gap Shelter as the clock closed in on 5:00 p.m. and we were shocked to see how fast we had hiked twenty-seven miles. It felt like a dream to look back and see how far we had come.

Crowded or not, we had decided we were going to stay in the shelter and when we arrived, there were three spots left. It took almost an hour of lying in our dry sleeping bags before we could function and cook dinner. Since we had hiked further than we expected over the past two days, we had an extra meal to spare, so that evening we ate two warm dinners to both lessen our pack weight and warm our chilled bodies.

It was one of the hardest days yet on the trail due to the weather conditions, and as we sat there talking about the day, we realized how effective we were in covering miles in such terrible circumstances. We could recall many other days when the weather was less than desirable and when our withering motivation made for slower miles despite the desire for the miles to be finished. That day, the stakes were high for our well-being, with the possibility of hypothermia more real than ever before, and there had not been room for error, for complaining, or for misbehaving. No one was going to get us down from those mountains other than ourselves, so while we were kicking ourselves for not packing proper rain gear, we at least found solace in our ability to approach the day's hike with extreme focus and discipline. We also considered ourselves lucky for making it through the day unscathed and decided that our gear needed some attention very soon. It was doubtful that the worst weather was behind us.

8 A MIXED BAG COMMUNITY

There was an undeniable presence of a lot of people on the AT, whether they were thru-hikers, sectioners, weekenders, day-hikers, or trail angels. There are so many access points along the way and the trail is in such close proximity to large communities that it's an inherently social trail. The shelters also play a big role in creating social gathering spots, so not only are there a lot of people hiking, there are also a lot of clumps of people in specific locations each day. Anyone looking to truly escape society may want to re-think an AT thru-hike because they will find themselves surrounded by people for much of the way. Even if thru-hikers get weeded out, there are still many different types of users along the entire trail. Yet, the AT is also unique because of the sheer amount of people that hike on its path each year.

The AT also draws all kinds of people who differ across the board, from age, to experience, to even citizenship. Since people come from such different backgrounds and lifestyles, they have different reasons for walking and different priorities while they walk. As thru-hikers, we had the opportunity to meet all those different people, some of which we related to better than others.

The next morning, our twelfth day on the trail, we left the damp, sunless shelter and crossed the Smoky Mountains Park's northern border, glad to have put that section behind us. I shuddered just thinking about what we went through the day before.

The only person ready before us was a hiker that we hadn't paid much attention to in our distracted evening of warming up and drying our clothes. His name was Whitney Houston and he wore a tattered, gray, cotton tank-top and mid-thigh length, navy running shorts, and he was tanner than any hiker I'd seen yet. His shoulder length, light-brown curly hair was tucked behind a bandana on his head, and his six-foot frame bounded down the trail with a small pack on his back and energy in his step, his hiking poles blurring in his speed. He looked like a strong hiker and I questioned how we had ever caught him in the first place.

Those thoughts about Whitney Houston stayed on my mind for a few fleeting moments, until I soon thought about the food available just a few miles away at the Standing Bear Farm, a hostel that also sold a small amount of groceries. We only needed a few items to get us through the next thirty-three miles to Hot Springs, North Carolina.

Upon arrival at the hostel, an employee politely showed us around and told us about laundry, internet, the kitchen, and groceries. As we walked around the hostel, we couldn't help but liken the scene to the morning after a frat party. There were empty beer cans strewn around the grounds, dirty cups and plates were placed under benches and on window sills, and the other hikers seemed to be in a daze as they milled about the hostel.

There was no denying that there was a part of the thru-hiker community that partied in towns when given the chance, so while it wasn't surprising to see the remains of a party, it was startling to see the effect it had on the appearance of the hostel.

The hostel employee walked in front of us as we approached the store, a small trailer at the top of several creaky wooden steps. He took one sideways glance to the left of the steps, after which his voice went flat with anger.

"You've got to be kidding me."

Just after he said it, a hiker ran up behind us and said, "I'm sorry! I couldn't make it to the bathroom in time. I was just going to clean it up."

The hiker had literally pooped outside the store entrance and without telling anyone, had walked away from it, leaving us to find it first.

"I'm allergic to wheat, and last night I had too many beers. I'm sorry, it just hit me so fast that I didn't know what to do," the hiker explained.

The employee had no sympathy and immediately handed him a shovel to clean it up. We let them sort out the details while we made our way into the store.

Running a hostel seemed like a hard job. While many hikers had good intentions of simply needing a bed, a shower, laundry and food, a handful of them crossed the line of decency.

Matt and I wondered if people were like that before starting the trail or if the freedom of the trail gave them the green light to let loose and live completely beyond their normal. While the trail did create a magical corridor of once-in-a-lifetime events, the trail could also create a false sense of exemption from the rules. It allowed for behavior with much more leniency, and at times, I too fell prey to the feeling of being more special than others.

We saw this predicament with hostels and hikers several more times, but it seemed more prevalent at the beginning of the trail, simply because there were more hikers who had not yet quit. According to the Appalachian Trail Conservancy, out of the 1800-2000 people that attempt an AT thru-hike each year, the chances of finishing are one in four. That is a lot of people that start and a lot of people that don't finish. While those first few hostels see it all, by the time the trail weeds people out, the party crowd is much smaller in quantity and doesn't have quite the impact it did in the beginning.

Later that day, while drying our gear out on the side of a forest road, two other hikers caught up to us who had shared the shelter with us the evening before. They too had found some of the hiking community's behavior unsettling and they voiced their concerns of the trail being crowded with the party community the entire way north.

Fortunately, we had PCT experience on our side, and we assured them that funds and motivation quickly waned with so much town time, and that they would get all the alone time they wanted very soon. By the time we made it to Oregon on the PCT, we saw few thru-hikers beyond a small group of five, and by the time we made it to Washington, I ached for the company of others. I didn't think it would get that sparse on the AT, but I knew that with nearly 2000 miles left until Mt. Katahdin, the trail was sure to weed many people out.

After we left the road we reached the top of Max Patch, a grassy, exposed bald that allowed for panoramic views. We finally thawed out from the day before as we walked across the open space with clear skies above us and temperatures in the seventies. Despite the lack of full foliage on the trees, the views of the hills surrounding us were a beautiful change in scenery from just one day prior. We were glad we hadn't hit the bald yesterday while frosty winds swept over the treeless top.

Atop Max Patch, we could sense the proximity to the town of Hot Springs and aimed to reach it the next day. It felt like the first real town stop because it actually had residents with homes and a grocery store, in comparison to the roadside Neels Gap and the limited Nantahala Outdoor Center.

That evening, after our hiking energy had been recharged by the hike atop Max Patch, our faith in the thru-hiker community was improved as well. We made it to the Walnut Mountain Shelter by early evening, with enough time to talk to the group of six men that had already set up in the full shelter. After I got a closer look at the shelter and realized it was missing a roof, I happily set up our tent. Something told me the shelter didn't do well a couple nights back during the storms in the Smokies. The hikers already set-up inside the shelter took pride the shelter's faults and spoke of their humble abode like it was a luxury condo in the middle of the woods. The company of those men that evening was some of the best on the trail, including that of Mickey, a hiker in his late fifties with a thick Boston accent and gear that looked like it had been purchased from a Coleman sale twenty years ago. Upon first glance at him, I thought, "How in the world did he end up out here?"

While the trail is well-known in many parts of the US, there are still plenty of pockets where the existence of the AT is so far off the radar, that even the activity of hiking is somewhat abnormal.

Still, Mickey had found out about the AT and there he was over two hundred and fifty miles in, with a tangible enthusiasm that was hard to ignore. Though he didn't look like the typical hiker, he was the kind of guy who I looked at and thought, "I bet he has a hell of a story to tell, maybe even hundreds of them." I wanted to sit back, pick a front row seat, and listen to what he had to say, if only to hear the accent and local slang.

We went to sleep in our tent that evening feeling better about the hiking community than we had just a few hours prior.

At the first sign of light, we left the shelter with town anticipation driving our legs. Pizza was the primary motivator, as it had been the choice of town food for Matt the first time around in 2000, and it could still satisfy eleven years later. It was less than thirteen miles to town, much of it downhill, and our footsteps were quicker and lighter than normal. It was a cool, clear morning and I was overcome with a feeling of happiness. I took full breaths of the brisk morning air and smiled back at an equally happy Matt.

The last two miles into town were filled with Matt's memories of hiking into Hot Springs with Animal. They too had stopped at the Walnut Mountain Shelter, with the plan of hiking into Hot Springs the next morning, just as we were doing then. But, Matt and Animal had the shelter to themselves and as the quiet evening surrounded them in the darkness, they felt uneasy about the shelter and didn't want to spend the night there. Rather than lie awake together in the shelter, they night hiked all the way into town, arriving at 4:00 a.m. Matt's memories of hiking downhill into town were that of seeing the lights of the town and its homes dotting the landscape as they descended switchbacks.

Once in town, their arrival unnoticed by the sleeping homes and businesses, they stretched out on the lawn in front of a business and were quick to pack up at the first stirring of the town. After that they spent the day in town and went about their day as if the prior evening's activities were already days behind them.

After hearing Matt's story, I was glad we had company at the Walnut Mountain Shelter and equally glad we didn't have to night hike into town. Instead of a view of the town's lights, we saw homes and farm buildings dispersed around the landscape as we made our steep descent into town. It was comforting to see signs of civilization again.

It was a typical town stop for us in Hot Springs, with the to-do list including pizza, ice cream, food for the next leg of hiking, and laundry. The town lived up to its name as the sun's heat radiated from the blacktop, making the air even warmer than the hottest day in the Smokies. We succumbed to the pull of the town and decided to stay the night, booking the last room available at the Alpine Court Motel. We ate a freshly baked cheese pizza as we sat on top of the motel bed and flipped back and forth between CNN and ESPN to see the current news. It was our thirteenth day on the trail and it marked our first shower. As I stood in the hot water, letting it wash off the accumulation of dirt, sunscreen, and sweat, I thought back to our PCT hike, where my first shower didn't come until twenty-one days into the trail. How I ever withstood that low of a degree of cleanliness, I'll never know.

During our resupply shopping, I created a solution for my blistered hands and fingers. I bought a pair of navy cotton socks at the Dollar General and cut off the toes and made a hole for my thumb. The thin gloves protected my hands and wrists from the sun and I never had a problem again.

We spent the evening lounging outside the motel room with Whitney Houston, who was staying in the room next to us. The first piece of information we wanted to learn was how he'd earned such a unique trail name. He explained that on his first day, he'd inexplicably had the theme song from the movie *The Bodyguard* in his head all day. When others asked him what his trail name was, the first thing that came out of his mouth was, "Whitney Houston."

The men that asked him about his trail name all had tough-guy names like Viper and Snake, and quickly corrected him, "You can't be Whitney Houston! That's a girl's name!"

Right then and there, Whitney knew he could *only* be Whitney Houston with a reaction like that, and he thought to himself, "Hell yeah, I'm Whitney Houston!"

As we listened to his story about how he came to hike the AT, how he got his trail name, and what he thought about the trail so far, all three of us shared a box of Snickers ice cream bars. We also found out that we had caught him because he spent most of his afternoons reading and hadn't considered the prospect of hiking all day. By the end of the night, after hearing about our hiking style, he seemed interested in trying out a different way.

That evening with Whitney Houston fulfilled my expectations of the first real AT town. The town to-do list had been finished, the evening had cooled off at dusk, and we had nothing to do but sit on plastic lawn chairs outside our motel room, with our feet up on the window sills as we ate ice cream bars and talked about life both on and off the AT.

It was perfect.

9 THE SWINGING PENDULUM

It was difficult to leave Hot Springs. It had been a wonderful rest stop and our packs were heavy with new food. To top it off, the weather forecast looked grim for the afternoon and the following day. We thought about staying until the storms passed but the predictions kept changing to later in the day for the storms' arrival, so we took our chances and left town around noon.

While we climbed out of town that day, I tried to take my mind off of town and looked for that familiar hiking rhythm that I'd lost in less than twenty-four hours. The weather forecast was on my mind and I kept an eye on the skies all day.

Despite leaving later in the day, our pace increased after the first climb and I was pleased that we managed to stay dry; leaving town in the rain was a letdown after doing laundry. Twenty miles passed without much effort and we arrived at the Little Laurel Shelter with plenty of daylight. In our company were Whitney Houston and California, and we enjoyed each other's company and conversation as a round of storms rolled in that evening. California was from…well, California, and he was quick to admit that he missed his wife greatly. I was reminded that evening of how lucky I was to have Matt right next to me each night and on every step of the trail.

The weather went from warm and humid to cold, windy and very wet. Wind blew through the cracks in the shelter walls and the rain fell sideways onto the floorboards at the mouth of the shelter. Despite our efforts to sleep against the shelter's back wall, it was shallow and didn't have much room to give. I lay in the shelter that night, already yearning for another clean, dry evening in town.

After an evening of strong winds and heavy rain, the cold trail was calling my name the next morning, and I did not want to answer. I was cozy in my bag and though it was only misting outside, I knew I'd get wet from the water dripping from the leaves above us or from the bushes bordering the trail. My motivation was low after I looked ahead at the guidebook and read that the upcoming section around Bearwallow Gap was "rocky and strenuous."

Once Matt started packing up, I followed, and we were indeed greeted with a difficult morning of miles. The trail was hard enough terrain to begin with and that much more difficult on wet rocks. Though I slipped on almost every step, I tried to stay positive. As much as I wanted to revert to the child inside of me that was ready to whine about the terrain, I listened to my logical self and stayed calm. I was surprised how quickly my mood changed based on the shifts in weather and terrain. I didn't know how to deal with the swinging pendulum because it never stayed in place long enough for me to get a hold of it and control its path. I was at the whim of factors outside of myself and I looked for a solution.

Smarter gear was high on the list. Other than gear, I knew the next best thing, which took more self-honesty than I wanted to acknowledge, was to simply deal with the conditions. They were all part of the experience and if I truly wanted the experience, I'd have to take the good and the bad. There would never be a magic cure-all piece of gear that would keep me dry no matter the downpour, no gear that would keep me warm yet not sweaty in cold, uphill hiking, and definitely no gear to keep me happy despite the amount of precipitation coming down around me. Gear also couldn't rid the trail of rocks. It was apparent that I would have to figure out the enjoyment factor from the inside-out, or it was going to be a long haul north.

These were important realizations as we walked twenty-five unmemorable miles that day. We finished the day's last few miles with Whitney Houston and camped just uphill from a highway at Sams Gap. There wasn't much social time that night, as it was raining and we were all in a hurry to nestle into our shelters for another night of rain. The bright side of camping so close to the highway was that we were able to call home on our cell phone from inside our tent while the rain poured outside. The line between a plush life of creature comforts and a stripped-down life of base existence was often so easy for us to cross that we could nearly be in both worlds at the same time.

The next morning we awoke to frost on our tent and we still had 1500 feet of elevation to gain. The game of staying warm and dry was getting harder to play each day.

Whitney was in no better shape than us, his hands frozen as he tried to pack up his hammock after a cold night of wind literally whipping right under his entire body. The bottom of his hammock was frozen and I smiled as I pictured the traffic warning sign that I saw so often while growing up in Ohio that said, "Bridge Freezes Before Road." The bottom of our tent had stayed comfy warm on the ground while Whitney suffered the consequences of a hammock suspended like a bridge between the trees.

We shot out of our campsite like rockets that morning, eager to warm up on the short uphill to a meadow. Upon arrival at the meadow, we experienced one of the most majestic scenes on the entire trail. I was uncomfortably cold, my hands were frozen, and my teeth chattered in spite of the red fleece hat on my head, but the meadow struck a chord in me with its beauty, and I no longer cared about the weather. A pristine blanket of frost covered every living thing, including the flowers, the trees, the branches, and the newly grown leaves. I video-taped our steps through the meadow because the scene was too beautiful and magical for only my memory to recall.

After we left the meadow we were focused on hiking fast and staying warm, especially since we were still gaining elevation. Five miles into the hike, we walked across the top of a bald, and even within the vicinity of the bald, we were blown sideways by a biting wind. At the top, we each used one of my hiking poles to anchor us to the ground. Once down from the bald and among the wind-breaking trees once again, the sun started to break through the clouds. We looked ahead in the guidebook and saw Erwin, Tennessee, a town that was still thirteen miles away. We debated whether to go in or not, and decided to not decide until we made it to the hostel situated at the road into Erwin.

The afternoon's smooth, fast trail was significantly easier and more pleasant than the morning's. I was thankful yet again for the pendulum swinging in my favor, as it must have sensed my breaking point on the cold bald that morning.

We reached the road to Erwin and learned that the hostel had a dinner shuttle leaving just fifteen minutes later that dropped us off in town for two hours while we ate dinner and grocery shopped, and then picked us up for a ride back to the trail. As we were served platters of Mexican food, with rice, beans, and veggie burritos, I wondered how we ever contemplated *not* going into town for that kind of a treat. The supermarket was also invaluable because it was cheaper and had much more variety than the typical general store or gas station right on the trail. While we tried to stick to stores close to the trail, in order to avoid hitching and to avoid losing the time it took to get in and out of towns that were further away, we still took the opportunity to shop at a supermarket if the logistics were just as easy as staying close to the trail.

That evening, we got back on the trail just as the sun was setting. We had promised to meet up with Whitney Houston just a mile or two into the trail, and while I would have rather been lying on the couch and watching a movie after dinner, we were still AT thru-hikers and we had Whitney Houston to camp with. It was dark within a mile of being back on the trail and we walked so close to homes that we could see interior lights and hear dogs barking. But, we couldn't find Whitney. It was impossible to find his dark green hammock among the trees and I felt like the swinging pendulum had caught us off guard in our satiated state from time in town.

"Whitney! Whitney Houston!" we called out in a hoarse whisper, chuckling each time we called his name. We tried to make noise without making *too* much noise in the proximity of the homes, but we never heard a response.

We walked on, assuming he had hiked further in, and then our whispers turned to desperate calls, and our calls to yells as we walked deeper into the woods, far from any lights. The trail was six-feet wide, a change from the normal single-track trail, and it resembled an old forest road covered in brown, dead leaves. Warning bells went off in my head when I realized the trail was different, and the fear of being off-trail overcame me. Matt felt the same way and we frantically searched for white blazes on the trees with our headlamps, but could find none. The trail followed a well-flowing stream that seemed like raging rapids in the silence of the darkness around us and the combination of limited sight and distorted sounds only added fuel to the fear of being lost. All I wanted to do was stop walking and find Whitney, two things that seemed impossible in the dark, and yet we weren't sure where we were.

Rather than turn back, we moved forward while one person walked with a light on the ground and the other looked for a blaze. We finally saw one as the trail started climbing uphill and were comforted to have solved one problem. The trail narrowed quickly as it continued to follow the stream, but became so narrow and steep that the hope of finding a decent campsite diminished with each step. Once I could no longer handle the unknown, I finally stopped and pulled out the guidebook to see where we were.

We opened the book to see that within a half mile or less was the Curley Maple Gap Shelter, and my heart rate settled as we finished our day's hike by 10:00 p.m. Within minutes, our tent was set-up and we were lying down in our sleeping bags, still recovering from the stressful night-hike.

"What a day," was all we could say in reaction to our sixteenth day on the trail.

10 THE IN-BETWEEN TIME

A stranger to life on the trail once asked me, "What do you do all day?"

"Well," I replied, "we literally walk for about ten hours from one campsite to the next, we eat, we sleep, and we meet other hikers along the way."

Without hesitation, she responded, "That sounds incredibly boring."

I thought about what she said as I waited to say anything. I'd never heard someone just come out and label it a boring lifestyle.

"Well, I guess you're right. It *can* be really boring at times," I said.

I went on to explain what we did in those ten hours, like think about future plans, talk to other hikers, and think about food, to name a few. As I described the trail life, I had to agree with this woman that much of thru-hiking could oftentimes be described as boring. There is always the in-between time, the days that seem to drag on, that aren't very memorable, and that don't seem worth the effort. The daily activities become tedious, some of which benefit from the efficiency created, such as breaking down and setting up camp, and others which beg for more variety, like eating the tenth Snickers bar in four days.

Those were the days when we really appreciated our iPods. While we didn't carry music on the PCT, we carried iPods on the AT and listened to music or lectures for two to three hours a day, particularly during the slump of the late afternoon hours. We'd play our power songs from artists like Green Day, Rage Against the Machine, Red Hot Chili Peppers, and even Kanye West, in order to keep our legs moving at a steady pace.

On the other hand, there are positive aspects of thru-hiking, like a sense of accomplishment from overcoming challenges, a sense of camaraderie among hikers, and an appreciation for towns and kind townspeople. Taking into account the pros and cons of thru-hiking, I believe the in-between miles are the ones that make or break thru-hikers. Anyone can get through the fun times. It's the tough times that define a person and their hike.

Part of the appeal of thru-hiking for me is the effort to find significance in that in-between time, and I could never put my finger on it until a stranger called the trail boring. She reminded me to avoid going on autopilot, just as I had in my previous corporate life, where I strung together months of insignificant days. I didn't want to let that happen on the AT. I realized I could find meaning in the in-between time by honestly recognizing the challenges and still wanting to experience them because I was aware of the benefits that came with those challenges.

Another aspect that Matt and I dealt with during the in-between time was learning how to play the emotions game. He had recently read a psychology book about the different states of emotions that people tend to shift in and out of throughout life, most notably the child and adult states. The child state is characterized by whining, irrational, and inconsolable behavior, while the adult state is rational and careful to avoid falling prey to childish thoughts and actions. It was very easy to regress into the child state while on the trail because of the physical and mental challenges, and the seemingly boring days were often prime breeding ground for a child state.

In the child state, we would snap at each other if we were hungry, we would believe the trail had a personal vendetta against us in its difficult climbs and terrain, or we would wish for the impossible, like an elevator to the top of the mountain. Because of the rawness of the lifestyle and the physical challenges that the trail provided, it was that much easier to revert to the child state and pout all the way north.

Much of our effort over the upcoming days, and many more days to come, was to stay on top of our emotions with a continuous, conscious decision to win the emotions game. We knew that true enjoyment of the trail happened when we were both acting accordingly for each situation. It never got easier to play the emotions game, but the fact that we were aware of its presence and the choice to play it, was a huge step in our progress towards enjoyment of the trail.

The next four days after we left Erwin, Tennessee, after the nerve-wracking night of walking through the woods and calling out Whitney Houston's name, could be described perfectly as in-between time. We had our sights set on the town of Damascus, Virginia, a place that held a gold mine of memories for Matt. It was the entrance to Virginia and I couldn't wait to reach it. The town symbolized real progress in our journey north, and while I looked forward to the creature comforts of town, I also wanted to see a town that was so memorable to Matt.

Yet, one hundred and twenty miles stood between our present location outside of Erwin and our future goal of Damascus. Though it was barely over four days of hiking, plenty of events still occurred in those four days that could hardly be called boring.

We woke up in a blur after the long night of frantically searching for both Whitney and a place to sleep. Our tent was in plain view of the shelter just up a small hill, about fifty feet away, and we felt exposed to the hikers who woke up and saw a tent that hadn't been there when they went to sleep. We packed up with ease, as we'd barely unpacked the evening before, and after we explained our prior evening to the hikers in the shelter, we started a long morning ascent.

Much of my memory that day was the expectation of being overtaken by Whitney Houston. He hiked a blistering pace of four miles an hour, even with a heavy pack, and we simply couldn't keep up. We had a feeling that we passed him somewhere the evening before and that he'd pass us as soon as we stopped for any significant break.

That moment came at our lunch break twelve miles into the day at the Cherry Gap Shelter. The morning fog had cleared just in time for the sun to shine on both the shelter and the picnic bench sitting out front. We had the shelter to ourselves and enjoyed the silence that surrounded the anticipation of a meal, coupled with the simmer of our stove. Halfway into our break, Whitney joined us in the shelter and we finally unwound all the details of the tangled mess that had been last night's hike. He was exactly where we thought he had camped, close to the cabins shortly into the trail, but he hadn't heard us calling his name and had no idea we hadn't showed up until he awoke the next morning. He assumed we had stayed in town, but that morning he talked to the remaining hikers in the Curley Maple Gap Shelter and was surprised to hear we were ahead of him.

While we enjoyed a hot lunch of ramen noodles at the shelter, Whitney snacked on an energy bar and peanut butter, his main staples. He didn't carry a stove and was not very creative with food beyond candy bars, peanut butter, and beef jerky. He was quick to get moving after eating his snack and we said our goodbyes, knowing the odds of seeing him again were just as good as not seeing him again.

Much of the rest of the day was spent in Whitney Houston's shadow. He was the first person we met that stuck with our miles and we had been around him for a week. Yet, he hiked the miles much faster, so we brought up the rear each day as we arrived in camp hours after he finished. Every person we met along the way asked us, "Did you meet that Whitney Houston guy? He's just flying through the trail with crazy miles!"

"Yeah, we did," we normally answered with a smile, though deep down our pride really wanted to say, "Yeah, and we hike the same miles as him."

As we followed in his wake that day, I asked myself why it bothered us to hear others gloat about him, when we in fact liked Whitney himself.

I didn't have many talents along the trail, as I was terrible at building fires and using our stove, and had never honed the ability to properly bear-bag our food. The only aspect I could control was our mileage and I tried to carve our niche in the small world of thru-hikers as the hikers that could cover big miles, no matter the terrain.

We weren't alone in that realm of big-mileage hikers and once we acknowledged that there was room at the top of the mileage scale for others beside ourselves, we found ourselves joining in on the conversations with wonder and awe at Whitney Houston's hiking skills.

"Yeah, he *is* crazy," we replied. "I don't know how he does it, and did you see how fast he hikes?"

To our surprise, we saw Whitney Houston near the end of the day, just before the climb up to Roan Knob. By then we had traded in our resentment for respect and enjoyed the evening with just the three of us at a campsite on the side of the steep hill.

The next day's weather started out beautiful with a brisk morning and a challenging climb to the top of Roan Knob. The day then gradually changed into threatening clouds heading into the afternoon. Matt and I spent most of the morning hiking alone, hopping from bald to bald, and as we climbed and descended each one, we crossed our fingers that the weather would hold out as we made our way over treeless, grassy tops that would have been impassable with lightning.

We were eating an early lunch nearly nine miles into the day at the Stan Murray Shelter when we met Red Oak. He was in his early twenties, of medium build with a thickly grown beard, and he looked low on energy. We only talked to him briefly before he packed up and headed up the trail. As I gathered my things twenty minutes later, I noticed a Steripen next to my pack. It didn't belong to me or the other hikers at the shelter, so we assumed it was Red Oak's. I kept it in my pack, hoping we'd catch him sooner rather than later. I didn't love carrying the extra pack weight, but I also knew how devastating it would be to lose a water purification system.

We made it four miles down the trail when we saw Red Oak stopped at a piped spring, feverishly looking through his pack. He saw us walk up, our smiles hard to hide as we slyly asked, "Missing something?"

"You wouldn't happen to have my Steripen, would you?" He said, joy rising up in his voice.

"Why, we do!"

He threw his arms up in excitement and we were suddenly better friends than we'd been after the short acquaintance at the last shelter. Matt hiked with Red Oak until we reached our destination, the Mountaineer Shelter, while I walked a slower pace behind them. It was rare for Matt to have one-on-one time with other hikers and it seemed like Red Oak was looking for camaraderie.

It wasn't until the next day that I truly appreciated meeting Red Oak, after I talked with Matt and heard Red Oak's story. On one hand, he was wrestling with low motivation to stay on the trail because of its difficulties, and on the other, he felt the need to finish in order to prove himself to his girlfriend. He had quit a job to hike the trail and was counting on the thru-hike to prove his staying power at a task and to prove to his girlfriend that he was good husband material.

I could relate with Red Oak in that wrestling match of the mind, with the desire to quit facing off with the need to continue. I wrestled with myself on a daily basis and the match never got easier. After I heard his story from Matt, I hoped that in the end, staying on the trail won each and every time he visited the idea of quitting.

We never saw him again after that night at the Mountaineer Shelter, and it was months later when the Appalachian Trail Conservancy published their list of 2000 milers of 2011 when I finally confirmed that he finished the trail. Though I'm not sure if he's with the same girlfriend, I imagine that every time he has a memory from the trail, he thanks himself ten times over that he finished the AT.

The next day, day nineteen, was focused on simply putting in the miles towards the town of Damascus, and we hiked another twenty-seven miles further. To our disappointment, the shelter and surrounding area of the Watauga Lake Shelter were completely full, so we pushed on past the shelter in hopes of a good campsite.

Our late-day effort to keep hiking was rewarded with a beautiful, large, flat campsite on the shores of the Watauga Lake. We had views of the lake just outside our tent door and we built a fire to celebrate the campsite as the clear evening cooled off. Though it was customary for us to just pick a flat spot and go with it, our primary motivator being sleep rather than scenery, we enjoyed the plush campsite that night. It hadn't been listed in the guidebook and the little things like flat ground and a fire ring were quick to raise our tired spirits.

We made a comfortable home that night out of our few belongings. Though we'd spent months of living outside with just a backpack of essentials, it rarely hit home at how good it felt to have such few things. Everything about that evening was cozy, from the weather, to our food, to the beautiful campsite.

We awoke the next morning with new energy and a rainy start. The town anticipation was still high and we set a lofty goal for a shelter twenty-nine miles up the trail, despite a hill to start the day. Later that day, after taking a break in a shelter while the sun poked through the clouds, we met Pajamas. He appeared to be in his early thirties and had a thicker build. We knew he was a thru-hiker when we spotted his blond grizzly beard and tiny pack covered in patches from other trails and adventures.

Pajamas also had his sights set on Damascus and he hiked much of the afternoon with Matt while they talked over adventure ideas, like canoeing down the Yukon River. I could only take on one adventure at a time, the AT being my primary focus, and was glad that Pajamas had come along to help pull us towards Damascus as we rolled over the easy afternoon terrain together.

We made it to the Abingdon Gap Shelter around 7:00 p.m. and were surprised to see the area full of nearly twenty-five other hikers. We had spent the last few days with very few people and knew that the pull of Damascus hit everyone that day, as the shelter was the last one within ten miles of town. There was a tangible buzz of energy around the shelter and surrounding tent sites, and an excitement only a town like Damascus could produce.

Damascus is a special town for hikers on several levels. It sits 465 miles into the trail, just before the milestone of reaching 500 miles, and it's on the edge of Virginia, the longest state on the entire trail. It's one of several towns that hikers literally walk right through, following the white blazes painted on telephone poles instead of trees, and it's an incredibly friendly town. The townspeople, the businesses, and the yearly festivities all welcome AT hikers and make them feel special, and while it's not a very populous town, it has everything a hiker needs. It's the epitome of a trail town.

We arrived at the shelter before Pajamas and since I was on water duty while Matt cooked, I walked the steep, rocky, .2 mile descent down to a piped spring behind the shelter. I was oddly happy with my duty, mainly because it was a rare moment of walking without a pack.

Once I returned to the shelter, I saw Pajamas sitting on the picnic bench, talking about pushing on to town. He may have wanted to push on, but his body language said that he was done hiking. He asked about water and when I saw him slump at the mention of a steep, .2 mile descent, I surprised myself and offered up our newly gathered water. Even Matt looked at me with a gaping mouth.

"Really? I can have your water?" Pajamas asked me, stunned that I would sacrifice so great an asset.

"Yeah, don't worry about it. We're not hiking on, and I don't mind going back down for more," I assured him.

At the time, I couldn't explain why I'd given him our water, but looking back, I took it as one of the few opportunities I had to give back while on the trail. Even if it was just a quart of water, it was the most anyone could have done for Pajamas at that moment to help his hike. Throughout the journey of a thru-hike, I was accustomed to taking a lot, whether it was trail magic, town services, or efforts from willing family and friends. It's usually not until after the trail that I can send out thank-you notes or give back to the next year's crop of thru-hikers in the form of trail magic.

I went to sleep that evening with a picture of Pajamas sleeping soundly in a hostel in Damascus, and I looked forward to reaching town the next morning.

Julie Urbanski

11 WELCOME TO VIRGINIA

The morning into Damascus started pre-dawn, thanks to a few early risers in the shelter. We slept in the shelter for a quick takeoff in the morning, but we weren't expecting to hear the opening of zippers or the rustling of plastic bags before sunrise. It was part of the trade-off of sleeping in a shelter versus a tent, the unspoken agreement with others that we were at the whim of a group schedule. I agreed to heed the extra-early wake-up call after the anticipation of coffee drove me to wiggle out of my sleeping bag, click on my headlamp, and pack up for the day.

As we began the easy, gradual descent into town, my legs were stiff and tired after a string of long days. I had also skimped on breakfast in order to take advantage of hitting town on an empty stomach. Breakfast was (and still is) undoubtedly my favorite meal and I wasn't going to mess it up by arriving with a stomach full of energy bars and peanut butter.

It was pleasantly misty that morning in late April, and after taking a quick picture at the Tennessee/Virginia border, excitement for town drove energy into our legs and increased our speed.

In 2000, when Matt and Animal arrived in Damascus, it was the Fourth of July and the town was bustling with people and holiday celebrations. They were also hiking with Rocketcop, a hiker who was finishing the second half of his two-part thru-hike, and who has been a good friend of ours ever since their meeting in 2000. The townspeople were surprised to see thru-hikers so late in the season, but Matt, Animal, and Rocketcop were undeterred by their late schedule and enjoyed the town's abundance of festivities and food. Most importantly, Matt remembered Damascus as one of his favorite towns because of how welcome he felt as a hiker.

We arrived in town by 9:00 a.m., just in time for the post office to open.

We had shared the post office address with friends and family and were giddy with excitement when the employee picked out five boxes from the pile of thru-hiker packages. We carried our good fortunes to a coffee shop nearby and soon unwrapped homemade cookies from a friend, specialty chocolates from my mom, and hiking clothes from Matt's mom. While I enjoyed a freshly baked cinnamon roll and a mug of coffee, I checked my email and uploaded photos to our online journal. At the same time, spitting rain came down outside the shop. My only regret that morning was that I didn't splurge for a second cinnamon roll.

Most of the day revolved around food and errands. We contemplated staying in town for the night, but after spending so many hours sitting and eating, we felt surprisingly refreshed. Damascus turned out to be as magnetic as I had imagined it to be, and as we left town later that afternoon, I already looked forward to returning to it in the future.

We put such little mileage pressure on ourselves that we only walked a mile out of town before setting up our tent for the evening. I joked to Matt that night that I was half-tempted to run down the trail the next morning for a cinnamon roll to start the day.

Our first official day in Virginia was beautiful, with blue skies and warm temperatures. We were twenty-two days into the trail and quickly approaching the five hundred mile mark. It felt like we had crossed a magical line. The grass appeared to be greener and the trees seemed to have grown leaves overnight. We encountered our first fence stiles, which I came to associate with the state of Virginia, along with cows and rolling pastures. I liked the pastures for the easy hiking they provided, but that ease was offset by the break in rhythm from climbing a fence stile. I also learned I have a fear of cows. They are massive animals and surprisingly scary up close, and we had to walk through herds of them. Their large poop piles were also fairly threatening.

The afternoon's hiking was more difficult than the morning, yet the scenery became more beautiful as we closed in on Mt. Rogers. I looked forward to reaching the Thomas Knob Shelter, just past the side trail to the top of Mt. Rogers.

As we walked uphill, approaching the shelter from about a quarter mile away, we saw a group of ten wild ponies galloping across the open mountaintop. Matt had been talking about them all day, wondering if we would see any, and there they were, just as he remembered them from eleven years ago. As he stopped and stood in a spellbound state, he said, "Look, they're wild ponies!"

He said it with the innocent, unabashed excitement of a child, and I should have recognized the sincerity in his voice. I confused his honest preoccupation with the ponies as sarcasm, and I thought he was joking with his tone. Instead, I glimpsed at the ponies, looked in the other direction at the shelter, which was within view, and said, "Uh, huh. Now let's get to the shelter."

"But they're wild ponies!" He exclaimed back, still lost in the wonder of their presence.

Within a split second, his excitement waned and my misunderstanding of him left him saddened. I hadn't been able to see that something was incredibly important to him, and because I wasn't there to share it, I ruined it for him. The passing moment that could only be paused for a brief second had come and gone, and I hadn't even noticed it. As we walked to the shelter in silence, I thought about our future together. I knew he wanted to have children at some point soon, and I wondered what kind of mother I would be if I couldn't even notice when my husband was genuinely excited. Would I do the same to my children, especially when they might find *everything* to be exciting? It had been my chance to practice sharing someone else's excitement, even if it wasn't inherently exciting to me, and I had failed.

While the evening in the Thomas Knob Shelter started out badly for us, it increased in excitement and drama throughout the night. We shared the shelter with Whitney Houston and Bravefoot, a previous thru-hiker out to repeat his favorite section. As we ate dinner at the picnic table outside the shelter, we noticed a hiker had left hundreds of pistachio shells on the ground. It seemed like such a blatant disregard for the cleanliness of the shelter, especially since the shells could attract rodents and animals. Yet, there wasn't exactly a garbage can to put them in or a great place to dispose of them, and no one seemed extremely concerned. All of us left the shells scattered on the ground and went to bed without giving it further thought.

A few hours after falling asleep, we heard crunching noises outside the shelter. In my half-awake state, I assumed it was another hiker arriving late, rummaging through his pack as he cooked dinner in the dark, being polite by not turning on his headlamp. As time passed, the crunching continued and no one ever entered the shelter.

After the crunching grew louder and moved closer to the shelter entrance, Whitney Houston yelled out, "Is it a bear?!?"

"No," Bravefoot answered plainly. "It's the wild ponies."

We clicked on our headlamps to see four wild ponies just outside the shelter entrance, their heads to the ground as they chomped on pistachio shells. One pony's head was practically in the shelter. It was licking the wood of the shelter entrance, right where our sweaty, salty legs had been sitting earlier that evening. I had a hard time falling asleep after that, listening to the crunching just three feet away from my head, nervous that they would step into the shelter. When we awoke the next morning, I was glad to have put the previous night's oddities behind us.

Our elevation of over 5000 feet made for a frosty morning with clear, blue skies. It was Easter Sunday, and though we weren't religious, it was still a special day for us because we often spent it with family. I missed my mom as I thought back to all my childhood Easters of painting pastel-colored eggs and hunting in our house for a basket full of candy. I smiled as I thought of how different that life was from the current one I was leading. A lot of strange twists and turns had led me up to that moment of starting my Easter morning on the Appalachian Trail, with my jacket zipped up to my chin to ward off the cold wind and an energy bar in hand for breakfast.

Though the weather bordered on being uncomfortably cold, we enjoyed the day's hike in the Grayson Highlands State Park. Matt correctly remembered it as a beautiful section of fairly easy hiking. The morning took us across an open, windswept section of trail with panoramic views. It was easy to follow the well-spaced intervals of white blazes painted on pieces of wood that stuck several feet out of the ground, surrounded by piles of rocks as a strong base. Two miles into the day was Fatman Squeeze, a short section through a rock tunnel that was wider than we expected, given the name, and easy to navigate.

About ten minutes after the squeeze, I had the funny feeling of déjà vu, and I turned to Matt as I stopped mid-stride and said, "Haven't we been here before?"

It looked oddly familiar and when I stopped to think about it, the sun was on the other side of us as compared to just twenty minutes earlier. We were walking backwards.

It had already been a slow pace that morning, despite the relatively easy terrain. My heart sank as I realized we had gone the wrong way through Fatman Squeeze, and I cursed the trail for having such a silly, useless section. Our enjoyment of it just minutes earlier was suddenly wiped away. Oh, how easily that pendulum could swing, especially when we didn't follow the blazes correctly and went the wrong way.

We quietly accepted the lost miles and continued on at a quicker pace, eager to make up the lost time. By lunch time, we had barely hiked ten miles and were exhausted for no reason, other than a mild lack of sleep. As we walked down the side of a grassy mountain, towards our next water source, with the exposed sun rapidly increasing the temperatures, we saw a large group of people camped out on the lawn next to the spring. They caught our attention and waved us over to their campsite. I hoped food was involved and crossed my fingers for trail magic.

The campers were previous thru-hikers who had set up a buffet table of food and were grilling out hamburgers, hot dogs, or anything else we might want. I promptly ordered a toasted egg and cheese sandwich and while I waited for it, I ate a plate of chips and salsa, fresh carrots and dip, and most appropriately, a chocolate egg. Over an open fire, one of the trail angels made my sandwich, and before I was even halfway through it, I ordered a second one. Whitney Houston and Bravefoot soon joined us as they made their way down the hill just as we did, surprised to be waved over to a campsite full of people and food. It was the morale boost that all of us needed after the evening's pistachio shell debacle and the morning's slow, bumbling pace.

That afternoon showcased trail magic at its best. It's hard *not* to be inspired to do the same for future thru-hikers when I know just how uplifting it can be to be offered a free burger and a cold beer, or in my case an egg sandwich and a soda. Trail magic was one of the aspects of thru-hiking that also left a lasting impression on Curmudgeon. While he'd heard about our PCT trail magic stories before hiking, he was still shocked each time he experienced the unconditional generosity of trail angels during his own thru-hike.

We left the group of trail angels so full of food that afternoon that we walked the rest of the day without touching our food bags. I felt new energy pumping through me once again after the fresh food and the inspiration from the trail angels. We tented that night at the Trimpi Shelter, our bodies still processing the plates of trail magic and our minds already contemplating the possibility of pizza the next day.

Our engines never stopped burning food and our minds never stopped thinking about it.

The next morning, we woke up to the thought of pizza, and we knew we could order it at the Mt. Rogers Visitor Center. We walked eleven miles of relatively smooth terrain and nibbled on food for most of the morning so we could time our arrival with the peak of our lunch-time hunger. You are probably doubtful or amazed, or both, at how much thought goes into meal time, but with our bodies burning calories all day, much of our logistics revolved around food.

Upon reaching the visitor center, we scanned the menus of the nearby restaurants, our mouths watering as we read about pasta, salad, pizza and breadsticks, and chose the restaurant with the most variety. We had almost arrived too early at 10:00 a.m. because the first restaurant we called had just opened up. When we called, we learned about the extra costs and hoops to jump through to order the pizza, but we didn't care what the requirements were. We just wanted food and we were willing to pay.

"Well, there is a minimum order of $25," they said after hearing that we were at the visitor center.

"That's fine with us," Matt answered.

"There is also a $5 delivery fee," they replied.

"That's totally fine," Matt answered back just as quickly.

"Since we just opened, it will be about an hour because the oven has to warm up," they concluded.

"That's great. We'll wait here," Matt said, in a hurry to put in the order and start the timer on our wait time.

After ordering food, I perused through the visitor center to pass the time and eagerly stepped on an available scale to see if I'd lost any weight. To my surprise and excitement, I weighed in at 118 pounds, a six pound decrease since the start of the trail. The lowest I ever weighed on the PCT was 110 pounds, and while I had no goals of getting that low in weight again, I wasn't going to complain if I was eating everything I wanted and still losing weight. I assumed the weight loss would continue after that point and promised myself I wouldn't hold back on any food put in front of me.

When the food finally arrived, it exceeded our expectations. To reach the minimum order, we purchased a large cheese pizza, a large Greek salad, and an order of garlic bread. We sat on the lawn as we moaned in celebration over each bite, rotating boxes of pizza, salad, and bread between the two of us as we gradually finished every bite. It was the second day in a row of eating town food while on the trail and we were at ultimate emotional highs.

As we packed up to leave, we looked at the weather forecast posted on the wall outside the visitor center and saw thunderstorms spanning the next few days. That particular day's forecast had just a twenty percent chance of rain. It was also a Monday. Though we'd had a bad track record with Mondays so far, we assumed we were safe based on the warm morning we'd just spent lying on the grass outside the visitor center.

As if in response to that doubt, the winds around us changed in both direction and strength. We first looked up at the sky, then down at each other, and didn't need to say what we were both already thinking. We nodded in agreement that it was time to pack up and leave before the weather hit us.

The weather turned from great to bad rather gradually and we walked eight miles in nothing more than a light, steady rainfall. Then we heard thunder in the distance and our pace picked up to a near-run because we could tell the storm was rapidly approaching us. A few miles away was the town of Atkins and we hoped to make it to a gas station before the storm really hit. The miles leading up to town took us across open fields and near power lines. We saw lightning in the distance and we knew the storm was closing in on us faster than we could run to shelter.

As we neared town, it felt like we were caught in a war zone. We ran across the exposed fields of high grass, crouched as low to the ground as possible while we timed our runs with the lightning. The rain picked up in intensity and within just a mile of town, the rain turned into hail. We wore shorts and short-sleeve t-shirts, and as the pebble-sized hail hit us with surprising force, we cried out loud, "I'm hit! I'm hit!" Our necks and forearms were red with welts. In the thick of the hail, we ducked under a patch of bushes for cover. We sat under the dripping leaves, unsure what to do next.

After sitting under the bushes for the bulk of the hail storm, our body temperatures dropped and we needed to walk or put on more clothing. We decided to run the rest of the way, no matter the rain or hail. Lightning was still off in the distance and the storm was moving out. The rain stopped just as we reached Atkins and walked towards a gas station. We had planned on going into the gas station for extra snacks, but in our current state, we were completely drenched and dripping water from our packs, our clothing, and our hair. It didn't feel right going into a business looking like that and trailing that kind of a mess in our wake. We stood on the outside corner of the building, frozen in indecision under the awning.

As we stood outside the gas station, a woman emerged from her car to offer us a towel to dry off with and dry t-shirts to change into. She had been waiting for the storm to blow over while she sat in her car and was shocked to see us walking in it. We thanked her for the dry towel and shirts and made our way into the gas station. The gas station attendant was understanding of our shell-shocked state. She let us sit in the closed restaurant section of the building in order to gather ourselves and dry off, and later told us of her admiration for the determination and perseverance of thru-hikers. I was just grateful she let us inside and was all the more flattered to hear that she liked thru-hikers.

While Matt called home and checked email, I dried our clothes with the bathroom hand driers and felt about as close to homeless as we could get. Before leaving, we picked up more food for the next few days, our best options being candy bars and bags of chips, and said goodbye to a gas station that had been a mini-resupply point. Gas stations weren't our top choice for groceries, but since it was right on the trail and made for the easiest logistical stop, we accepted the trade-off of proximity to the trail for a plethora of unhealthy choices. Now that we go to gas stations for the sole purpose of gas rather than groceries, we look at the aisles of food and ask each other, "How in the world did we grocery shop from these places?"

Hunger, that is how.

That night, we camped with Whitney Houston at the Davis Path campsite, where he'd been in his hammock for hours and had not even noticed the storm. We had been through our personal version of a war zone while Whitney had barely noticed rain drops on his hammock's rain fly. By sunset, we were exhausted from all that had transpired that day. We also went to bed fearing the upcoming string of weather. If a day with just a twenty percent chance of thunderstorms had turned out like that, I was scared to find out what kind of weather would we get with an eighty or ninety percent chance.

Julie Urbanski

12 THE PUSH

Out of all the feelings that will get a person up and moving, fear has to be one of the strongest motivators. We had come to fear the thunderstorms on the AT and had already found ourselves in precarious situations that we were in no rush to repeat. Mondays had proven themselves to be notoriously bad weather days, yet we knew the other days of the week were not off-limits.

The big news on the trail was about the predicted storms on Wednesday night. It was Tuesday morning when we walked away from the Davis Path campsite, and not only did we have fear of the storms driving our legs, we had the town of Pearisburg to fuel the fire, a town eighty-five miles away. The guidebook elevation remained relatively steady and the terrain allowed for swift, easy footing. A plan was put in place as we contemplated the next few days of hiking.

We called it The Push and made it our goal to reach the Wapiti Shelter by Wednesday evening in order to stay in a shelter in case the impending thunderstorms amounted to their predicted proportions. The shelter was sixty-eight miles from our starting point and only seventeen miles from Pearisburg. It seemed like the ideal plan in order to secure a shelter from the storm and to reach town within two and a half days. The plan was to hike thirty miles one day and thirty-eight the next to make it to Wapiti.

One thing to be noted here is that we often created plans in order to spice up the routine on the trail. While we never *had* to hike big miles, or *had* to push to town, we enjoyed creating a new challenge out of every day, whether that challenge was to avoid impending weather, meet a post office deadline, or time a restaurant meal. Whatever the reason, we usually came up with a plan to increase our motivation to cover the miles, and most of the time, it worked.

The thirty-mile day before the Wapiti Shelter was easy hiking and the weather held out as we made our way across exposed, windswept pastures. The wind was so strong in some sections that four-foot high grass lay flat on its side, like it had finally given up and succumbed to the wind. Overall, it was an uneventful day of miles that ended at the Jenkins Shelter, where we were greeted by twelve other hikers, including Whitney Houston. Only the possibility of rain and the proximity to town could explain such a large group around a shelter, and after eating a quick dinner at the picnic table outside the shelter, we retired to our tent for an anticipated night of sleep.

The first day of our plan to push to the Wapiti Shelter was complete, but our odds of doing it again the next day, with an additional eight miles, seemed slim. It was unlikely that we'd make it with how tired we felt after just thirty miles, but we decided to aim for it, knowing we could stop at the Jenny Knob Shelter twenty-four miles away if the day was going poorly. The only problem with that plan was that the Jenny Knob Shelter only fit six people, and we were surrounded by twelve hikers also headed north, who would most likely aim to hike twenty-four miles rather than a shorter fourteen miles to a shelter .3 miles off-trail. Every day was a numbers game with the shelters and the number of hikers around us, and we doubted there were many of them planning to hike thirty-eight miles to the Wapiti Shelter. We at least knew Whitney Houston was in the mix, as he seemed able to handle any mileage, and handle it fast.

The Push was still in effect the next day when we woke up and started hiking before dawn. We wanted to give ourselves a chance to make it to the shelter before sundown and before any rain. With better odds of reaching the shelter, the prospect of being in town by lunch the next day was also becoming more likely. According to the elevation chart in the guidebook, the day looked easy, but we knew that could get us in trouble by assuming too much.

We agreed to make it a nose-to-the-grindstone kind of day. All whining was off-limits, even if the inevitable foot pain set in before the day's hiking was over. We both wore running shoes that already had a few hundred miles on them before hiking and we were nearly six hundred miles into the trail. Most runners and hikers only put around five hundred miles on a pair of shoes, but we wore them until they fell apart. We wanted to squeeze every possible mile out of them before throwing them away. It was also hard to convince ourselves to spend money on new shoes that would immediately get wet, muddy, and worn down by the trail.

The morning miles were easier than we expected and our legs found their cruise control before the morning fog even burned off. While we planned on taking as few breaks as possible, it was imperative that we stop momentarily at the crossing of US 52, the road into Bland, Virginia. We arrived at the road at 10:00 a.m. and as we paused to tip our hats to the town, Matt recounted the story which explained why Bland will forever be tattooed in his mind as the most memorable town on the AT.

Matt and Animal shared a tent at the start of their hike but sent it home by Damascus and relied solely on the shelters. They were still hiking with Rocketcop in the section around Bland, and one evening, Rocketcop felt like hiking further while Animal was done walking for the day. Matt joined Rocketcop in going further, knowing he would cowboy camp in the open air in whatever spot they chose. The weather had been clear for the last few days and the skies didn't show any sign of rain.

After sleeping for a few hours, Rocketcop in his one-person tent and Matt in the open air, Matt woke up to pouring rain. He huddled under a small tarp not much bigger than his sleeping pad, and was entirely soaked after an hour, despite every effort to stay dry. Night hiking in the rain seemed like a better option than sitting under a tiny tarp. Matt packed up and headed for the next shelter to spend the rest of the night's rain under cover. As he hiked, his headlamp lit the way and bugs flitted around the light on his forehead. Soon after he started walking, he stopped in a sudden panic. A moth that had been hovering around his headlamp flew straight into his ear.

He stood frozen in fear and thought, "What the hell do I do?" After the initial shock of the moth flying into his ear, he tried everything he could to get it out. It was not only alive, but also flapping its wings on his inner ear every few seconds. First he shined his headlamp into his ear, hoping the moth would follow the light. Then he tried using tweezers from his small Swiss Army knife to grab the moth from his ear. When that didn't work, he cupped the mouth of his water bottle to his ear as he tipped his head over and tried to wash the moth out with an influx of water. Nothing worked, and with each vibration of the moth's wings on his ear drum, Matt was driven a little crazier. For hours, he could think of nothing but the moth in his ear and the torture of its wings fluttering against his inner ear every thirty seconds.

He hiked on to the next major road crossing and decided to hitchhike into town and get to the nearest hospital. That road was I-77, and that town was Bland, Virginia. He passed up US 52 because of the lack of traffic on the road and he hiked a mile further to the interstate, where he was sure a car would pass him. The first car to pass him as he stuck out his thumb was a police cruiser, but Matt didn't care what the laws were. It was around 5:00 a.m. and in the earliest of morning light, Matt desperately pleaded with the policeman to take him to a hospital, "Please, you've got to help me! I have a bug in my ear and it's driving me crazy!"

The sight of a dirty hiker is enough to turn heads on any roadside or in any town, but the sight of a hiker nearly mad with a story about a bug in his ear must have convinced the policeman that Matt had a real emergency. He let Matt climb in the back of the car as he radioed to the main station, "Uh, I've got a hiker here with a bug in his ear. Is there anyone who can take him to the hospital?"

A nearby volunteer ambulance picked up Matt and took him to the emergency room, sirens blaring and lights flashing. Once at the hospital, a doctor flushed the moth out with a turkey baster tool. After the moth finally plopped out into a dish of water, its wings still flapping with life, the doctor sarcastically asked Matt, "Would you like to keep it?"

Matt was finally relieved of the moth, and after such a stressful ordeal, he enjoyed the plush hospital bed and the free breakfast-in-bed. The same doctor that removed the moth had just finished his shift, so he took Matt back to the trail. Matt recovered his backpack from where he left it, behind a crop of bushes. He hiked on for a few hours that morning and upon reaching the Jenny Knob Shelter, he fell asleep in exhaustion until Animal and Rocketcop showed up around lunchtime. Rocketcop hadn't known that Matt left in the middle of the night and woke up confused by the empty space where he'd seen Matt the night before. Animal had no idea that anything out of the ordinary had happened.

Though the story of the moth in Matt's ear has grown more entertaining over the years, it was a traumatizing experience when it happened. After that night, anytime Matt hiked, he wore a bandana around his ears. He wasn't taking any chances, whether it was day or night, and even now he covers his ears if a moth is near. His story became legendary on the trail and his name was nearly changed to Moth Man, but he preferred to put the experience behind him and continued to be called Optimist.

As we passed Bland, Virginia, that morning on our thirty-eight mile day, Matt shuddered as he remembered the feeling of the moth's wings flapping in his ear. The town held a memory for Matt that was anything but bland. (I couldn't resist.)

After the moment to remember the moth story, we pushed past Bland and didn't let up again until we made it to the Jenny Knob Shelter, twenty-four miles into the day. It was only 2:00 p.m. and we had plenty of energy and daylight left for the remaining fourteen miles. We rewarded ourselves with an hour lunch break as we prepared ourselves for the next push to the Wapiti Shelter. The weather showed no signs of immediate storms, but the wind felt more questionable than just a breeze, and we knew the kind of storm that it was carrying our way. We had already tented in one too many storms, so we continued on that afternoon, hoping there was room at the shelter. It only fit six people and we knew both ourselves and Whitney Houston were headed for it, so that only left three little spots for any other hikers that were already ahead of us.

The remaining miles were even easier than the morning as we followed a smooth, wide trail that hugged a stream for miles. The wind picked up as the afternoon turned to early evening and we feared that we would arrive at the shelter too late. We made our way along quiet logging roads just before the shelter, the silence of the woods unsettling to our nerves. The forest was so dense that the wind couldn't penetrate it, or maybe it was the calm before the storm. We held our breath as we walked up to the shelter from behind it, and as we peered around the corner of the side wall, we exhaled a sigh of relief as we saw just four other hikers inside.

Whitney Houston and three other hikers had already cooked dinner and built a fire before we arrived at 8:15 p.m., and we immediately claimed our spots along the inside wall of the shelter. We weren't taking any chances of someone else arriving to take our places. The first priority as we sat on the shelter floorboards was to take off our shoes. My shoes seemed to be glued to my feet and disrupting the equilibrium that they had found hurt more than I had expected. We went to bed with surprisingly clear skies and increasing humidity. I lay awake for some time, nearly too exhausted to sleep, the pain in my feet increasing with each pulse of blood that pounded through them, and I wondered if the forecasts would prove to be correct.

At 1:00 a.m., we all awoke to a storm gathering strength and speed as the lightning and thunder quickly met each other right on top of the shelter. All six of us were lined up across the shelter floor, our heads facing out towards the mouth of the shelter. The lightning was so bright that I could look down across the line of people and see their faces watching the oncoming storm. We stayed still as the drizzle of rain turned to a downpour and as the claps of thunder drowned out all other sounds.

Just as the storm was at its worst, the wind changed directions and pebble-sized hail blew sideways, halfway into the shelter. In unison, each one of us hurried to pick up our sleeping bags and crouched at the back of the shelter, protecting ourselves with our sleeping pads as shields from the hail and rain. I didn't know whether to laugh at the comical picture we made of ourselves, huddled together at the back of the shelter with our sleeping pads as our makeshift shields, or to cry in fear that the storm could get even worse than it was.

After the wind died down and the storm moved on, we swept the hail out of the shelter with a broom, a common sight in most shelters, and tried to go to sleep. As I lay there next to Matt, my eyes wide open in shock as I stared above me at the shelter ceiling, I said to Matt, "Thank goodness we pushed to get here."

Julie Urbanski

13 THE PEARISBURG EFFECT

The previous night's storms cut through the heat and we woke up to frigid temperatures. Pearisburg was just seventeen miles away and our motivation to walk was high, despite having to leave our warm sleeping bags and face the cold morning. We felt a strong sense of camaraderie as all of us in the shelter recounted the unforgettable 1:00 a.m. wake-up call of hail. We planned on sharing a hotel room with Whitney Houston and saw in the guidebook that there was a Mexican restaurant in town. Chips and salsa were calling my name and I let the thought of food once again push the pace.

Water covered much of the trail as we made our way uphill, the water cascading down towards us like we were walking upstream. We gave up on dry shoes after the first mile of hopping from one dry edge of the trail to the other, and soon walked right through the middle of the trail where the water flowed the deepest and the swiftest. We knew we would dry our shoes in a warm hotel room that night, so we traded wet shoes for faster miles. The icy water felt good on our sore footpads and I actually enjoyed the ice bath on my feet and lower legs. We'd only stopped walking just ten hours before, allowing for little recovery time.

Aside from difficult footing around Angels Rest, the last high point before we descended 2000 feet into town, the rest of the miles clicked off quickly under our feet. I let the downhill carry me into Pearisburg, some sections so steep that I slid down the trail, and Matt called his Dad from our cell phone once we were within a mile of town.

The main topic of conversation was our indecision about whether or not we would attend the upcoming family vacation in mid-June in Myrtle Beach, South Carolina. We had already paid for a week-long vacation in a condo by the beach, but had made the plans before the trail ever came into the picture, and well before quitting our jobs was on our radar. On the other hand, we had never taken a complete day off while thru-hiking, including the PCT and the current AT, and we weren't sure we wanted to start. The other factor in our decision was the fact that the trail was actually going quite well. We were averaging about twenty-three miles a day and we estimated a finish time of early July if all stayed on course. The last remaining long-distance trail on our minds was the Continental Divide Trail, the CDT. It would be a late start for the trail, but with already having our hiking legs and hiking mentality, we considered hiking the CDT directly after the AT. Taking a week off at the beach would delay our start on the CDT, therefore jeopardizing our ability to finish it before the cooler fall weather arrived in the mountains. It was the first time we'd voiced the plan to anyone other than ourselves and it was a little scary for me to hear it out loud.

Matt's dad was surprised to hear the plans, but like any other time he heard Matt propose one of his ideas, he took it in stride, asked a few logistical questions, and let the subject change, knowing nothing was final until we actually made it happen. No decisions were made about vacation or the CDT that afternoon.

We walked into Pearisburg at 1:00 p.m., just in time to meet Whitney Houston at the Mexican restaurant for three baskets of chips and salsa and three large, oval plates loaded with the typical Mexican fare of burritos, rice, and beans. While we sat in the restaurant, we had our first update in days on the news in the real world. CNN was broadcasted on every TV in the restaurant and the headline story was about the destructive tornadoes in Alabama that touched down the prior evening.

Several thoughts crossed my mind upon watching the news. First, I was shocked that we had just slept outside in the tornadoes' peripheral storms. I didn't doubt the possibility of a tornado on the trail and realized that the storm last night was a little too close for comfort.

Next, even though we'd only been on the trail for less than a month, a drop in time compared to the other twenty-nine years of my life, I already felt far removed from the world portrayed on CNN. I was so deeply entrenched in the trail life that watching the news was like hearing about events in another country. It was hard to equate the lives of those on TV with our own lives of walking all day and sleeping in a tent.

Lastly, I thought about Curmudgeon and wondered where he had spent the night of storms. I knew he avoided sleeping in shelters because of the symphony of snorers, as he called them, but I hoped the forecasts had convinced him to opt for a shelter over his tent.

At that point, he had just passed Erwin, Tennessee, three hundred miles behind us. He too had heard about the intensity of the upcoming weather and spent the night of the Alabama tornadoes at the Cherry Gap Shelter. Ironically, while we were sweeping hail out of the front of the shelter, he was sleeping soundly with overcast skies that never amounted to even a drop of rain.

I later found out that Curmudgeon still had his fair share of storms to speak of, most memorably the one atop Clingmans Dome. Even he can't explain why he did it, but through sixty to eighty mile per hour winds, in dense fog with little sight-distance, and in heavy rain that hurt when it hit him, he climbed to the top of the Clingmans Tower, *above* Clingmans Dome. He doubted his chances of ever returning there and as he walked the ramp to the top, he pulled himself up by the handrail, both hands tightly clenched to the railing while he leaned into the wind. Halfway to the top he met another hiker on his way down that delivered the news that rangers were advising everyone to stay off the mountain and seek shelter. Regardless of the advice, he was determined to get to the top, even if he couldn't see a damn thing once he made it there. He finally reached the top of the tower and he'll never forget the circumstances surrounding that moment. Nor will he ever regret it.

During our twenty-four hour period in Pearisburg, we consumed A LOT of food, whether in a restaurant, from the grocery store, or from one of the care packages we received from friends and family. I had to loosen my hip belt as I waddled out of town the next day. For the first time in days, I wasn't anticipating my next meal. I didn't even want to think about food because I felt so uncomfortably full.

The hiking was fast outside of Pearisburg. After a quick gain of about 1600 feet, we walked atop a ridge for the rest of the day's miles and cruised through twenty miles until we dipped down to the Pine Swamp Branch Shelter. By the time we arrived with the setting sun, the area around the shelter was already dimly lit. The shelter sat on the side of a hill, the area choked by the surrounding trees, and I couldn't tell if the area ever received daylight with all the foliage above it.

The next day, we realized two things: we no longer appeared to be thru-hikers and I did not pack enough food.

With the oncoming heat of summer, the increasing temperatures seemed exponentially hotter to Matt. He'd grown a full beard in his month on the trail and the heat, the itchiness, and the feeling of a lack of cleanliness were worthwhile reasons for him to shave it off in Pearisburg. He wasn't quite sure it was acceptable thru-hiker code or not, but he didn't care what line he crossed in not only shaving off the beard, but in also carrying a razor so he could shave more often. Two rules were broken in shaving the beard and carrying unnecessary pack weight, but a continuously clean-shaven face was invaluable to Matt. He loved the new look.

The result of his lack of facial hair was that no one knew where to place us on the hiker spectrum. Our clothes kept getting dirtier, our head hair grew longer, and our gear appeared filthier, but his face rarely showed more than the stubble of a few days' worth of growth. Were we really clean thru-hikers or really dirty weekenders? Our status fell from, "You must be thru-hikers," to "How long you guys been out here?" The assumptions turned to open-ended questions as we approached others on the trail and in town. It was oddly satisfying to be mysterious to people who didn't quite know what category to put us in.

Another effect of our Pearisburg time was that I ate too much food. I was so full of food by the time we resupplied that I couldn't imagine eating another bite. I didn't want to look at food, much less shop for it, and I skimped on my resupply. By lunch time on the day after Pearisburg, I knew I wouldn't have enough food to reach the next town of Daleville, about sixty miles away. My rations got smaller and smaller as I enviously eyed Matt's food, knowing he'd packed plenty for himself. While we made joint decisions about the meals we carried, we chose our snacks as individuals because we tended to have such different tastes.

We awoke to our thirtieth day on the trail, May 1, to a misty, foggy morning. I was already in a bad mood because of my lack of food and I didn't feel like walking in damp weather. Nine miles into our day, we passed the Audie Murphy Monument, a monument for the most decorated American soldier of World War II. There was a dense, low-lying fog all morning and we couldn't see more than twenty feet ahead of us. Being a Sunday morning, more people were out on the trail and a group of middle-aged runners ran past us, enjoying their Sunday morning run along the trail.

I was slightly jealous of them as I remembered our life in Washington. We'd run so many Sunday long runs on the trails in Forest Park in Portland, Oregon, for the last few years, and I missed the freedom and lightness that came with trail running. My pack seemed to weigh more after watching them glide over the trail with quick, effortless steps. We kept walking as I reminisced about life in Vancouver, the negative memories fading as I looked back on my favorite aspects of the life we had made there.

Later that day we climbed Cove Mountain, which is well-known for its .1 mile side trail to Dragons Tooth, a stone monolith, which normally held incredible views. Our foggy, misty day not only blocked out any possible views, but it also made for difficult hiking on the slippery, rocky trail. We chose to skip the side trail to Dragons Tooth, and unfortunately, it's another extra step that I regret not making on the AT. We stood by our adage that we avoid hiking extra miles, and I regret not seeing a place that I may never be in a position to see ever again. I don't want to repeat that climb up or down Cove Mountain any time soon, especially since it had metal handles in the vertical rock surfaces, and though the views may have been less than stellar that day, I could have made the effort to find something of significance in them.

Dragons Tooth was one of those places along the trail that others excitedly asked us, "Did you go to Dragons Tooth?" and we replied, "No, we didn't want to do anything extra." I wince even now when I picture the disappointment in their expressions. I used to be an extra credit person who made every possible effort in school, necessary or not. If there was an opportunity to go above and beyond the call of an average student, I never missed the chance. What changed about me? What was it about hiking that made me so lazy and unable to see future effects of my present efforts?

These are difficult questions to answer as I sit at my kitchen table, under a roof, and look back at a day where I was cold, wet, and tired from hiking difficult terrain. While I understand the more challenging situations of the trail versus the comfortable environment at home while I ask myself these questions, I still end up puzzled and angry with myself. These are questions I'd like to sew on my pack as I prepare for future hikes so I'll remember to ask them of myself in the most difficult of moments.

That evening we arrived to a crowded Catawba Mountain Shelter. The town of Daleville was less than eighteen miles away and after seeing only two other hikers all day, we were suddenly among a group of ten thru-hikers. We set up our tent on damp, squishy ground as the day's fog finally cleared for a beautiful sunset.

We spent the evening eating much of our food. I played sad eyes to Matt over dinner because I didn't have any extra snacks to spare and barely had enough for the next day. He reluctantly tossed me a Little Debbie Star Crunch like I was a pitiful puppy that had gotten the better of his logic. I felt guilty taking his food, but I also knew that a hungry Julie was not a nice Julie. Matt knew that too.

The next morning was sunny and the shelter was buzzing with talk of McAfee Knob. If you've ever perused through photos of the AT, you've most likely seen McAfee Knob, one of the most photographic points along the trail. We were lucky to wake up to clear, blue skies and perfectly warm temperatures before heading up to the scenic overlook.

The hike to the knob was ridiculously easy as we cruised over a smooth path that felt like pavement on our trail-tested legs, and our excitement for Daleville increased with the easier hiking. As we enjoyed the views up top and snapped a few photos, my grumbling stomach was quick to remind me that food awaited us in town.

Matt's first memory of Daleville from 2000 was the view through the trees of the red roof of Pizza Hut as the trail approached the road, and that memory was solidified when we faced the exact same view as we reached town. We crossed the road and immediately ordered two large pizzas for the two of us while Whitney Houston, who had arrived an hour before us, continued his three hour binge on the buffet of soup, salad and bread sticks.

While sitting in the booth, awaiting our pizzas, Matt recounted his other memory of Daleville from 2000. After pizza, he and Animal made the mile trip out of town to the post office to pick up care packages. Being mid-July, the summer was almost at its peak of heat and humidity, and they were uncomfortably warm. They walked out of the post office and noticed the backyard of the house next door, particularly the pool in the backyard of the house next door. Reasoning with each other that they had nothing to lose, they knocked on the front door and asked the homeowner if they could swim in the pool and cool off.

The woman at the door was more than happy to oblige and she served them ice-cold lemonade as they swam in the pool. We have a photo of them bobbing on the surface of the pool in inner tubes, glasses of lemonade in-hand, their expressions showing tickled disbelief. Their smiles were stretched wide under patchy beards that only nineteen-year-olds could grow. It is an image I will never forget, that symbolizes all that is inspiring about thru-hiking, from the generosity of strangers to the genuine happiness with life's serendipitous fortunes.

After Matt and Animal had cooled off in the pool, they headed back up the trail to the Fullhardt Knob Shelter, just five miles out of town, where Rocketcop had gone instead of the post office. He knew something was up by the grins that Matt and Animal wore as they approached the shelter that night.

"You won't believe what just happened," Matt said to Rocketcop, as many trail-legendary stories often began.

We followed the footsteps of Matt's 2000 hike later that afternoon as we walked out of Daleville and camped outside of the Fullhardt Knob Shelter for our thirty-first night on the trail. My pack was heavy with several days' worth of food and it made me happy to know I could eat until I was full, and then some. We packed out extra pizza from lunch, I carried soda in my water bottle, and we enjoyed a little piece of town on the picnic bench that evening. The shelter's location atop the mountain overlooked the twinkling lights of civilization in the valley below, and I felt intensely happy. Whitney moaned from his hammock, too full to move, while I looked forward to the next day's rations, knowing I had packed plenty of food.

We looked at the next few days of hiking in the guidebook that night and saw that we'd soon enter the Blue Ridge Parkway, a section I'd only heard about, but couldn't envision. I felt overwhelmingly positive as we fell asleep that night, happy with our short but eventful pause in Daleville.

14 THE BRP

There is a reason Virginia came to be my favorite AT state, and a part of that is because of the Blue Ridge Parkway (BRP). It is a road that winds through the mountains while the trail zigzags over it, crossing it several times a day for nearly a hundred miles, and something about it was magical to me. Each time we emerged from the trail to cross the road, I stopped to inhale the view of the road disappearing at a bend and into the landscape, as if the possibilities were limitless beyond that bend. The views never got old and I looked forward to every road crossing.

Matt and I have taken numerous road trips in our lives, including five cross-country drives on different horizontal highways, countless trips up and down the East and West Coasts, and a tour of the southern states. We have covered much of the US on foot, on a bike, or in a car, and while we love our bodies as the engines, we also love our car and the freedom it gives us. The Blue Ridge Parkway's smooth, open road represented that freedom, and we appreciated its presence. Many hikers balked at the intrusion of civilization running right through the trail, but we welcomed the sight of something we could relate to so well. I was more motivated to keep going for the sheer desire to finish, go home, pack up our car, and come back to drive the parkway.

The terrain eased up considerably as we crossed the BRP several times that first day, and each mile increased the enjoyment I found in hiking that section. Twenty-seven miles into our thirty-second day and almost 750 miles into the trail, we arrived at my favorite shelter, the Bryant Ridge Shelter. It was a fairly new shelter with two levels and a covered porch that wrapped around half the shelter. We set up our sleeping bags on the top floor, which we had to ourselves in the twenty-person capacity shelter. Only three other hikers joined us that night, including Legion, a name I'd already heard tossed around among other hikers.

He looked to be in his late-twenties and was energetic with shoulder-length, curly hair, frizzy with the humidity. His eyes bulged slightly as he talked about the trail with an excitement and unconditional love that I had yet to see on the trail. He was also a little rough around the edges, with a personality that I had a hard time warming up to.

Legion had already been at the shelter when we arrived, and before we even loosened our pack straps, he asked us several questions about us and our hike. Not that I didn't want to answer those questions. I just wanted a chance to sit down and take off my shoes before I had to think much further than dinner. Even though we gave off the vibes that we weren't in the mood to talk, he prodded us for conversation as we set up our space in the shelter.

At first, I was annoyed with Legion's enthusiasm and in-your-face social tactics. The reason I came to look past his traits and toss aside the rumors was silly, but the moment I tried to see Legion beyond the surface was when he gave me a Double-Stuffed Oreo. It was the smartest way to make a friend. Give me food.

And it worked.

After that, I listened to everything Legion had to say. I barely got a word in on the conversation, but it gave me more enjoyment to just sit back and listen, which I doubt many hikers had patiently done. As I sat there listening, I saw a guy who had found something he loved so much that it was hard for him not to share it with others. He loved everything about thru-hiking, about the AT, about the community, the food, the lifestyle, and even the crazy weather. I admired his unconditional love and the way he wore it like a loud logo across his chest. I would say I was even a tad jealous of his love and honest passion.

Whenever we met other hikers down the trail who talked about Legion, I refrained from adding fuel to the rumors and talked positively about him and his love of the AT.

The next day's skies started off gloomy. The previous night's thunderstorms, which we watched from the comfort of our top level in the shelter, had once again brought in cold, foggy weather. As I lay in my sleeping bag, I wondered how Legion could love a trail that had such extreme swings in weather and terrain. I was so comfortable in bed, with the smell of freshly damp wood around me, that it was hard to get moving. No one else in the shelter showed any signs of movement, nor had anyone taken their morning pee break. It was hard to get ready when I didn't even hear the rustle of another sleeping bag.

Like other cold, damp mornings, when it was hard to find motivation, I counted on my food to get me going. I had packed so much food that I estimated about 4500 calories worth of food per day, a jump of at least 1500 calories per day from the previous resupply. The stretch from Pearisburg to Daleville had instilled in me a real fear of hunger, and I assured myself it wouldn't happen again.

I started my day with a blueberry toaster pastry as I packed up, and we left our comfy shelter for an uphill climb of 2200 feet over the first five miles of the day. The morning miles were slow and hours passed before we crossed my new favorite friend, the BRP. An upside to the day was when we crossed the BRP midday, only to be greeted by a trail angel who'd brought donuts from Daleville, courtesy of Peanut, another thru-hiker just ahead of us. The trail angel had been handing out donuts all morning, and since she was driving home after she met us, we finished off the box of the six remaining donuts. At that point in the hike, we considered it a small snack.

The donuts couldn't have come at a better time that day because the trail's elevation was much more of a roller coaster than the previous day. Even the weather fluctuated greatly, from hot to cold and from clear to rainy, and each side of the mountain revealed a different weather pattern. I stopped at least ten times to put on my rain jacket, only to take it off less than a mile down the trail because I was sweating so profusely and was soon wetter from sweating than from the misty rain coming down.

We crossed the James River footbridge later that afternoon under white skies, as a heavy fog had moved in. As we made our way to the Johns Hollow Shelter, we quickly saw that we wouldn't be camping alone. A group of twenty-five boys, ranging from ten to fifteen years old, along with four adult leaders, had already set up long tarps spanning most of the open space near the shelter.

While I wasn't excited to see so many kids, I also didn't want to hike further than the twenty-seven miles we'd already covered. We chose a campsite a good distance away from the group of boys and the selfish side of me hoped they had extra food. Groups that were out for short hikes were known for bringing extra food and thru-hikers tended to benefit from their overzealous packing.

Matt introduced himself to the leaders as I set up the tent and we found out that they were part of a wilderness summer school, out for a week on the trail. The leaders also established that they were about to begin cooking a pot of pasta and veggies, and offered to make extra for us. My ears perked up as I listened to Matt's conversation and kept a distant interest in the progress of their dinner preparations.

Twenty minutes later, another thru-hiker showed up, who we'd recently seen in the journals just ahead of us. Shorts was an eighteen-year old kid from Maine, out hiking before starting college, skinny as a pencil, with youth radiating from his pale skin that had yet to encounter a wrinkle or even a sprout of facial hair. Fittingly, he wore shorts, and he was quiet, with quick, brief answers to our questions.

We shared that evening with Shorts and the group of wilderness school boys, eating their pasta, which in all reality, was terrible. They had forgotten to bring a strainer, so when they poured out the cooking water, half the pasta went with it, directly onto a bed of dirt and pine needles, and the dehydrated vegetables had been put in so late that they were still rock-hard. It was far from gourmet, but we ate it anyway. The parmesan cheese tasted so good that I piled it on to enhance the meal. Since it was dusk by the time dinner was ready, I avoided shining my headlamp into my bowl so I wouldn't see how much dirt I was actually eating.

Being around the kids had a strange effect on us. We felt a sense of duty to act the part of expert thru-hikers. At the very least, we had to be adults who didn't swear, who stayed logical, who problem-solved when pasta was spilled, and who spoke positively about challenges such as hiking the AT. Being on my best behavior took more effort than I expected; yet, I appreciated the chance to play that role because I knew what an effect it had on the kids' outlooks on life and on the trail.

I tried my best to be positive around them and to answer the wide array of questions they had about living outside for several months. Most of all, I didn't want to negatively influence their decision when it came to enjoying the hiking trip. They were at a young enough age that someone else had made the decision for them to be out there, yet they were old enough to know if they liked the results of that decision. While others may have assured them the outdoors was a fun place to be, just as we did that night, the realities of rain, sweaty clothes, tired feet, and inedible food could have easily made them doubt that claim. Talking with those kids, on a night when I could have just as easily chosen to be anti-social in the tent, rewarded me with yet another perspective on the trail.

When we started walking a 2000 foot ascent the next morning, all I could think about were those young kids making the trek up the mountain, their packs heavy with old, rented gear, and their minds unsure about what they were doing and why they were doing it. It fascinated me to think about how different kids' perspectives were, and I often thought back to the one and only hike I could remember as a kid in the Smokies. Had someone told me then that people hiked for months at a time, it would have been so far from my suburban life in Cincinnati that I wouldn't have believed that kind of life existed.

The rest of the day held only one crossing of the BRP and I missed my comfort blanket of seeing the road. Our mileage choices were also slim. The shelter twenty-four miles away was .6 miles off-trail, and the next shelter was ten miles further, for a total of thirty-four miles away from our starting point. Neither option was appealing. We often aimed for the shelters because they had the most reliable water sources on the trail, but when they were more than .2 miles off-trail or were simply too far for the day, we stealth camped. That day, we settled for a flat spot after thirty miles, at an unmarked campsite thirty feet off the trail. We camped alone for the first time in days and enjoyed the silence of the woods as we fell asleep.

Two strange sounds woke us that night. First, I awoke to what seemed like the middle of the night and saw that it was barely 9:00 p.m. when I heard Shorts pass us in the evening as he pushed on to the next shelter. Our fear subsided when we realized it was another hiker. Then, about an hour later, we heard strange snorting noises just outside the tent. Up until that point, we'd only seen one bear's backside as it ran away from us while we hiked near Pearisburg. Other than that, we'd only seen squirrels and deer. Our food was hung in a tree nearby and we half-expected to hear it hit the ground any moment, a bear successful in its attempt to get our food. Instead, we heard several animals rustling through dead leaves, snorting at a high pitch. Once we made enough noise from within the tent, yelling into the woods surrounding us, the animals went away. We later found out that the mystery snorts came from deer, and however unwarranted our fears may have been, the creepy sounds were still disturbing.

We passed Shorts four miles into the next morning, our thirty-fifth day, as he slept in the Seeley-Woodworth Shelter. The talk of the day was the upcoming hike up to The Priest, and while the climb up the mountain was surprisingly easy, I was more fearful of the miles *after* The Priest. The trail descended 3000 feet in order to cross the Tye River, only to hike 3000 feet back up to Three Ridges Mountain. It was the roller coaster aspect of hiking that my legs still had difficulty adapting to.

The weather held out for our hike up and down The Priest and I was fatigued by the steep, slippery footing as we made our way downhill on loose rocks. My legs barely had time to shift gears at the Tye River from the quad-beating downhill to the hamstring-straining uphill. We took a break halfway up the climb to Three Ridges Mountain at the Harpers Creek Shelter, situated just off the side of the trail, across a creek and set back deep into the shade of trees. As we sat in the shelter, an eerie change in the wind blew through the shelter and kicked up the leaves from off the ground. It was time to get hiking. Looking back, I don't have a good explanation for why we felt the need to *leave* shelter rather than seek it when there was a change in the weather, but something about sitting in a shelter and waiting for a storm to arrive simply felt wrong.

The climb continued after the shelter and the wind grew stronger as it ushered in the rain, thunder and lightning. I became more fearful the higher we ascended. Trees dropped in numbers, our trail turned to large rocks and boulders, and the closer the storm moved to us, the more exposed we were on the mountain. We reached the top just as lightning was coming down around us and we hunkered down behind boulders while the worst of it passed. When there seemed to be a safe moment, we ran down the trail to get off the mountain. The trend of running from a storm was unsettling and I never got used to the fear that drove us forward.

Our nerves were shot as we passed over the remaining miles of the day, surprised by another pop-up thunderstorm. Though most of the afternoon was too cold to stop for a break, the sun broke through the clouds just as we walked our last two miles into camp, making for a beautiful sunset on an otherwise dreary day. We were back within earshot of the BRP and I felt secure as we walked over the flat, wet, rocky trail just below the road.

The next morning started out with a biting wind and rocky terrain, a combination that typically brought me down, but we only had fourteen short miles to the town of Waynesboro, Virginia. I was determined to enjoy the day. We walked with very little effort to keep up the pace and arrived at Rockfish Gap by noon, just in time for lunch. A trail angel gave us a ride into town as well as a brief overview of Waynesboro, including the history, the layout, and the hiker hot spots. While my pre-trail self would have said, "Nah, I'll skip the tour. You can just drop me off at the hotel, thank you," at that moment, I was perfectly content sitting in the back of the trail angel's Subaru for the tour around Waynesboro. The day was young, we had already planned on staying in town for the night, and all we had on the to-do list was a restock of food and a call to home.

I went to bed that evening in the comfort of clean sheets as I said goodbye to the Blue Ridge Parkway, thanking it for being so good to us, and as I looked forward to our next section of Virginia in the Shenandoah National Park.

15 THE NATIONAL PARK EXPERIENCE

Thru-hikers are accustomed to a freedom like no other. We visit restaurants in a state of borderline-acceptable hygiene, smelling so pungent that it's no surprise when we're seated in our own corner, far away from other patrons. We walk the boundaries between private property and public land, often stepping foot in one to get to the other. We eat copious amounts of food without hesitation and it doesn't matter whether a stranger gives it to us or whether the food is from a car, a cooler, or a cupboard. The normal codes of conduct are fuzzy for thru-hikers, and I would say that hikers even get spoiled with all the perks that come with thru-hiking, not to mention bold in our behavior, especially if it's hunger-driven. I have made brash decisions with my stomach guiding me that I look back on and think, "I can't believe I thought that was ok!" Yes, I admit it, I ate someone else's dessert in a restaurant on the PCT after they paid their bill and left the table. In my defense, the dessert was untouched.

When it comes to national parks, the lines that cannot be crossed become crystal clear and Federal law trumps that of the typical thru-hiker code of conduct. Thru-hikers simply aren't that special in a national park. Rules are established and those rules know no difference between a day hiker and a thru-hiker, no matter what kind of special privileges thru-hikers think they have. I know I questioned just how special I actually was as I read the Shenandoah National Park rules in the guidebook while we lounged in our hotel room in Waynesboro. I was so surprised by them that I repeated them out loud to Matt.

"It says here we have to carry a backcountry permit on our pack the entire time? Wait, we *have* to stay in a shelter? And if we want to camp, it has to follow these distinct bullet points? What about thru-hikers? Do we really have to follow these rules?"

Matt wasn't surprised to hear the rules, though he was a bit intimidated by the four bullet points that our campsite had to fulfill in order to meet the guidelines of a legal campsite. We shook our heads in disbelief but agreed to follow the rules as we crossed the Shenandoah National Park boundary the next afternoon on our thirty-seventh day. We filled out registration forms and attached them on our packs in plain view for anyone looking for them.

I was not excited to enter the Shenandoah National Park and dreaded the upcoming days of forced sheltering, mainly because it controlled our mileage options. I wanted to be on the northern end of the park so we could be free again, but I could not have been more wrong in how I approached the park or how I predicted my enjoyment of it.

First, we traded the Blue Ridge Parkway for Skyline Drive, an equally enchanting road that bent in and out of view as the trail crossed over it several times a day. The liquid black pavement was smooth with a recent coating of blacktop and the bright white and yellow lines mesmerized me in contrast to the deeply black road. My first impression of the park was much better than I expected and the idea of a future road trip on the Blue Ridge Parkway extended to include Skyline Drive.

In the twenty miles that we hiked that day to the Blackrock Hut, we crossed Skyline Drive a whopping nine times. The elevation chart was witness to the high number of crossings, as we never strayed far from the elevation of 2700 feet. It was gloriously easy hiking and I tossed aside my initial concerns about the park before we completed our first day of hiking in it.

That evening was spent around a crowded shelter of thru-hikers, sectioners, and weekenders, all following the same rules. We gladly tented in one of the few flat spots left, and while we normally avoided stopping after just twenty miles for the day at a shelter .2 miles off-trail, it seemed like a minor inconvenience to trade for such a pleasant walking experience.

As we lay in our tent that night, looking ahead at the next few days in the guidebook, I asked Matt, "Do you think we'll stop at any waysides?"

The answer to that question greatly impacted the quality of our hike through the remainder of the park. I flipped to the informational pages of the guidebook for clarity on what a wayside was and saw that the upcoming waysides had meals, groceries, and a soda machine. Jackpot!

"Sure," Matt said. "Let's see what they have if they're close to the trail."

We hadn't counted on the waysides to replace any meals in our resupply, so we viewed them as bonus meals in addition to our regular meals. We proposed to each other that if the wayside was within a half mile, it was worth visiting. Over the course of the next three days, we traded packaged meals for fresh vegetarian chili, potato chips for salads, and candy bars for blackberry milkshakes. The waysides were an immensely satisfying perk within the park, and we were on a food high the entire way.

With each passing day and wayside, stuffing ourselves on town food never got old, and the hiking was so easy on our legs that we could have walked in our sleep. We hiked a three-day string of twenty-nine, twenty-seven, and thirty-four miles, which included at least two to three hours of breaks each day at the waysides. We were delirious with happiness through that section. The sun also never saw a cloud in the sky and the temperatures barely crested the seventies. It was the most comfortable state of hiking that I have ever known, and all the while I kept a loving eye on Skyline Drive.

We also had the company of Pete, Peanut and Handstand as we made our way through the park, three hikers we'd been around for several days. We spent time with at least one of them each day as we all took different meal breaks. Our last night in the park, we camped with all three of them at the Byrds Nest #3 Hut, 930.2 miles into the trail. We spent the evening sitting around a picnic table, sharing stories as the sun set in the background. I was disappointed when we all retreated to our tents or to the shelter for sleep, ending one of my favorite days on the trail. It was a rare moment of genuine happiness that overcame me that evening and I can still feel the happiness in that memory today.

Looking back, it's hard to believe we spent less than four days in the park, when upon entering the park, I thought the days would feel like an eternity until we exited it. Instead, I was sad as we crossed its northern boundary the next day, our fortieth day on the trail. We reached the last shelter in the park, the Tom Floyd Wayside, twenty-eight miles into the day. It was 6:00 p.m. and our bodies felt fresh. The shelter was slightly dumpy and the hiker already inhabiting it struck us as a questionable person, so we hiked on, hoping to find a flat spot a few miles up the trail. Yet, the miles wore on and just after the park boundary, the trail shifted dramatically from a woodsy setting to people's backyards as we approached the road that led to Front Royal, Virginia.

Once we crossed the road, we entered a wildlife sanctuary as the sun was setting, and the fear of not finding a campsite crept into my thoughts. I was reminded of the evening spent searching for Whitney Houston outside of Erwin, Tennessee, and I didn't like where the night was headed. The densely forested trail followed a well-flowing stream, and the sound of it drowned out our voices. The combination of the loud stream, the oncoming darkness, and the suffocating trees affected me so greatly that I nearly hyperventilated with fear. My logic escaped me as I imagined the possibility of hiking all night, never finding a campsite or a shelter. The trail also climbed 800 feet in an instant, and the energy that I spent on fear was no longer available for my legs to use in powering me up the hill. Things fell apart very quickly.

It was close to 8:00 p.m. when we saw headlamps in the distance, a few switchbacks up the hill. I ran to the sources of light, craving company with the hope that other people meant a campsite. Upon reaching them, we learned that they were thru-hikers headed to a campsite about a mile up the trail. After telling us what side trail to look for, they let us lead the way. We walked faster than them and within just a few minutes, we found ourselves alone once again in the dark, silent woods. After twenty minutes, we wondered if we'd missed a turn. We were at least following white blazes, so we knew we were on the trail, but I wondered if we missed the side trail to the campsite. I soon let the fear of walking all night repeat its unproductive, vicious cycle.

Matt walked quietly behind me as he watched my emotions get the better of me. The illogical fear of walking all night drove me to angrily dig my hiking poles into the ground with each step. I couldn't explain why I was having a breakdown over finding a campsite, when it wasn't even 9:00 p.m. I also couldn't get a hold of my emotions. I couldn't stop the child inside of me from having a temper tantrum in the middle of the trail like I was a two-year-old crying in the middle of a grocery aisle. At that moment, Matt was the parent that walked behind me in disbelief, unable to pacify me as my downward spiral continued.

I believe now that I was upset by the sudden shock of our plans falling apart without any sort of fallback to turn to, on a day that we didn't need to hike such big miles. We had hiked past my mental deadline for the day, in both miles and time, and the Stopwatch inside of me couldn't find a way to deal with it other than with intense fear and anger. I was perfectly fine going another hour past the last shelter in the park, but three hours was more than I bargained for, and I handled the situation very poorly.

Once we finally found the campsite, we hastily cooked dinner among four other hikers and retired to our tent. The miles and my outburst had exhausted us both and we fell asleep that night in a state of shock on several levels. There was the shock of haphazardly hiking thirty-four miles, a relatively long day that ended in night hiking, one of my least favorite activities. Then there was the shock of the lack of a campsite for six miles, hinting that we had taken for granted the previous ease in finding a flat spot. Lastly, the biggest shock of all was the severity of the storm that raged within me and the toll that it took on Matt. I had acted like a child and he seemed saddened to see me revert to that state. It hurt to see the disappointment in his eyes, knowing that I had failed to act like an adult when a challenge had called upon me to rise above my past-self. That night, I was embarrassed to be myself.

It was not the conclusion to the Shenandoah National Park that I had envisioned, especially after I loved our entire experience in the park, and the evening held a strikingly dramatic finish to such a tranquil section of hiking. The contrast could not have been any greater as I looked back over the last few days, already reminiscing about memories that could never be repeated, and regretting actions that could never be taken back.

Julie Urbanski

16 THE RAIN BEGINS…AND CONTINUES

In the spring of 2004, Matt's brother Jeff, aka Rawhide, started his journey on the Appalachian Trail. Though Jeff was an incredibly different person than Matt, he followed similar footsteps of hiking the trail after leaving one college and before continuing at another. The biggest difference in their hikes, which greatly affected Jeff's odds of finishing, was that it rained nearly every single day of Jeff's hike. It sprinkled, poured, or misted when Jeff woke up, while he walked, and as he went to sleep.

If he is ever asked about his hiking memories, he can describe them in one word: rain.

A hiker already has to deal with so much physical pain caused by the simple act of walking all day that the addition of rain to a thru-hike makes things all the more uncomfortable. By the time Jeff was just a week into the trail, his hip bones were rubbed raw and his feet looked like he'd slept in a bathtub for two days. His solution was duct tape. Each morning he went through the ritual of taping his hips, his feet, and any other hot spots that were rubbing with the never-ending supply of precipitation. Hence the trail name, Rawhide.

Jeff did not finish his AT thru-hike. By the time he made it to Harpers Ferry, he couldn't handle being so wet for such a long string of days, and he had already decided on the school he wanted to attend in the fall. While he would have liked to finish the trail, the possibility of suffering through a thousand more wet miles with a roll of duct tape as one of his few comforts was enough to justify quitting the trail. Even when he recounted his trail memories years later, I often replied in awe, "I don't know how you made it through so much rain."

On the other hand, I was accustomed to a PCT amount of rain before we started the AT. Out of the one hundred and nine days that we spent on the PCT, it rained just five of them, and I thought that was miserable. Fast forward to the AT and we had already walked through more rain than we were prepared to experience, and we weren't even halfway through the trail.

The day after we left the Shenandoah National Park already seemed like a world away from our cushy thru-hiker life of waysides, runnable trails, and ideal weather. We were quickly approaching the West Virginia border, and therefore the Roller Coaster, a fourteen-mile section characterized by numerous ascents and descents, one after the other. There was a sign posted at the beginning of the section, warning hikers about the section they were about to enter, and though the sign was a little cheesy for my tastes, I took the sign as a challenge.

I refused to acknowledge the difficulty of the section and I approached each climb and descent with a vengeance. Our late afternoon push through the Roller Coaster worked and we surprised ourselves with hiking thirty miles that day. We camped near a stream just a few miles from the end of the section, and though mosquitoes inhabited our campsite, we went to sleep in the tent so quickly that it didn't matter. The skies looked clear as we went to bed, so the nightly debate of sleeping with the rain fly on or off ended in the decision to leave it off. We were confident it wouldn't rain.

At 2:00 a.m., I felt a drop of water on my forehead through our mesh roof, and within seconds I was pulled out of my deep sleep and into a fully alert state. I wasted no time in slipping on my sandals and headlamp, and hurried to put on the rain fly. Matt woke up shortly after me and quickly popped out of the tent to help. While we knew it could just be a drizzle passing over, we also knew how quickly a drizzle could turn to a downpour, and we weren't taking any chances.

Within two minutes we were back in our sleeping bags, listening to the rain hit our rain fly, the sound always worse than the reality. It was easy to fall back asleep knowing that our tent would keep us dry for the rest of the night. What we didn't know, and at that point didn't question, was just how long the rain would last.

It would be a long time before we ever slept without a rain fly again.

As I had suspected, the rain wasn't finished by the time we got moving the next morning, just after 6:00 a.m. Even though it was sprinkling rain, I drew motivation from the fact that the town of Harpers Ferry was on the horizon, and I was excited to reach it. In 2000, Matt, Animal, and Rocketcop stopped there and took three days off to see Matt's parents and to visit family and friends in Washington, DC. All three of them shared a hotel room, with Matt's parents in the room next to them. Matt's most vivid memory of those three days was walking into their hotel room, after they'd been gone for the entire day, and smelling the sharp scent of a thousand miles' worth of three hikers' funky stench. Even Matt's mom can still vouch for it today, and she didn't even have to enter the room to smell it.

Just a mile into our forty-second day we crossed Snickers Gap, at VA 7 and 679. Cars' headlights reflected off the slick, wet blacktop in the pouring rain. Because it was the middle of rush hour traffic, the headlights spanned across several lanes of cars that were backed up until the road rounded a bend, the cars crawling forward at a commuter pace. The road was difficult to cross because of all the cars, and as we scampered across the road, illuminated by the cars' morning headlights, I was briefly taken back to that world of commuting to an office. I could immediately picture myself driving to an office in the chilly, early morning darkness, lulled into a meditative state by the sound of the windshield wipers as I sat in traffic and sipped my coffee. I shuddered at the thought and we were glad to disappear from the drivers' sight and into the woods, as if we were mere visions to the drivers as we crossed in front of their cars.

We were shaken by the road crossing because we hadn't been that far-removed from that world in terms of time and we didn't feel like we were truly detached, like we could still re-enter that world at the simple click of a button. Yet, we were currently part of such a different world that I doubted any drivers would believe that we could eloquently explain the differences between an IRA and a Roth IRA. We could play either role, a hiker or a corporate worker bee, and because of that, we somehow felt like phonies because we could so easily slip into either role and be completely different people, with vastly different skill sets, applied to incredibly diverse goals, to-do lists, and daily routines.

With these thoughts of such diverse lifestyles colliding into each other on an AT road crossing during early-morning commuter traffic, we crossed the West Virginia border. The trail eased up considerably while the rain continued to fall around us and we stayed focused until we reached the Shenandoah River. I had hoped for a beautiful crossing with sweeping views, but instead my thoughts were drowned out by loud bridge traffic and my views were blocked by a heavy mist that blanketed Harpers Ferry. We visited the Appalachian Trail Conservancy (ATC) and had our picture taken in front of the building, just as so many hikers do when passing through.

To our surprise and delight, the ATC had photo books dating back to 2000, and Matt was able to locate the picture taken of him, Animal, and Rocketcop, all together as they stood in front of the same building so many years prior. All three of them looked dirty, thin and exhausted, but most of all, they looked proud. It was a special moment for Matt to see that picture and to see himself as a nineteen-year-old on the trail, with friends that he's kept through the years, and to see himself eleven years later with a wife, two degrees, a career, and a retirement fund.

The ATC also gave us a chance to weigh in. There was a scale in the bathroom, and Matt and I promptly took off our wet clothes and each stepped on the scale. It was the old-school kind of scale, where we manually adjusted the number until the scale balanced. Matt excitedly dropped the number to 138, an eleven pound loss from his pre-trail bloated weight of 149. I stepped on the scale and put the marker at 120, expecting to adjust it down. Instead, it didn't budge, so I tapped the marker *up* the scale, one pound at a time until it balanced. I was shocked when the scale finally balanced at 124, right back where I started, and I cried out in disbelief.

"What? I gained six pounds!?!"

I had gained weight on the trail and we were hiking twenty-five to thirty miles a day. Matt was even deflated because he could no longer celebrate in his weight loss if I was sulking in my weight gain.

"I'll lose weight after the trail," I said as I stepped off the scale.

It was the irony of all ironies, for a thru-hiker to say they will lose weight after they're no longer exercising ten hours a day. We both had a good laugh at my promise to lose weight after I was finished walking a marathon a day, and I made no vows to change my eating habits or increase our mileage. I was going to continue taking advantage of every opportunity to eat the food of my choice at my own discretion. Matt was relieved.

I shivered as I put on my wet clothes again, suddenly embarrassed by my nakedness because it was six pounds heavier than I had expected it to be, and therefore appeared that much fatter in the mirror. I looked back at where I'd gone wrong over the past few days and I had to admit that I had been pushing the limits of my caloric intake. My new favorite dessert, at both lunch and dinner, was the combination of a four-pack of Soft Batch chocolate chip cookies, topped with a spoonful each of peanut butter and Nutella. Every bite was glorious and I had no shame in stuffing my face with that combination two times a day. Apparently its caloric count of six to eight hundred calories, twice a day, contributed to my weight gain as a thru-hiker.

The town of Harpers Ferry was quiet and empty as we walked on its damp sidewalks, and after picking up care packages from family and friends at the post office, we headed out of town. It was a Friday afternoon and our sights were set on the next day with a planned visit from Matt's parents and brother. We enjoyed the smooth, flat walk on the C&O Canal Towpath out of town, our memories sent back to the time we lived in Maryland and ran on the towpath often. The rain seemed a little less bothersome when we had memories to entertain us as we walked.

We tented just outside the Ed Garvey Shelter that night, surrounded by a new crop of sectioners and second-half hikers who had gotten on at Harpers Ferry, and we went to sleep anxious for the next day's visit from family. I knew Matt's mom was bringing cookies and brownies and had plans for each guilt-free bite I was going to take of them.

As we expected, judging by the slow drip of rain when we went to sleep, it was still raining the next morning as we packed up. However, nothing could have brought us down, because thirteen easy miles was all that stood between us and a car with a cooler full of food.

We finished the day at 10:00 a.m. at the Washington Monument State Park and felt relieved with the knowledge that we weren't going to walk again until the next afternoon. Our family was still en route, so we enjoyed the slow passing of time on a picnic bench as we waited for them. When they arrived, it was still raining and not ideal for an outside picnic, so we drove to Hagerstown, Maryland, where we had two hotel rooms booked and plenty of time to pass.

After a mandatory shower, I put on freshly laundered khaki pants, a cotton t-shirt, and a hooded sweatshirt, all clothes that Matt's parents had brought from Ohio. Once I was clean, I was allowed to touch the cooler of pasta salad, pesto sauce, fresh veggies, and cheese and crackers. We ate lunch on the hotel beds, watched TV, and talked about the trail. I appreciated the break with family and it felt like we'd been there for days when we finally checked out the next morning.

It was a peculiar feeling to get back on the trail that Sunday afternoon, our forty-fourth day in that life. We'd been well out of the radius of the trail corridor in Hagerstown, in a town that seemed far removed from the AT, and I even wore civilian clothes for a day. We hadn't seen a soul the day before on the trail, no one knew we had plans of getting off at the Washington Monument, and no one saw us get back on the trail. We seemed to be in a pocket void of other thru-hikers, and it was like the question of a tree falling in the woods. Does it make a sound if no one hears it? Did we really leave the trail if no one saw us get on or off? It felt like we had never left and I was sad not to share our town tales with anyone else.

We finished the day sixteen miles later at the Raven Rock Shelter, my new shoes already muddy and saturated with rain. Our cleanly laundered clothes were soaked through and we didn't have a soul to tell about our day feasting in town with family. I felt homesick after tasting a piece of home, but was still motivated to continue with Pennsylvania quickly approaching. I also had mixed feelings about our next state because of the journal entry from a southbound section-hiker that I read in the shelter that night.

It read, "Goodbye boulder fields of PA!"

The feeling of homesickness didn't last long. By the next day, our visit in Hagerstown already seemed weeks behind us and we looked forward to another visit that day from Brian, a friend from Annapolis, Maryland. Matt attended graduate school in Annapolis from 2005-2007, and in that time, we made two genuinely good friends, both of which became our roommates at different times, and one of which shared an interest in the outdoors. Brian always had the dream of thru-hiking, but could never put together the time off or the money to afford it, so visiting us gave him a taste of the lifestyle.

We had twenty-three miles to hike before meeting Brian at 3:00 p.m. that day in Fayetteville, Pennsylvania. Though it rained throughout the morning, the afternoon cleared considerably for the first time in days. We easily made the deadline and even arrived a little early to our meeting point. I wondered if all the fuss about rocks in Pennsylvania was really true. Our first day in the state went almost too smoothly. With the crossing of the Pennsylvania border also came the feeling that the trail had changed. We crossed a lot of roads, skirted a lot of towns, and our phone signal worked nearly every time we tried. I felt like we'd temporarily exchanged the mountains for the backyard woods, and was curious to see how long that feeling would last.

For three hours that afternoon, we spent time eating pizza and ice cream with Brian and talking about life outside of hiking. It was refreshing to see a friend from a life we had lived years ago, and even more satisfying to cover subjects that extended far beyond the trail. Though Brian was a quiet guy who rarely opened up to people, we had known him for so long that it was effortless to transition from the superficial catch-up conversation to the questions that really mattered to all of us. He was at a point in his life where he was in his early thirties, happy with his routine of work and triathlon training, but he knew he wanted more, and couldn't quite put into words what that was, let alone make it happen. I could fully relate with him, myself quickly nearing the age of thirty and not yet confident in what I really wanted to do in life. It was a position I was gradually realizing that many, many people were in, no matter their age or life situation.

We didn't come to any great conclusions that day with Brian, but I felt renewed as we watched Brian drive away from the trail. With less than three miles to go to the Quarry Gap Shelters for the night, and with threatening skies above us, we picked up the pace to avoid another downpour and made it to the shelters just in time for the rain to start once again. We met three other thru-hikers in one of the two, four-person shelters, and realized that the other shelter was completely empty. It was the first time we had a shelter completely to ourselves and hoped it would stay that way for some much needed couple time.

Our hope didn't hold out long, as we heard the unmistakable crunch of footfalls outside the shelter opening just a few minutes later. Another hiker arrived, soaking wet from getting caught in the downpour that we missed by mere seconds, and he looked sad beyond measure.

"How's it going?" Matt asked tentatively as the other hiker sat on the edge of the shelter and stared at the ground.

"Oh, not so good," he replied as he removed his wet shoes and socks. "I said goodbye to my girlfriend just now at the last road crossing. She's off the trail."

"Oh, I'm sorry to hear that," Matt replied, unsure of what consoling remark to make and hesitant to ask too many questions, for fear that the hiker was too upset to talk about it. Only a few seconds passed before he opened up and told his story.

The hiker's name was Rabbit and his girlfriend was Tortuga. She had been having terrible knee pain and didn't want Rabbit to slow down for her. She had dropped him off at the trail and headed to Duncannon, a town further north, so they could see each other one more time before she headed home.

We felt bad for him. It was apparent how dearly he already missed her. He had to transition from being part of a couple to being alone in crappy, rainy weather while she headed to town. The reality of hiking alone seemed to have set in. I could see the wheels of doubt turning in his mind in regards to the health of his own thru-hike, but he said he was resolved to keep hiking. He also hoped the time off for Tortuga would allow her to get back on the trail with him.

As we lay in the shelter with Rabbit, I thought about my hike from the perspective of being part of a married couple on our second thru-hike together. We too were tired of hiking in wet, miserable weather, but we at least had each other. Our companionship was the one consistent bright side to comfort us during the most challenging moments. The more I imagined Rabbit's situation, the more I doubted my ability to face the trail alone, without Matt by my side. It wasn't the first time and certainly wouldn't be the last time that I realized how deeply grateful I was for Matt's presence, patience, and friendship.

We looked at the guidebook together that night, as we did every night, and came up with our next plan for a two-day push to Duncannon. Town was sixty-two miles away, but the elevation was pancake-flat and we needed to find the motivation to hike if the rain was going to continue. We had a feeling the rain clouds would still be around the next morning and we doubted that we would want to leave the comfort of a dry shelter to walk on muddy, wet trails once again. We felt well-rested from the previous days spent with family and friends, and our plan stood to offer a jolt of excitement to start walking the next morning. Rabbit's interest was piqued as he listened to our plans, as he had calculated three days to town. He decided to join us in our mileage in order to surprise Tortuga by arriving a day earlier than she expected him, and we all went to sleep with a thirty-three mile day awaiting us the next day, rain or shine.

Julie Urbanski

17 HALFWAY IS ENOUGH

The two-day challenge to Duncannon started off like the four previous mornings. It was very, very wet. But, our motivation was undeterred and we were determined to get in the miles. We clicked off the miles in spite of slick, rocky terrain, our pace aided by the lack of both bugs and breaks. The bugs seemed to hate the rain more than us, so we hiked without fear of mosquitoes buzzing in our ears or flies circling our heads. Also, breaks were not only short, but they were few and far between. The breaks were kept to a maximum of ten minutes because only shelters offered true coverage from the rain, and that day there were only two that were directly on the trail. Even if we took breaks in the shelters, I rapidly lost body heat from being so damp and couldn't sit for longer than fifteen minutes. We walked quickly, ate quickly, and stayed focused on our efforts.

My spirits were relatively high considering how long I had been cold and damp in the endless precipitation. Our morning brought us past the AT midpoint, where an elaborate sign announced that we had covered 1090.5 miles. While we would have liked to pause for a long break at the sign, the pouring rain decided otherwise. I tried to celebrate the completion of the first half, yet not think too much about the second half. We'd already been through so much that it was intimidating to imagine what was to come. We were in our fifth straight day of rain on our forty-sixth day of hiking, and I hadn't heard a glimmer of hope in the weather forecasts. I had heard rumors about how hard the northern states were and wondered what kind of weather and terrain were in store for the next thousand miles.

Shortly after the halfway point, we arrived at the Pine Grove Furnace State Park's general store. The store was only open on the weekends and it was a Tuesday afternoon. There would not be a half-gallon challenge for us that day. The challenge was to see how fast a hiker could polish off a half-gallon of ice cream of their choice.

I had already heard Matt's famed story from 2000 about his successful, yet painful attempt at eating a half gallon of cherry jubilee ice cream on a hot, humid day near the end of July. He triumphed in eating all the ice cream, but felt so ill by the time he finished that he lay in his sleeping bag on the front porch for hours in order to recover. Meanwhile, Animal sailed through his half-gallon like it was a snack and proceeded to eat a full meal afterwards.

It was a different story as Matt and I stood in front of the store with a chilly mist falling around us from the permanent grey skies.

I was glad to have the half-gallon challenge decision made for me. Within five minutes of stopping at the store, I was shivering. At the same time, I also knew my weakness for ice cream, no matter the situation. However self-punishing it may have seemed, the possibility of putting myself in a hypothermic state was worth the risk if there was ice cream available for mass-consumption. Instead, we cooked lunch on a picnic bench under the front porch and the break for warm food re-energized us. We pushed on for the rest of the day, never stopping for more than five to ten minutes every two hours. It was efficient hiking at its best, thanks to the rain, and we easily covered thirty-three miles, well before sunset.

Rabbit didn't fare as well as us. He had been accustomed to lower mileage, hovering around the low twenties, and the rain was taking its toll on his feet. Blisters covered most of his feet and the resolve that he'd shown just the evening before was wavering. He arrived some time after us at the Alec Kennedy Shelter, just as the evening cleared during a momentary lull in the rain. He assured us that he was still going to push for Duncannon, especially since he was more than halfway there, but he looked tired. I hoped his idea of squeezing three days into two wouldn't be detrimental to his overall hike.

The next day's hike could potentially be classified as epic, mainly because of the volume of rain that fell from the skies. We started the day with a demoralizing slog through wet, squishy cornfields. Runoff from the road created swirls of oil on top of the water in the fields, and I crinkled my nose at the thought of my feet soaking in oily water.

That day, we crossed one road after another, climbed only two hills that required extra effort, and noticed an increasing number of rocks that crowded our path and slowed our progress. It was dreary beyond comprehension, and Matt and I agreed that if there was anywhere to stay in Duncannon, we would take it. Anything that would get us out of the rain and let us dry out for a short period of time was worth it to us.

Out of the few lodging options available in Duncannon, one of the most famous establishments that had the most buzz among hikers was the Doyle Hotel. Matt stayed there with Rocketcop in 2000, and he remembered sleeping on top of the bed, in his sleeping bag, in a room with a piece of the window broken out. It was cheap and bare bones back then and I expected no different eleven years later. But, when the bar was set so low in comparing the hotel with a roof to a tent in the rain, the Doyle suddenly moved up on the quality scale.

With just a few miles left until town, the day had gone considerably well. We were closing in on 5:00 p.m. on a twenty-nine mile day in wet, rocky, flat terrain, and we felt pretty proud of our efforts. All at once, two things happened to derail our progress as we descended into town. First, the terrain became much more difficult to maneuver, with sharp piles of rock sporadically covering the trail. Our smooth strides were replaced with short, well-placed footsteps, and our concentration centered on the ground directly in front of us. Second, the weather ushered in an intense thunderstorm and a heavy downpour soaked us. The storm came on suddenly and powerfully, and as the trail became more exposed along the side of the mountain, we scurried down the loose rocks as fast as possible, unable to see through the thick wall of rain.

As we made our way closer to town, I repeated in my head, "Please let there be room at the Doyle!" There was a real possibility of the hotel running out of space with so many other hikers also looking to get out of the rain, and I laughed at the irony of holding out hope for a hotel that was famous for all the wrong reasons. The storm heading into Duncannon pushed me to my limits of discomfort and I was willing to take any respite from the rain.

We finally arrived in town just after the storm had passed, the street drains still clogged with the sudden influx of water, and the cars moving slowly over the flooded roads. Everything on us was dripping wet and as we walked up to the front door of the Doyle, we felt comfort in the warning sign of "Smelly Hikers" posted on the door. We stood outside the door, contemplating if we should somehow dry off before entering, but we didn't have to think for very long. As we stood there, the hotel owner opened the door and told us to go to the side door, where she had towels and a room key waiting for us. She let us clean up and set down our stuff in a room before we even paid or told her our names. It was exactly what we yearned for, the feeling of being taken care of after such a disturbing descent into town through yet another thunderstorm.

The Doyle was everything the rumors lived up to be; it was a far cry from even a Super 8, but we didn't care. It was dry, the owner was nice, and the food was good. It took the humbling experience of living outside through consecutive days of rain to make me appreciate a base standard of living that at least included a roof and four walls, and I had no qualms about cozying up for the night at the Doyle.

Curmudgeon had a similar experience while dealing with the rain in Virginia. While in Pearisburg, Curmudgeon admitted to staying in a dirty hotel room with cigarette burns all over the furniture, the carpet, and the bedding. He didn't even turn down the sheets and slept on top of the bed in his sleeping bag. His reasoning for taking such a dilapidated hotel room? "Anything was better than the ground that night."

That afternoon, we randomly met Tortuga as we sat down next to her at a restaurant and started talking about the trail. Rabbit still hadn't arrived, so we were careful not to spoil the surprise. She admitted feeling better about hiking and said she was ready to get back on the trail. It was good to hear; we knew how much Rabbit had missed her. Just as we paid our bill, Rabbit showed up in the doorway of the restaurant, sopping wet, limping with blisters, and in tears upon seeing Tortuga. Though it was a little dramatic (all it needed was an 80's movie theme music in the background to round out the scene), it was still touching to see them reunited after we'd heard both stories separately.

A few hours later, we saw Rabbit and Tortuga together, giddy with happiness and holding hands as they walked down the hotel staircase.

"So are you getting back on the trail, Tortuga?" Matt asked, assuming nothing other than a yes.

"Nope." Rabbit answered. "We're both getting off and buying plane tickets back home to Texas. We've decided we're both done."

They seemed happy with the decision, but it was surprising for us to hear it after talking to Tortuga. It was always hard, no matter the situation, to hear that someone was quitting the trail. Whether it was for better or for worse, it still meant someone wasn't able to complete a journey they had set out to finish. Each time I heard about someone quitting, I was selfishly thankful that it wasn't me. I thought about quitting at least every other day, but I never thought it would ever become reality. So when talk became action, even if it was other hikers quitting, it was unsettling to hear that the AT had weeded out yet another person, leaving fewer and fewer people on the trail. The rain undoubtedly affected their decision as well, and since the rain was soaking hikers up and down the entire trail, it was possible that quite a few people were reaching their limits of discomfort.

The interesting aspect about Rabbit and Tortuga was that they were quitting as a couple. It was a completely different dynamic to hike as a couple on the trail. Two people's needs had to be considered in all decisions and one person could either bolster or crush the motivation of the other. I imagine that as Rabbit sloshed alone through two days of rain, he pictured his life back in Texas with Tortuga, and weighed the pros of going home with her versus the cons of staying on the trail alone. He had probably decided to quit by the time he arrived in Duncannon, and since Tortuga was already on the fence, she was easily swayed to revert back to her original decision to get off the trail.

As a couple, the decisions seemed like they could go either way. While it was easy to commit together, it was oftentimes easy to quit together, and Rabbit and Tortuga were a prime example of that. I often found motivation to walk because Matt seemed to have an endless supply of it. On the other hand, if there were ever days where he wanted to stop in town or stay at a shelter before reaching our goal, I was quick to toss the plans aside and adopt his new one in an instant.

If he had ever said, "Let's quit," I'm embarrassed to say it, but I believe that in a split second, I would have said, "Ok!"

The couple dynamic is fascinating even in real life, so it is all the more interesting to see it in action on the trail, in a challenging situation that's hard enough as an individual. Seeing another couple struggle actually strengthened Matt's and my resolve to stick together and always talk out our issues before ever deciding to quit.

Julie Urbanski

18 GREAT EXPECTATIONS

Expectations are all over the place at the start of a thru-hike. You expect the experience to be challenging yet rewarding, life-changing, even if it's only in the sense that you now carry the distinction of an accomplished thru-hiker, and body-altering. Walking 2200 miles has to do something to your body, and you simply hope it's not just to break it down, but to build up muscle, melt away fat, and leave you in the best shape of your life by the end. The expectations are different for every person, and they are all the more unique when taking into account a couple hiking together.

Not only do couples have to think about what hiking means to them as individuals, but also what it means to the relationship. The trail experience and the relationship's health are intertwined, woven tighter and tighter together over the miles, with one affecting the other all the time. Even the strongest relationships are put at risk over the course of a thru-hike because the trail brings out the best and the worst in a person, and there is always another witness to those worst moments. The other half sees your bad moods, smells your ten-day old stench and listens to your hungry whining. Also, there is always another person to blame for shortcomings, for mistakes, and for decisions that were made as two people. Even if you agree on a decision, if the results of that decision turn out badly, it's almost natural to instantly blame the other person. It somehow becomes incredibly easy to treat the one person closest to you, with whom you spend all your time, worse than anyone else on the trail.

I have had my highest and lowest emotional states while thru-hiking and Matt has been there to see every one of them. I can only imagine what he thought when he saw my first breakdown nine days into the PCT in 2007, when all the starry-eyed hopes of the first few days had faded, and I was no longer on my best behavior. He must have been ok with what he saw, along with the other times I behaved like a child and blamed him for the decision to hike, because he not only married me, he also agreed to join me on another thru-hike. He's even been there to see me unexpectedly poop my pants and still helped me clean it up. However, I am not proud of those moments when I treated him the worst and when I questioned our relationship and wished it had ended with the thru-hike. Thankfully, the wishes that I made while in the heat of anger, hunger, or stress were never granted.

Stretch and Zippers' journey on the AT found its roots early in their relationship. They had been dating for two years before embarking on the AT and in their first summer together, they hiked the John Muir Trail (JMT), a 211 mile trail that spans three National Parks in California, including Yosemite. The short trail was a trial version for future long-distance hikes and they were both thrilled to learn that each of them had a desire to hike the AT.

Matt and I hiked much of the JMT in 2007 when it followed the same path as the PCT, and though it was our favorite section on the entire PCT because of its beauty, it was also the most difficult section. There were numerous climbs and descents, several thousand feet at a time, and we hadn't packed enough food to account for all the calories we burned over such taxing terrain. Things turned very sour once the hunger kicked in. I had one of my worst moments at the end of that section because I was so upset about missing the post office hours that I entertained the idea of quitting the trail. Hunger was doing the talking, but I didn't restrain it, and it nearly broke our relationship that day in Yosemite.

Considering Stretch and Zippers hiked the JMT together, their success as a couple on the AT seemed more likely than the norm. In addition, they each had individual motivation behind them. Stretch grew up hiking the AT around Maine and New Hampshire, and though the idea of a thru-hike seemed like an adventure perhaps too long in length, he knew he loved being outside. The thru-hike brewed in his mind for several years and he knew it was possible based on his enjoyment of the JMT and on the experiences of friends who had thru-hiked. The draw of spending a long time outdoors with an ultimate goal of a thru-hike accomplishment was what led him to start the hike and what kept up his motivation to keep hiking, even when it waned at times.

Zippers' dream of hiking the AT stemmed from her own father's dream, passed down like an heirloom that never got used, except Zippers finally cashed it in for what it was worth when the timing was right. She had thought about hiking for at least a decade, but had never aligned all the pieces to make it work. The thought of hiking alone didn't appeal to her, so when she found out Stretch shared the same passion, the plans to hike together quickly evolved.

While both Stretch and Zippers had a shared dream of hiking, the expectations of what the hike meant to them as individuals and as a couple were very different. Stretch knew he wanted to attend graduate school in the fall of 2011, a typical step for a person going on twenty-five years of age, a few years removed from undergraduate school. He saw the trail as both a capstone to his last several years of employment and a spring board to the next adventure of graduate school. He had the savings, so he merely gave up a summer job to hike. Before starting, he expected the social aspect of meeting so many people along the trail to be a dominant experience. Stretch wasn't looking for the grand, life-changing experience that the trail is often portrayed to be. It was simply a logical time in his life to complete a challenge that he felt prepared to endure.

Zippers was at a point in life that many a near-thirty-year-old has often found themselves in. She had been in a job where she felt like she had maxed out its possibilities and was holding on to it for the security that it offered. For years, she had started projects but never finished them, and was ready to buck the trend. The AT was a possible restart button in Zippers' life, in which she saw herself coming out on the other end as a person with the clarity that she hadn't yet honed. As any other female would relate, me included, she hoped to leave the trail thinner than when she started, an outward symbol of the new life she hoped to make for herself. Lastly, Zippers saw the AT as an opportunity to build the foundation of her and Stretch's life together. Her sights were set on a much bigger journey than the AT, much longer and perhaps harder. The differences in expectations left them starting on very different paths before the trail had even begun.

Going into the journey, they both knew what a challenging situation they were putting themselves into, so they expected both high and low points on the way. There was no illusion on either part that they would walk over 2000 miles without bearing a few scars, or without arguing over seemingly simple things.

On a damp, foggy day in mid-March, two weeks before we started our own AT journey, Stretch and Zippers stepped foot on the start of the Approach Trail at Amicalola Falls. Eight miles later, they made it to Springer Mountain, the official southern terminus of the AT. Though the weather was drab and made for a boring start to such an exciting undertaking, they were bounding with energy and enthusiasm.

Each day, they ended their miles with a regimented stretching routine and attributed much of their injury-free status to their loose muscles, which they were adamant in maintaining. Stretch believed it allowed them to hike longer days in the beginning, and it soon became his name when Zippers suggested it one night at camp. The name fit, especially given that he was a tall person to begin with, and Stretch became Stretch. In contrast to Stretch's calm, quiet demeanor, Zippers' vibrant, passionate personality could rarely be contained. She overflowed with energy, often bubbling over from one pot to the next without attention to the details of which pot, and she often forgot to close her zippers all the way on her pack. The trail name was born in their first few days of hiking once her inability to remember to close the zippers on her pack surfaced as a common theme. She loved the trail name and fully embraced the meaning it held for her energetic personality and her struggle with attention to details.

By the time we were barely a few days behind them, they had been on the trail for two months. They already had their fair share of trail magic, rainy weather, challenging miles, food binges in town, and hunger-induced arguments. Two spats in particular had involved a Snickers Bar at one point and a chocolate cupcake at another. It was usually hunger doing the talking, but there were snippets of truth in the jabs they made at each other when exceptionally difficult days of hiking stripped them of their censors. There were usually undertones of dissatisfaction in how one person was treating the other, or in the lack of completely open, honest communication.

So far, it was only jabs that had been thrown. A punch could do real damage to both the relationship and the hike. On a thru-hike as a couple, it's pointless to throw the emotional punches at the other person. While it may feel rewarding at the time, the punches only lead to hurt feelings in an environment where there is little escape from each other. Still, even the smallest jabs weighed on Zippers' mind as they covered the miles together. She questioned their future together nearly every day, wondering if she'd been kidding herself from the first step at Amicalola Falls. With each high and low moment, she grabbed on to each one and inspected it for a deeper meaning and for answers to their relationship.

By the time we closed in on them, Stretch and Zippers were in the same rocky, rain-drenched state of Pennsylvania that we were in, and which Rabbit and Tortuga had been in when they quit. The beginner's party was over and we were in the Wednesday of the work week, looking forward to Friday night, but knowing there were plenty of miles that would reveal both our best and worst true selves before it was all over. As we made our way north, I saw how everyone dealt with the challenges of the trail differently, and would soon learn much more about Stretch and Zippers and their journey to Mt. Katahdin.

19 FIELDS OF BOWLING BALLS

As we walked out of Duncannon on our forty-eighth day, leaving Rabbit and Tortuga behind us in return for the pursuit of Stretch and Zippers, it was still raining. A heavy mist lay on the bridge over the Susquehanna River and I tried to stay positive even as the rocky ascent out of town reminded me of my heavy pack full of food for the next five and a half days.

The mist turned into a heavy downpour just as we tucked inside the Peters Mountain Shelter, eleven miles into our day. As I looked out at the rain from under the shelter's roof, I was amazed by its persistence. I had never imagined my thru-hike to include such a large amount of rain for such a long period of time. We waited out the rain with two other thru-hikers in the shelter and kept walking once it let up. After that break, the rain never paused long enough for another break for the rest of the day. Very little about that day was exciting except that we were able to hike twenty-five miles out of town, a relatively high number considering we didn't start until 10:00 a.m., over three hours later than a normal day. We camped alone at a clearing near a stream, happy to dry out inside our tent and curl up in our sleeping bags, one of the few items in my pack that could still comfort me. We went to sleep with our wet shoes and socks outside the tent, under the rain fly's vestibule, the stench too great to keep in an enclosed space. There was no longer hope of drying them out; that hope was tossed aside when the heavy clouds above us settled in days ago.

There was no sign of the rain letting up.

The next morning, we were still surrounded by moisture and we went on strike against the rain. Normally, the sun was our alarm clock, but we decided to pull our sleeping bags over our heads and sleep in. Our plan was to play the waiting game with the rain and we were optimistic that if we just waited long enough, maybe the rain would stop before we started hiking. We later found out that Curmudgeon was so wet and tired one day that he stopped walking at 3:00 p.m., set up his tent, and read his Kindle for the rest of the day. That morning, we snuggled in our sleeping bags all morning and ate a breakfast in bed that included energy bars and instant breakfast drink. By 10:00 a.m., the rain won the battle. It had outlasted us and we were ready to get hiking, no matter the precipitation around us. We slipped on cold, wet shoes, and I squeezed into my damp sports bra like an icy sponge against my warm core. It never seemed to dry, even in the most perfect conditions.

The thought that pushed me out the tent door was the fact that twenty-two miles away sat the 501 Shelter, a famed shelter from which hikers could order pizza delivery. Once again, food convinced my achy legs to get moving and we warmed up into a steady pace after just a few miles. It was still fairly easy hiking, with little change in elevation, and my concern over the rocks switched to a concern for blisters from hiking for so many days in wet shoes and socks. We both had tough feet from running long distances, but I rarely had wet feet for more than a few hours. My morning routine of applying Vaseline to hot spots was increasing in length with all the new hot spots, and increasing in frequency, as I reapplied Vaseline at least once each day after it washed away with the rain. It was a growing concern for all the hikers and another reason we hoped the rain would soon pass.

Just as we arrived at the 501 Shelter, another hiker was on the phone, ordering a pizza. Our packs didn't even get unbuckled before we looked at the menu and picked out a pizza to include in the delivery order. The timing could not have been any better and we settled into the enclosed shelter with eight other thru-hikers.

Because it was an enclosed space, the combination of ten hikers' body heat and all their wet gear created a dank, stuffy environment inside. There were socks, shorts, shirts, and bandanas hanging from every possible ledge, rope, and corner in an attempt to start the next day as dry as possible. I followed the other hikers' examples and promptly covered every inch of our bunk beds with wet clothing. It surprised me how quickly and easily the hope to dry out clothing and gear returned each and every night for nearly all hikers, even if the possibility to dry things out was fruitless. In a subtle way, it said something about the determination of a thru-hiker.

Matt and I enjoyed a large, hot, cheese pizza, while I sipped a twenty ounce bottle of Pepsi. I looked back on the morning and realized that I held no regrets for giving myself the chance to sleep in, to take the impulsive break, and to finish the day early for pizza. It had been an out-of-the-ordinary day, and I was grateful for every moment of it.

I was still full from pizza the next morning as we lazily eased into another day's hiking of wet, rocky terrain. The only saving grace in the terrain was that it was flat. I laughed at myself as I mentally tallied the pros and cons of the hiking, reminding myself that there would always be cons to go with the pros. I was amazingly positive despite my surroundings, which was largely attributed to the previous evening's pizza.

Later in the day, the sun came out as we made our way downhill, into the town of Port Clinton. We stopped suddenly in an open patch of grass just to close our eyes and absorb the sun's heat. I felt like I breathed in new life as I stood there taking in the overwhelming warmth of the sun. We had missed the sun and didn't realize just how much until we saw it for that brief moment from behind the clouds. As we stood on the edge of town, we contemplated stopping for the evening, simply because it was a town right on the trail. But, the little bit of sunlight had recharged us and instead, we pushed on to the next shelter.

Had we stopped, we would have met Stretch and Zippers, who had stopped there the day before with a few other hikers to tour the Yuengling Brewery. They filled up on beer while they feasted on soft pretzels and cheesy dipping sauce. The rain had finally pushed them to their limits and the timing of the town and the brewery allowed for a much-needed break. We unknowingly passed them that day while they took a day off at a friend's house.

In the last six miles of the day, the sun sadly gave way to the clouds. Around 6:30 p.m., we strolled into the Windsor Furnace Shelter to finish our fiftieth day after a relatively easy thirty miles. We also met Tigger, another thru-hiker who had just hiked out of Port Clinton that day. He was tall, thin (who wasn't by then), in his early twenties, with chin-length brown hair and a positive energy about him that seemed to give him a permanent smile. He had just made his dinner of peanut butter and tortillas, a cold dinner since he'd already sent his stove home, and was quick to make conversation with us. We first talked about pack weight, as Tigger was pushing to make any cuts he could to make the hiking easier, and the conversation hopped from topic to topic as early evening changed to night. We were happy to have met him; it was refreshing to be around a positive person who wanted to talk about solutions to the conditions rather than complain about them. Admittedly, I didn't find myself in his position often and I admired his optimism.

The next day's hiking looked easy on paper, so we decided to aim for a shelter thirty-three miles away. Tigger joined us for some of the hike, but with his long legs and my slower pace, he didn't stay with us for very long. That day was when I started to believe the rumors that Pennsylvania was rocky. I had already walked over my fair share of boulders and maneuvered over a characteristically rocky trail, but that day was the real beginning. We walked over narrow sections of rocks, each side unforgiving of missteps with steep drop-offs, and the boulder fields that I had read about in a journal just a week before finally came to life. Coupled with the constant rain and mist, it was like walking on wet bowling balls and my hiking poles barely helped me without any ground to grip into. They were more of a hindrance as they slid off the surfaces of rocks and stuck awkwardly into crevices, more difficult to remove as my energy levels dropped. I kept my eyes focused on the ground in front of me, my hat bill shading my eyes from the never-ending boulder fields laid out ahead of me. I even watched Tigger nearly do the splits as his legs slipped out from under him, and I felt a little better knowing I wasn't the only one who had problems walking on wet rocks.

The boulder fields slowed our pace considerably and we thought about staying at the Bake Oven Knob Shelter, twenty-seven miles into our day, only to push on because it was just too crappy, even for our standards. It was dirty from other users' trash, damply cold from so many days without sun, and inherently dark because of its construction. One side of it backed up into a hill and I could already imagine hearing the pitter-patter of mice feet scurrying across the shelter floorboards, in search of our food. We moved on with Tigger for a few more miles, only to camp in a water-soaked, grassy patch of ground just off the side of the trail near Lehigh Furnace Gap. It was not an ideal campsite, but we were all tired of walking after thirty-miles of boulder hopping.

I went to sleep with the mantra, "Rain, rain, go away!"

With no surprise, we woke up to rain the next morning and packed up in a hurry to save the few dry things from gathering any further moisture. We said goodbye to Tigger as he finished packing up, letting him know where we planned to finish that day, and headed up the trail for another day in the rain.

Awaiting us that fifty-second morning was the Superfund Trailhead, just outside of Palmerton, Pennsylvania. It is the site of former zinc smelting operations that contaminated the soil with heavy metals, eventually causing a collapse in the ecosystem. Plants couldn't grow across a 3000-acre area, soil eroded into nearby water sources, and a lengthy cleanup process has been in place for decades. Before reaching the trailhead, we were hiking on a lush trail surrounded by trees, and as soon as we entered the Superfund area, we were climbing a barren, windswept ridge covered in huge boulders. There were several moments on the uphill where I was frozen in fear, scared of losing my grip or slipping on the wet, smooth rock faces. The wind whipped around me, threatening to pull the hat off my head as the whir of highway traffic in the background drowned out my thoughts. I was shocked by the difficulty of the climb, constantly wondering how older people could manage such parts of the trail if even I struggled at half their age. It also surprised me that Matt hadn't warned me about the terrain. It seemed like a memorable section that he would have had from 2000, but even he found himself saying, "I did this?"

Back in 2000, Matt hiked the Superfund at 4:30 a.m. with Rocketcop. They both wanted to catch up to Animal, who was scheduled to hit the town of Delaware Water Gap that same day, so they awoke early to cover the thirty-seven mile stretch in order to reach town and Animal. It was a full moon as they climbed the Superfund section, and the reflection from the moon made the rocks appear white, like they were literally on the moon. As they climbed up the mountain's white face, the rocks were still warm from the previous day's hot, late-July sun. Only the memory of the moon-like, warm surface of the rocks stuck with Matt, not the difficulty of the climb. Based on the slow progress we made that day, I was continually amazed that Matt and Rocketcop covered that kind of distance over that kind of terrain.

Once at the top of the climb, as I tried to shake off the fear of climbing the wet boulders, we arrived to a densely foggy, other-worldly-like trail. All traffic noise disappeared once on top and it was void of any sound at all. The bright green grass was a stark contrast to the grey fog, and we could barely see ten feet ahead of us as we walked through it. I half-expected aliens to emerge from the clouds as we made our way over the treeless, clumpy ground. Our speed increased over the easier trail and I looked forward to a change in scenery.

A few miles later, as we made our way slowly over large rock steps, we heard the booming bark of a dog. I looked up and saw a large, heavy black lab ten feet away from me, sitting at the top of several rock steps, each rock a foot or more in height. Two middle-aged women appeared shortly afterwards, their rain jackets soaked through and their glasses fogged up with the arduous effort of rock scrambling in the rain.

"Winston! No barking; it's just other hikers," one woman said to the dog.

I immediately fell in love with the fat, black lab named Winston. Once the dog realized we weren't a threat, he continued hiking, but whined after looking down at the sight of the huge rock steps ahead of him. He was a far cry from a sprightly puppy that bounded with energy, and the lab part of him that loved food had contributed to his pudgy weight. We could tell he was struggling over the rocky terrain, and I thought back to the terrain that we had just gone through in the Superfund. "If this dog is struggling here," I thought, "there's no way he'll make it down the Superfund."

"How are the rocks coming up?" one woman asked us.

We quickly advised that they take the detour down the Superfund or get a hitch out on the upcoming road. In giving advice like that, we tried to do it tactfully. We were genuinely concerned about their dog and wanted to be completely honest about the difficult terrain, without implying that they themselves weren't capable of hiking it. It was a hard tightrope to walk, but they seemed to consider their options after looking down at Winston's sad face. He had taken the opportunity to lie down and rest while we talked about their options.

After leaving them to weigh their decisions, we moved on and I hoped for Winston's sake that they listened. I have wondered to this day what those women did after leaving us.

By lunchtime, we were drenched and exhausted, despite the flat line of elevation in the guidebook. The closest shelter was .2 miles off trail, which we weren't willing to walk, so in an effort to boost our morale, we set up our tent midday for an hour break out of the rain. We cooked a warm lunch of buttered noodles and it gave us another boost of energy to continue hiking for the rest of the day. The day ended after twenty-six miles, on a day that took the energy of a thirty-five mile day, and we set up the tent for the evening on a flat piece of ground just outside of Wind Gap.

We never saw Tigger that day or ever again on the trail. He never caught up to us during any of our breaks, and while it surprised us, we assumed the rain had dampened his spirits enough to give into a town over the course of the day. But, we could only assume. Later down the trail, we found out that he was so stricken with Lyme disease that his jaw clenched shut. He had trouble eating and had to let the medicine move through him for several days in Dalton, Massachusetts, before he could move on. It was sad news for us because we really enjoyed his company and hadn't expected to lose it so abruptly. He was one of the many genuinely good people that we were fortunate enough to meet along the way.

As we started our fifty-third day on the trail, we were damp but excited to start walking. The trail was still rockier than anything I had ever experienced before, but we took our time, knowing that the town of Delaware Water Gap was fourteen tiny miles away. Our spirits were elevated with the thought of town and the day before had been so difficult that it made the present one pale in comparison. There was no question of stopping in town, as I was completely out of food, with merely a collection of empty plastic bags to speak of. I ate my last energy bar six miles into the day and I knew I was hungry when I could smell Matt's bar while I walked six feet behind him.

"You're eating an apple pie bar right now, aren't you?" I asked Matt, jealous he had rationed his food better than me.

"Yeeesss," he said slowly.

"Don't worry, I don't want any. I just wanted to know the flavor," I assured him. I knew he was fearful I would ask him to share it.

We were pleased with easy hiking for most of the day and arrived in town by noon, with a total of 1285.3 miles behind us and just under 900 miles ahead of us. The sun partially poked its head out of the clouds during our last technical miles descending into town, and I took a deep breath of gratitude as our feet hit pavement. My hunger felt satisfied just by arriving in town and seeing civilization again.

The question of staying overnight in town had been debated all morning. We knew we'd arrive early and have plenty of time to enjoy town and hike out, but the pull of staying dry for an evening, under a roof, was strongly magnetic. We waited to make a decision until we scoped out the hotel and food options in town.

By the time we reached the local bakery, where the overwhelmingly powerful smell of baked goods engulfed us as we entered the store, we were sold. The vast array of pies, cookies, and pastries was enough persuasion for me to stay. I wanted to consume ten things in just one glance, but we promised to pace ourselves and only have two pastries each to start. After that, we bought several mini pies to-go, with plans of returning once those were polished off. We then booked a hotel room down the street and settled in for an afternoon of food and relaxation.

It was the comfort we'd been missing over most of the last twelve straight days of rain and we savored every minute of it. While in town that night, the plans of hiking the CDT directly after the AT continued to evolve, and we ordered maps, guidebooks, and a few new pieces of gear for the next trail. It was hard to believe that we still wanted to keep hiking after sloshing through hundreds of miles of muddy, rocky trails, but the reward of town had left us in optimistic spirits. We were also sitting at the border of Pennsylvania and New Jersey, and I looked forward to the next day's hike, where we'd put Pennsylvania behind us.

"Goodbye boulder fields of PA!" was the new saying as we went to sleep that night.

What we didn't know then was that we should have added, "Hello swamps of New Jersey!"

Julie Urbanski

20 BUG WARS

New Jersey. The sound of the state was music to our ears as we left Delaware Water Gap. The sun was shining, we'd made it through the rocky state of Pennsylvania, and the guidebook still showed flat elevation. We turned a new leaf, a dry one at that, and it felt like we were finally making progress north, even though all we did was cross the Delaware River.

The area had several memories for both Matt and me as individuals and as a couple. Not only had Matt hiked there back in 2000, but he'd also hiked the trail up to Sunfish Pond with his sister in 2002. Just a year after that, we day-hiked the very same trail to Sunfish Pond with Rocketcop, then Matt's third time on it, and there we were, hiking once again out of the Delaware Water Gap, up to Sunfish Pond and beyond.

Our motivation soared with the rising temperatures and we shared the smooth, gradual, uphill trail with several day hikers. Once we arrived at a swollen Sunfish Pond, the trail became more difficult to maneuver over the rocks surrounding the shore, and we spotted a few snakes in the water. Every other creature must have been holed up for the last twelve days of rain, because every one of them was out on the trail with us that first day of sun. We saw more wildlife on that first day in New Jersey, including eight snakes, than we did on the entire trail leading up to it.

Past the pond, the dwindling number of trees made for an exposed trail and Matt talked on our phone with his sister while we took quick, energetic steps over the semi-rocky terrain. I soaked in all the sun's energy and felt life come back to me. It was a great beginning to a new state. Because of that, I was undeterred by the record number of snakes we encountered, along with the surprising amount of rocks still present. I didn't know why I thought the rocks would end at the state's border. It was wishful thinking, but I hoped New Jersey's terrain would be dramatically different from that of Pennsylvania.

Since we didn't leave until early afternoon that day, we had a shorter day to cover the miles. The heat was surprisingly draining and though I started off with a full tank of enthusiasm that morning, it had subtly waned all day. I realized that I was starting to drag when we sat down for a break.

As we sat on the side of the trail, with panoramic views of the green valley, the foliage fully grown in by then, I said to Matt, "I feel kind of down."

I couldn't pinpoint what hit me, nor could I express exactly what I was down about. It was like the batteries had been losing power all day and I hadn't been monitoring them until the flashing red light had caught my attention. Then it was nearly too late to recharge them.

We talked about my mood as we sat crouched on the side of the trail, and I even had a little cry. I hadn't cried yet on the trail and it felt good. I sobered up when a group of twenty teenage boys passed us and saw me crying. We chalked up my mood to having spent so much time in the heat that day, something we weren't accustomed to because of the cold rain. I also had high expectations for the easiness of New Jersey. In all of Matt's stories from 2000, he had never mentioned much about New Jersey, most likely because he couldn't remember much, but I believed it was because it was such an easy state. I should have drawn on the Superfund climbing experience to know that his memory didn't work like that.

At around 5:00 p.m., we found a clearing off the side of the trail and called it home. It was early to stop for the day, but we assured ourselves that the motivation would kick in the next day. The temperature was slow in cooling down and the air stood still as we set up our tent among the trees. Our first official sign that the rain had ended and the sun had come out also made an appearance that day: mosquitoes. And there were many of them.

Our mesh tent was a safe haven from the mosquitoes as they buzzed around the tent, searching for any holes in our armor. It was hot and stuffy in the tent without a breeze to keep us cool, but I didn't care. I sat in the tent, read the guidebook, and gnawed on an eight ounce bar of milk chocolate that Rocketcop had sent us in a care package. We had traded core-chilling rain for bug-buzzing heat in just one day, and we contemplated which would be more challenging. After the fact, the rain of Pennsylvania had been many blessings in disguise.

The next morning, I heard the mosquitoes before I saw them. I expected to have at least two hours without them to start our day, but I knew from the first moment of waking up that it would be a battle with the bugs from the very beginning. While it had crossed our minds that the bugs would come out again with the sun, we hadn't expected that they would be out in droves. They were also very hungry.

Walking in New Jersey was like being on a different trail with the sudden onset of heat and bugs. The water sources were also concerning in both quantity and quality. They dwindled in number and many of them were orange or brown in color. Even though we trusted bleach as our water purification system, neither of us could stomach filling up our bottles with orange water. We found ourselves very thirsty in New Jersey, a sensation we hadn't felt in quite a while.

We also passed by several swamps whose rain-bloated banks of thick, grey ooze crept onto the edge of the trail. The swamps were both disgusting and fascinating to look at. The trees seemed stuck in the cement-like water and it felt like very few life forms could survive there, causing a stillness about them that scared me. Mosquitoes called the swamps home, so even though the swamps were interesting to observe, we passed them as quickly as we could because the bugs were guaranteed to swarm us if we stood still.

Later that afternoon, after chugging nearly a half gallon of water at a water spigot outside the High Point State Park, we hiked on to finish the day at the High Point Shelter. The shelter was full of a group of weekenders out to hike the state of New Jersey, so we camped on the soft ground just below the shelter. In the short time that we set up our tent and cooked dinner, ominous clouds rolled in and we heard the rumble of thunder. The sense of irony doesn't do justice in describing my happiness in hearing that thunder. All I wanted was a break from the heat and the bugs, if only for the evening and possibly the next morning, and I knew rain could deliver it.

With such sudden thunderstorms, I realized that the swinging pendulum of weather, terrain, and my mood was back, and that I needed to be aware of any changes in my emotions. I also had to admit that the pendulum never really left; it had just been stuck for twelve straight days of rain in Pennsylvania.

The previous night's thunderstorms, which rolled out of camp as quickly as they came in, only knocked out the bugs temporarily. The mosquitoes were persistent in their pursuit by the next morning and I felt my motivation dropping just as fast as the temperature was rising.

That morning, on our fifty-sixth day, the trail took us through pollen-laden fields of waist-height grass. The grass choked the trail and our feet struggled to find the narrow trail, our view of the path covered by the grass. My clothes were caked in the dusty, light-yellow pollen, and because there was just enough morning dew on the fields to dampen it, it clung to my clothes and was difficult to remove. After the gauntlet of fields, we then walked along private fence lines, so close to homes that we could pet their dogs in the backyard or look straight into their window to watch them eating breakfast. I felt just as exposed as the homeowners probably did, like we were a rare breed of animals that were rarely seen "in the wild" while walking on the trail.

We crossed several footbridges that morning and each one seemed more mosquito-infested than the next. We had wised up and covered our ears and necks with our bug bandanas, as we called them, but we couldn't cover much more of our bodies. It was the choice between walking in the sweat-box of rain gear, nearly bug-free, or that of walking in our thin running clothes and losing the battle with the bugs. I liked New Jersey less and less the further we walked, and looked forward to New York already, hoping the states were very different.

Eight miles into the day, we were worn out from fighting the bugs and pulled off the trail for food at the general store in Unionville, New York. Even though the trail continued to be in New Jersey, we crossed into New York briefly that morning by walking a mile down the road to the store. As we lounged on the front porch of the store, we noticed a complete lack of mosquitoes. It was completely bug-free and it baffled me as I sat there undisturbed. The mosquitoes seemed to be unique to the woods, where we spent the majority of our time.

We lounged on the front porch with another thru-hiker, Squash, whose name we'd seen in the journals for some time. When we mentioned how difficult of a morning we'd had with the bugs, he replied with a confused look and said, "Huh, I didn't see any bugs this morning."

"What!?!" we responded in unison. We sat up so quickly in our rocking chairs that we nearly tipped over in shock.

He had treated his clothes with bug repellant and walked mosquito-free on the trail. We had completely overlooked a prominent piece of the trail and had only ourselves to blame for being in the middle of New Jersey without any kind of bug remedy. A solution was in order, but unfortunately, the general store didn't have any bug spray. Rather than lament the lack of bug spray, we focused our attention on a more pressing matter at hand, which was the store full of food behind us.

I will not list all the food I ate that morning, but I crossed the line somewhere in the middle of eating an entire Entenmann's coffee cake. Even Squash said he was surprised by the sheer quantity of high calorie food that I put down. By the end of our binge, Matt was full but comfortable, and I was miserable. As we walked the downhill mile back to the trail, I left my hip belt unbuckled and whispered to Matt, because it was too painful to talk, "I hate myself."

I asked him to never let me eat that much again and suffered through the next few miles of forgivingly flat trail. The term "food coma" didn't begin to describe how sleepy I felt as my toes crashed into rocks and roots because of lazy feet that scraped the ground, and as visions of curling up in my sleeping bag clouded my logic. It was a relief when I finally felt digested enough to tighten my hip belt and take a full stride.

Later that afternoon, I talked to my mom on our phone as we climbed the large, rocky steps up Wawayanda Mountain, and I tried to hide the fact that I missed her and missed home. Though the trail wasn't handing out challenges that we weren't already accustomed to, I was feeling the real desire to quit. It wasn't a feeling that I could truly voice, but it was heating up below the surface and slowly reaching a boil. I had imagined the states beyond Pennsylvania to be a refresh button on the trail, and instead, they only brought on different challenges. I missed the comfortable trails of Virginia and didn't know how to accept new challenges without wishing I was back in an easier state. I had no solution at the time and didn't want to vent to Matt, so I kept quiet and hoped the desire to quit would swing out of focus before I made any impactful decisions.

Our campsite that night at the Wawayanda Shelter was tucked deeply into the trees, with such stuffy, still air that it was hard to breathe. The mosquitoes thrived on any chance they had, and I couldn't blame them, for they were the definition of opportunists. Matt knew something was on my mind as he watched me silently stare at the mesh ceiling of our tent, but he didn't ask many questions. He hadn't forgotten the sudden rush of tears that had hit me just two days earlier.

He too was struggling with the lack of improvement in the trail experience after the rain had ended. It was an entirely different trail with mosquitoes and we weren't prepared for the consequences. We'd been lucky in the past and avoided disasters in spite of a lack of proper gear or preparation, but it felt different, like our luck had reached its allotted limit.

With eight hundred miles left to go, I could barely convince myself to sign up for the next day of hiking, much less another six weeks. A disaster of a different kind was bubbling under the surface, ready to erupt, and it was only a matter of time before we felt its effects.

Julie Urbanski

21 DISASTER STRIKES

I once heard another hiker describe the passing of one day on the trail as the equivalent of four days in real life. I completely agree with him. When there is less on the daily to-do list, time inevitably passes slower than a day packed with meetings, errands, a visit to the gym, and TV shows. In real life, the days go quickly and we don't have time to think about our lives because we're so busy living them. On the AT, we had nothing but time to think about life. Time passed slowly over the course of each day, and since we walked an average of ten hours a day, all that time allowed for a multitude of thoughts and emotions to cross our minds. At the end of those days, it felt like an eternity since we'd packed up camp that morning, based on all the stories we could tell about who we met, what we saw, what we thought, and how we felt. The distractions were few, such as an iPod or a Kindle, so it was up to us to face the time with a purpose rather than let it mindlessly pass. It would take at least four days of normal life to dilute the potency of just one day on the trail.

The difference in the passing of time between normal life and trail life is the only reasonable explanation I can come up with to explain how I went from ordering new gear for a CDT thru-hike while in Delaware Water Gap, to waking up three days later with the desire to quit the AT. Three days in normal life equated to twelve days in trail time. Only seventy-two hours passed between crossing the Delaware River into New Jersey and crossing the official state line into New York, but a switch was flipped in my mind, and I was finished walking.

I woke up in a wretched mood on the morning of our fifty-seventh day on the trail, and could already feel the cloud of mosquitoes waiting to pounce once I left the tent. The sun was shining, but it was hard to see through the dense forest we slept in the night before, and the upcoming elevation appeared ridiculously easy. Once we were out of the forest and atop ridges, it was slow progress over huge boulders that made for awkward footing. My foul mood continued as I grew frustrated with the increasingly difficult terrain.

Just after the New Jersey/New York border, we stopped for a break on Prospect Rock. Something inside of me snapped. I pulled out the guidebook, anxious to see where the next town was, with the thought, "What is the fastest way off this trail?"

"I'm quitting," I said to Matt. We both knew the conviction in my voice was telling the truth.

Within three miles was a side trail to Greenwood Lake, New York, and even that seemed too far to walk. I wanted off the trail immediately. As Matt sat there in disbelief, I called the local bus company for a schedule out of Greenwood Lake and made plans to go home. Before I called our parents to tell them I was on my way home, he stopped and asked that we spend time in town first in order to talk about our options. I wanted nothing to do with him or the consideration of my decision. I'd had enough of the bugs and couldn't take the discomforts anymore.

Looking back, even I can't fully explain how I went from talking about two thru-hikes in one summer, to a resolute decision to quit the AT, all in three days. Going into New Jersey, I believe now that I knew in the back of my mind that I was setting myself up for disaster if I thought the trail was suddenly going to be easier after Pennsylvania. I really thought that the rocks would end, that good weather would come back, and that the terrain would allow for the effortless thirty-mile days we hiked in Virginia. Matt's lack of memories from New Jersey and New York had tricked me into believing that he didn't remember them because they were so uneventfully easy. The unexpected intensity of the bugs was also a huge slap in the face and my response to the challenges was to give up.

That morning, I was mad at myself for being so foolish over the last few days, for holding out such false hope, and I was mad at Matt for being such a relentlessly strong, good person. There was no possible way he was quitting, even though he'd already hiked the trail once before. He had set out to do something and he was going to finish it. He wouldn't quit with me and in making the journey home alone, I knew the repercussions of my actions would be deeply damaging to our relationship. It would be more than just a physical separation from each other if I left him to hike alone.

Matt had the character of the person I could only hope to be, and I felt like I was living a lie that I had as much character as him. Quitting the AT felt like I could finally give up the facade that I was an outdoorsy, worldly, enemy-loving person who thrived on challenges like the AT. In all honestly,

I didn't particularly enjoy great views or wildlife, I loved settling into the comforts of home, and I found it very hard to be nice to everyone. I didn't thrive on the AT. Instead, it beat me down so hard that it appeared that I thrived because I could only go up from the bottom.

To keep hiking was not thriving for me. It was surviving. For me, to thrive would have meant living in the present moment and finding significance in that moment, no matter the quality of it. I had merely been surviving, and it wasn't enough for me to continue.

A few miles later, we silently left the white blazes of the trail as we turned right on the Village Vista Trail, where we followed blue blazes for the first time. It was a steep side trail that fed us into Greenwood Lake, just .8 miles later. Matt had wanted to continue on another two miles to where there was a road with just a slightly longer walk to town. He wanted to avoid the steep hike back up to the AT the next day, but I had none of it. I wanted off the trail and was taking the fastest possible escape. My only concern was that I would never step foot on the trail again. Even now I find it unforgivable that I didn't care what kind of trail Matt had to face alone the next day.

We walked into a hot, busy town, on the Saturday before Memorial Day. Flags hung from telephone poles, angled into the streets, and there was a content feeling about the town. We could tell it was a three-day weekend just by the atmosphere. I was happy to be off the trail as we sat on a park bench and looked at our lodging options.

After calling a few hotels, with zero vacancy, we walked to the edge of town, to Anton's on the Lake, a hotel with a B&B feel and a reputation for being friendly to hikers. The wife of the couple that owned the place saw us walk aimlessly over the grounds, looking for the office with clueless looks on our faces. She had been sitting down, working in the garden, and saw us walk up before we noticed her.

She called out to us as she walked over the grass to approach us, "Can I help you?"

"Yes, we know it's a holiday weekend, but do you happen to have a room?" Matt asked with little hope in his voice. I stood in the background with a lump in my throat as I tried to hold back the tears.

She stayed silent as she crossed the lawn, a pair of hedge clippers in one hand and gardening gloves in the other. Once she reached us, she leaned forward, and in her English-accented half-whisper, she smiled and said, "Well, you're damn lucky, because I do!"

We both exhaled a sigh of relief that we hadn't realized we were holding in. In my mind, a hotel stay meant that I could spend time with Matt for the rest of the day before I left the next morning. For Matt, it was precious time to convince me to stay on the trail.

I couldn't help but pour my heart out to the hotel owner as we sat in the air-conditioned office and paid for the room. The first time I told her that I was quitting, I nearly choked on the declaration and could barely get it out. She seemed well-versed in talking hikers back from the ledge, because she went into motherly-comfort mode immediately.

She didn't tell me what to do, or what not do to, and let me vent about the hiking. She also assured us that I wasn't the first to struggle through the New Jersey/New York section. I felt much better after talking with her and agreed that I wouldn't make a final decision until the next morning, after I'd had a good night's rest.

She also told us there were two other hikers scheduled to arrive that day, as they had reservations: Stretch and Zippers. Our ears perked up immediately and I felt a glimmer of hope. I thought it might do Matt and me some good to be in the company of another couple that had gone through the same rain, the same terrain, and the same bug-infested trail, as we just had over the past few days. Until they arrived, Matt and I sat in our room and talked about solutions.

At first, I was hesitant to show any interest in a solution. I had found my solution and it was quitting the trail. But, once I was off the trail, I was able to step outside of myself and see how my decisions affected the rest of Matt's hike. He would have to carry all the pack weight that we currently shared between the two of us, and he would hike completely alone.

It seemed like a small form of a separation for our marriage as we talked over the consequences. The negative side effects of my solution were growing, and I hated to admit that I was the cause of every one of them. We sat in our room and debated our solutions for hours. I was tucked under the bed covers as Matt paced the floor in front of me.

I knew exactly when it hit home that I couldn't quit. Matt asked me to do something for him before he got back on the trail the next morning. He asked me to write a trail obituary for our blog, so I could explain to everyone why I was quitting. We had a small following of family, friends, and even strangers on the blog, and he wanted the story to come from me, in my words, so there would be complete transparency as to why I had quit and what truly happened. He knew that I wanted to just slink away and go into hiding at my mom's home in Cincinnati, and that I didn't want to admit to readers that I was weak and couldn't handle the challenges of the trail.

In other words, he wasn't letting me get off that easily.

I hated him for it. I hated that he knew me so well that he could see three steps ahead of me and block the path I so desperately wanted to run down. I also hated that he was such a good person. He always did the right thing, the moral thing, the thing only a person with a strong, unquestionable character and clear sense of judgment would do. I wanted to have that strong of a character, and oftentimes I did, but my choices didn't always align with the high standards that he abided by so staunchly.

And yet, I hated that he was so damn right.

I couldn't say no to him and just leave, and I couldn't say yes. I couldn't write my trail obituary, just like I couldn't quit the trail. I didn't have a great reason for quitting, other than I simply didn't want to be so uncomfortable any more. I couldn't write, "Sorry folks, this is just too hard and I'd rather be at home, watching TV and eating a sandwich." I wasn't quitting because I was injured or because I'd run out of money, or because of anything I couldn't overcome with enough determination. My reasons for quitting wouldn't be justified enough for readers, and therefore they weren't good enough for my conscience.

That evening, a two part plan was hatched. First, we bought bug spray. Full on, 100% DEET; we weren't messing around and we each carried a four-ounce bottle. Second, we dropped pack weight. We'd been carrying a three-season, free-standing tent that had been one of our luxuries on the trail. But, it weighed a whopping five pounds and there were plenty of shelters to sleep in, so it was tossed in the "send home" pile. Our stove, its fuel, and the pot also weighed at least four pounds combined, so we opted for cold food, as it was called on the trail, and gave up our warm, cooked meals. Along with the tent and stove, we shed a few other random items that seemed unnecessary, like a razor, dental floss (probably should have kept that), and flip-flops.

The manner in which we dropped pack weight may have not been the best decision, to the point of being "stupid light," as we'd heard it called, but if it meant saving the hike, then it was worth it. We weighed our packs that night, and mine dropped from around thirteen pounds to just eight, and Matt's from about sixteen pounds to eleven. Without food or water, my pack was smaller than most day packs. I had to admit that the dreary day behind us was fading quickly, and I went to sleep thinking, "This was by far the worst day yet on the trail, and it can only get better from here."

I hoped I was right, because I couldn't handle many more of them.

We spoke to Stretch and Zippers early the next day, after we'd made our plans and revived our spirits. We talked a little about the trials and tribulations of the trail and my desire to quit. Zippers was shocked to hear that I'd already completed a PCT thru-hike and still had thoughts of quitting the AT. Yet, they were quick to concede that they too had been hit with the hiker blues after rainy, rocky Pennsylvania, only to be greeted with ninety-degree weather and bugs in New Jersey and New York. The weather had greatly affected their moods and had recently pushed them both to grouchy states. Zippers admitted to also being bored, saying she had lost some of the fun she'd previously found in hiking because of the new challenges that New Jersey and New York presented.

After meeting them, I also felt better knowing I wasn't the only one that had noticed the astounding amount of rocks still present. Zippers even described the first few miles in New York as "downright grueling," and I felt true validation in those words.

It was a short conversation among the four of us, but we covered all kinds of topics, from the ever-present majority of men that rarely allowed for girl-talk among females, to the amazement in the quantity of food they'd been able to eat over the course of the trail. Just to name a few, their eating feats involved an entire birthday (sheet!) cake and a box of Life cereal and a quart of milk. Both times, they ate all the food in one sitting. Despite their increase in food consumption, Stretch had already lost so much weight that at one point, he put his underwear on backwards and didn't notice it until he went to the bathroom to pee. He came out of the bathroom with a smile and said to Zippers, "Honey, it's official – I have no ass."

The one piece of trail life that we differed greatly on was our resupply preparations. They were on top of things while we lagged greatly, and we were slightly embarrassed when we found out how much smarter they'd been in preparations. They had set up a mail drop schedule for the entire trail well ahead of time, having dehydrated about seventy-five meals for the two of them. The meals accounted for nearly two-thirds of their food along the trail, and they bought the rest in towns along the way. We had yet to send ourselves any boxes and relied solely on the towns we passed through, or on the surprise boxes our family and friends had sporadically sent. Oftentimes, gas stations were our grocery store and town often meant pizza and ice cream. We were vegetarians, but I couldn't remember the last fruit or vegetable I had consumed as we stood there learning about their wholesome, dehydrated meals.

They had taken a huge piece of the trail, food resupply, and planned it out well ahead of time, to take the stress of resupplies out of the current equation. They were essentially eating healthy, nourishing, home-cooked meals of dehydrated stews, bean dips, and fruit. We were setting off from Greenwood Lake with a bag of chips for each day, candy bars, and jars of peanut butter.

It almost felt like a no-brainer as to why I'd been so unhappy on the trail, because I was eating so much junk all the time. They attributed a large portion of their success on the trail to their diligence in preparing and eating high calorie, healthy food along the way. Matt and I admired their ability to prepare so well for the trail, and wished we had done better, knowing it could have enhanced our trail experience. We knew something would have to change regarding our resupply strategy if we were ever going to take on another long hike.

Stretch and Zippers were the final push that I needed to get me back on the trail. I felt reassured about our hike after just ten minutes of talking to them. Zippers had an energy that was fun to be around and Stretch seemed like the engineer-type that knew how to get things done. Unfortunately, they had planned a day off at Stretch's mom's home in Albany, so we would inevitably get ahead of them on the trail. I hoped they would somehow catch us so we could be around such positive, realistic, and driven individuals, and so Zippers and I could have some much-needed girl talk. I hadn't realized I was even missing it until we breached the topics of sports bras and periods, after which the conversation died because Matt and Stretch stood there in an awkward silence.

I took a deep breath as we set out from Greenwood Lake that morning and made our way up the steep side trail that I was sure I'd never see again. I kicked myself for caring so little about Matt's hike the day before, because the least I could have done was hike further so that we would only have a road walk or a hitch back to the trail. Instead, there I was, paying for my bad behavior. However, the steep uphill was less noticeable because of the sheer lack of pack weight on our backs. I hardly felt my pack on my hips and shoulders and was immediately grateful for our decision to leave the tent and stove behind in Greenwood Lake.

My outlook changed as we continued over the rocky terrain that day. The heat didn't let up and the rocks didn't disappear, but I realized that maybe it was possible to both hike the trail and still hate parts of it. I let myself hate the rocks, the rolling terrain, and the lack of excitement in the state of New York. I also let myself love the time with Matt, the chance to burn calories and therefore eat without regret, and the ability to wake up each day without a trip to the office. I had been living like it was all or none, and I felt like a poser on the trail if I secretly hated certain aspects of it. I thought that I had to love everything if I was going to be a thru-hiker. Meeting Zippers and Stretch gave me the freedom to stay on the trail because they too had parts of the trail that they didn't enjoy, but there was no question that they were continuing on. They took it all in, the good and the bad.

After admitting that I loved and hated the AT all at the same time, it allowed me to laugh at some of the ridiculousness of the trail. There were some sections that had special names for no reason other than they were the only cubic-zirconium in the rough. One such example is the Lemon Squeezer, which was a tiny section of trail through a tight rock formation. The trail could have simply gone around it, but it went through it, and while it was sort of interesting to walk through such a section, it was slow and paled in comparison to so many other great parts of the trail. Sections like the Lemon Squeezer weren't even worthy of being a diamond, but they were better than the surroundings, which held little views, few rewards for the difficult hiking, and very little excitement. I had to laugh at those types of sections and nearly felt sorry for them. I'd already been blessed with walking through Yosemite, and I was supposed to find significance in a short, tightly squeezed section of trail through rock walls. I found that being angry with such a meaningless little blip of a data point along the trail did nothing to help my mood, and that knowledge was comforting.

The first night without a tent and a stove was an adjustment. Our normal routines were greatly altered when I no longer had a tent to set up and Matt no longer had a meal to cook. We were left with cold food and a space on the floorboards of the Fingerboard Shelter. Yet, our spirits were hopeful because we were excited to have such light packs and to test our new way of hiking. Dinner was an assortment of potato chips, peanut butter, and chocolate. I wasn't fully satisfied from the meal and I only stopped eating because I was simply tired of chewing. The shelter was hot and buggy, and while we had DEET to save us, I wasn't ready to smear it all over my face. I chose to sweat under my down-filled sleeping bag, out of the mosquitoes' reach.

I refused to be discouraged after just one day and vowed to continue the experiment of giving up comforts in order to carry a lower pack weight. As we went to bed slightly hungry and sweaty, we questioned our decisions, but we were both ready for another day, which was another day further than we expected me to be.

22 THE SHELTER LIFE

Casting aside our tent created a few side effects that we hadn't expected, or at the very least, hadn't taken very seriously. First, our mileage was fixed. There wouldn't be a day where we just didn't feel like hiking anymore, out in the middle of the woods, where a nice looking flat spot could be our campsite. We were stuck with whatever mileage challenges the shelters created, which meant we had to be content with covering eighteen miles one day and twenty-eight the next, rather than two twenty-three mile days.

Also, we were suddenly competing for shelter space. Before, it never mattered what time we arrived at a shelter, unless there were predictions of crazy storms, and if there wasn't room at the inn, we had our tent to fall back on. Without a tent, precious shelter space could be filled by people that stopped hiking much earlier in the day than us, or by groups that were passing through. Taking into account this dilemma of supply and demand, we agreed to each other that if we ever arrived at a full shelter, we had to be mentally and physically prepared to move on to the next one, no matter how tired we were. Basically, there would be no bitching from either of us if we had to walk extra miles. That clause was mainly, and rightly so, directed towards me.

Lastly, there was nowhere to hide. We had to be social. Normally, once we arrived at shelters, I set up the tent and I changed my clothes in our tent before coming out for dinner. Our tent allowed for the privacy to change and to unwind before socializing with others. The shelters were an inherently social environment, so we had to adapt to that environment once they became our official home. I was already not an extremely social person by nature and I liked my personal space, so it took more effort on my part than Matt's to uphold this part of the contract with the shelters.

Yet, the shelters allowed us to drop five pounds of tent weight between the two of us, and they were dependable, even if the space inside them wasn't. I eventually looked forward to them as they became our permanent residence each night, and I was grateful for being part of that unique aspect of the AT. They also lead us to meet amazing people along the way, which we may have never met had we been zipped inside our two-person tent.

I was ready to get moving by the next morning because I was hot under my sleeping bag and I welcomed the morning walk in the cool, foggy clouds. We hadn't seen fog for a few days and I was ashamed to admit that I had missed it. It temporarily knocked out the bugs and we walked the first few miles of the day in a sort of daze. At the first stream we crossed, we met Squash, who we hadn't seen since my gluttonous coffee cake day in Unionville, for which I still hadn't forgiven myself.

Squash walked with us for the next two miles and soon after, the trail popped out into a clearing to reveal the William Brien Memorial Shelter, a dark, musty shelter set back into a rock wall. As Squash started heading towards the shelter, he turned around to face us with an enticing question, "Coffee break?"

We looked at each other, and Matt looked as indecisive as I felt. We didn't normally take impulsive breaks, but the sound of warm coffee on a foggy morning on the trail was so inviting, no matter how crappy that shelter looked.

"Hmm…ok! We'll do it!" I said. "And we'll trade you dark chocolate for coffee, if you'd like."

It was a deal, and we sat in the old, beaten-down shelter, with holes in its floorboards and trash in the corners, talking about the challenges of the trail over cups of hot coffee and squares of dark chocolate. Though I didn't outwardly say it to Matt, my motivation to stay on the trail was still wavering. The aftershocks of my breakdown in Greenwood Lake had lingered and I had my doubts about staying on the trail, knowing there was an upcoming train station on the trail that could take me to New York City.

We hiked most of the late morning with Squash, sprinting across the Palisades Parkway together and climbing the well-maintained trail up to Bear Mountain. Once at the top, we toasted vending-machine Fantas at the Perkins Memorial, surrounded by crowds of people who'd driven to the top, off work for Memorial Day. The sun was out, the day was warm, and it was nice to be around people on a holiday. When we were in the middle of the woods on a holiday, far from any town, we just couldn't celebrate the holiday the same as the rest of the country.

All three of us had lunch together in the recreation area at Hessian Lake, after which we said goodbye to Squash at the Trailside Museum. He was headed to town the next morning for a package and was going to camp near the lake. I was sad to see him go, like I was with so many hikers in the past, including Zippers and Stretch. I counted him in the category of hikers that I knew could make my trail experience that much better because of their presence.

The rest of the day was sleepy with oncoming humidity, but we took our time with the miles, knowing we had plenty of daylight to hike. Just before our destination shelter for the day, we crossed a road with a market and indulged in packing out a pint of Ben & Jerry's ice cream to take to the shelter for dessert. If we were forcing ourselves to stay in the shelters, we were at least going to find ways to improve our living space, which usually happened with food. We arrived at the Graymoor Spiritual Center with an hour of daylight left, and met just one other section hiker occupying the shelter.

It wasn't the typical AT shelter, as it lacked walls, but there was a roof over our heads and folding tables to sleep on. We went to sleep for a second night with mosquitoes buzzing around us, never touching down on our chemically covered body parts.

Our sixtieth day on the trail started with a strong desire to start walking. It never cooled down enough to decrease the bug activity and neither of us had slept very well. My fear of rolling off the folding table had also kept me awake. I knew how much I rolled over from my side to my back over the course of a night and was hesitant to test the width of the table.

The day's mileage choices were either eighteen or twenty-eight miles, but rather than make an early decision, we started walking without a destination in order to account for the terrain. We walked over small rollers all day while the sun increased the temperatures, and our lack of sleep eventually affected our energy levels. The day became brutally hot by late afternoon and the air was thick as we approached the RPH shelter, our end point for the day. Though it was only 3:00 p.m. when we stopped for the day, knowing we could have easily hiked ten more miles to the next shelter, we were ready to finish. The empty shelter was different from the normal shelter because not only was it a fully enclosed space, it was also bug-free. We both took a short nap in the shelter, the afternoon heat lulling us to sleep. I lay under my sleeping bag, clammy from the humidity, yet chilly in the shade.

Another hiker soon entered the shelter and woke us up. We quickly fell into conversation with him as he cooled off in the shelter, soaked in sweat from hiking during the heat of the day. His name was Marathon Mouse, and though he was a northbound thru-hiker, he had to be creative with his miles because of upcoming schedule conflicts in real life, so he was headed southbound at the moment. We'd seen his names in the journals and had assumed he quit since he disappeared from the regular entries of northbounders, so it was satisfying to put a face to the name and to hear that he was still on the trail.

It didn't take long for the conversation to reach the topics of my desire to quit in Greenwood Lake and my inability to fully shake that desire. He jumped right into talking some sense into me when he heard I had wavered.

"Don't quit," he said flatly. "You may think it's a good idea now, but three months down the road, you'll regret it."

I knew he was right and it was helpful to hear it from someone other than Matt.

He also admitted, with no shame in his voice, that he thought about quitting every day. But, he didn't succumb to the desire because he knew he couldn't go back to his family and friends having quit.

It was good for me to hear. He didn't sugar coat anything, he agreed that many parts of the lifestyle were not fun, and he made me realize I needed to finish what I started. I was so grateful for whatever sixth sense made us stop early that day, because meeting him pushed me over the final hump that I needed to put the idea of quitting behind me.

Once I thought over what he had to say, taking into account what I learned from Stretch and Zippers, that other people simply made the choice to push through the hard stuff and concentrate on something else, I said with surprise, because I hadn't truly processed what came out of my mouth next, "Maybe I just need to nut up!"

The words felt utterly inappropriate as I said them, because though I was known to let a few cuss words fly, I never *actually* talked like I was a guy. But, the sentence couldn't have summed up my sentiment any better. I'd been a cry baby for too long and was tired of telling a sad sob story that only made me feel sorry for myself. I needed to stand up straight, tighten my pack straps, live with my choices, and just keep walking.

From then on the evening only got better. We ordered pizza delivery to the shelter and enjoyed a bug-free night of sleep after an evening of conversation with Marathon Mouse. Most importantly, we came up with a plan to motivate us over the next several days. We called it the Beach Body Push.

23 BEACH BODY PUSH

One of Matt's tactics to motivate people to do something, especially kids, is to make a game out of it. The night that we camped with Matt's sister and her two young boys, on the eve of our AT hike, we built a campfire. We inevitably had to gather wood for the fire, and the two boys inevitably wanted to do whatever the adults were doing. At first it seemed like a hindrance to have them following us around, trying to be a part of the fire in any way they could, until Matt made a game of it.

"Let's see who can collect the most sticks in the next five minutes!" he said to the boys, and their eyes lit up with the chance to be useful and to compete against each other.

Matt showed them the types of sticks to pick up after Austin, the five-year-old, tried to carry an entire branch to the campfire. We couldn't blame him for going for quality over quantity.

Beach Body Push was the motivation game that we needed. We were closing in on our vacation with family in Myrtle Beach, South Carolina, which was due to start on June 10, and the date of the evening with Marathon Mouse was May 31. We had nine more days of hiking to get in as many miles as possible before vacation, and to burn some calories in hopes of looking better on the beach. We liked the satisfaction that came with hiking big miles, with finishing a day tired yet proud of our efforts, and with pushing ourselves to our limits, and possibly, beyond them.

We set our sights high with a goal of reaching Rutland, Vermont, which could have been either 255 or 273 miles away, depending on the road we reached. As it stood, we needed to average twenty-eight miles a day to arrive at the first Rutland crossroad, and thirty miles a day to reach the next. It seemed attainable, especially given the miles we were able to walk when our motivation was at its highest.

We looked at the next few days' miles with Marathon Mouse in order to get his input on the difficulty of the miles since he had just hiked them. The push looked fabulous on paper, and though we were a little scared of the mileage numbers, we were excited to have a new plan and to have vacation just over a week away.

Day one of the Beach Body Push and day sixty-one on the trail started off with clear, cool, sunny skies. The goal for the day was simple: get out of New York. I wanted the state behind me because the one prominent story that came out of the state was my desire to quit the trail. The Connecticut border was twenty-six miles away and the shelter beyond that was three and a half miles further. Even though the elevation looked easy, we'd been fooled by it before. We started early, vowed to go late if necessary, and kept the breaks to a minimum. It felt good to push ourselves, especially after being softies over the last few days with all my emotions getting in the way.

Except for a few highlights, the day was far from memorable, considering it was the start of such a focused effort. The sign for the Connecticut border came up quickly and we finally put the state of New York behind us. We had a new purpose, crossing a border felt like a fresh start, and our optimism was renewed that sunny, warm afternoon. I realized over and over again what a downer I had been to myself, to Matt, and to our relationship. I no longer wanted to negatively affect the hike with my personal issues. I wanted to contribute to the hiking experience, for the better, and to make both our hikes that much easier despite the continuing challenges.

Shortly after the border, after hiking in heavily wooded forests, we arrived at the Ten Mile River Shelter, which we shared with three other people. Day one of the Beach Body Push: success.

Day two began with a beautiful start to the miles. It was chilly, the perfect hiking temperature in the strengthening morning sun, and we were the first ones out of the shelter. Our love for the cool, quiet, summer mornings had been rejuvenated. There hadn't been many mornings like that on the AT as compared to the PCT, and we missed it. The mornings were our time to work through all our thoughts without many interruptions, before the trail traffic, and before the heat or the bugs could join us for the day.

The trail was slightly rolling, but the footing was smooth and we covered the first nine miles of the morning without much effort. After those nine miles, we arrived at CT 341, the road into the town of Kent, our next resupply point. We were in such good spirits from the tranquil morning that we actually *wanted* to walk the extra .8 miles into town. It was the most beautiful way to enter Kent. One moment we passed by rolling fields, and the next, just after crossing a bridge, we saw an impeccably manicured lawn at a school on the edge of town. Next, we saw pristine streets with well-maintained buildings that had an old style but a new feel. It was the most majestic town I'd seen yet on the trail.

In a span of just a few hours, we spread out our hunger over pastries and coffee, sandwiches, and Chinese food. The local supermarket was a beacon of light after eating chips and chocolate for the last few days, and we scoured its aisles with unmatched excitement, trying to uncover healthier meal options.

Just as we headed out of town, Squash came in. We last saw him before we met Marathon Mouse, and because we had such a different outlook on our miles, it was like meeting him for the first time all over again. We were excited to share our plans with someone we'd known from "the past," at least that's what those bad days already felt like. Since he had just arrived in town, we knew it was doubtful that he'd catch us, but we told him about our Beach Body Push, in case he got a fire under him to speed up and hike with us. Another part of playing games to motivate ourselves was learning how helpful it was to include others in the games. It was that much harder to quit the games when other people depended on our participation.

The afternoon heat never rolled in and we covered the next seventeen miles with surprising ease, making our way through beautifully wooded forests and sun-soaked fields along the banks of the Housatonic River. Our adrenaline was pumping as we pushed to make it to a shelter before dark, and we arrived at the Pine Swamp Brook Shelter just as dusk was settling in. We shared the shelter with two New Yorkers who were out for a small section. My body and mind were tired from such a full day that included a resupply stop, but I already felt my batteries recharging as I ate dinner in the enclosing darkness, my headlamp focused on the Ziploc bag in front of me. We were intensely satisfied with our progress over the last two days of hiking, and it took us a while to calm down from the exhilaration of pushing to the shelter before dark. I went to sleep excited to start the next day.

The next day's mileage was a little trickier because we had the choice between twenty-one and thirty miles, and neither option sounded pleasant. One was a tad too short and one was a tad too long. We wanted the Goldilocks version of one that was just right, so we pushed the decision off until later and headed up the trail with a full dose of determination to start the day. Both of us knew that we were capable of covering the thirty miles, even on a tough day, so we gave up trying to gauge the day's difficulty by the guidebook and just kept walking.

The only time we got turned around was near Falls Village, Connecticut, where the AT crossed the road twice. There wasn't a white blaze in sight. We passed by a school, looking confused as we looked up at the trees and telephone poles for a sign of the trail. For one of the first times, Matt even got a little snippy when we couldn't find the path. He had the ability to stay calm during the most stressful situations, but once he was in the position of being turned around, he grew frustrated and annoyed. It didn't happen often on a trail that was clearly marked with white blazes, but when it did, an unexpected side of Matt was revealed. Maybe he's human after all. We were also feeling the mileage pressure of the last few days, so each minute that passed without seeing a blaze wore on us. We eventually found a blaze on a telephone pole near the school, which we hadn't seen because it was mostly covered by overgrown trees. Matt's grumpiness subsided and we avoided any major blow-ups once we finally got back on the trail.

The second half of our day was steady, with a couple of difficult climbs and increasing heat. We decided to reach the shelter thirty miles away and with eight miles left in the day, we put in a hard effort to reach the top of Bear Mountain, only to be followed by an even more challenging ascent up Mt. Everett. Marathon Mouse had warned us of the two climbs, and rightly so. They were two of the hardest climbs we'd seen in several days. Once near the top of both of them, the trail changed from hiking through smooth forests to climbing up steep slabs of rock. The two climbs unexpectedly wiped us out, and we shuffled into The Hemlocks Shelter, already half-asleep with exhaustion. Day three of Beach Body Push had finally done some damage. Though our mental motivation was still fairly high, our physical energy had been drained. I was so tired that I could barely muster up the desire to eat dinner. I had a feeling that our bodies weren't recovering as fast as they did with lower mileage and I feared that my body wouldn't be so eager to start the next day.

The hard effort at the end of the day took place in the first few miles of Massachusetts, just over 1500 miles into the trail, and we laid our heads to rest with a strong sense of accomplishment. Not only had we covered the miles, but we had also checked off another state.

As if the previous day's shelter locations hadn't been spread out far enough, with nine miles between them, the next day took the spread to another level. We had the choice between two shelters that were either twenty-one or thirty-five miles away. The shelter thirty-five miles away was special because it was the Upper Goose Pond Cabin, complete with bunk beds, mattresses, porches, canoeing, and best of all, but only a rumor, a caretaker that cooked pancakes and brewed coffee for hikers.

It wasn't the pull of a town with a B&B and a diner, but it was enough to let our stomachs be our guides on our sixty-third day. We sleepily peeled ourselves off the shelter floorboards for another day of hammering out the miles. It was remarkable what the mere rumor of pancakes and coffee did for our motivation, especially since it was thirty-five miles up the trail and twenty-four hours away.

I'd like to say I remember a lot from that day, but in all honesty, the focus on the miles is what I remember, as well as the feelings Matt and I had. Sometimes people criticize others who hike big miles because they say the hikers are going too fast to notice their surroundings and are missing out on scenery. I was certainly going slow enough to notice the trees, the flowers, and the endless amount of footbridges, streams and ponds, but the scenery wasn't as memorable for me as the feeling of concentrating so hard on a goal with Matt right there with me, pushing over the same terrain. We worked together and kept each other's spirits up, and for me, that was more satisfying than any scene in nature.

That day was particularly memorable for Matt because it was the same section his dad had hiked with him in 2000. They too had stayed at the cabin and celebrated Matt's twentieth birthday. It was a special day for Matt, especially as we walked the final miles to the cabin as the sun was setting. It looked just how he remembered it from eleven years ago and he swelled with pride and emotions at the sight of the porch, where he remembered sitting with his dad. It made me tear up just to witness the memories passing across his eyes like he was watching clips of a movie as he stared at the porch. All day, he had pieced together the memories of his hike from 2000 and the miles with his dad like they were a puzzle. He already had the edge pieces and a few moments of clarity snapped him back in time to where suddenly he had entire sections that revealed a clearer picture. By that evening, many more memories and stories had come back to him and we were both happy we had pushed to the cabin.

We went to sleep in separate bunks in a hot, crowded shelter, worn out from the four consecutive days of high mileage and hopeful that pancakes would be a part of the next morning.

In keeping up with the trend of days that started with a three, at the first sign of daylight we awoke to the plan of another thirty-mile day. We packed up and headed downstairs to the caretaker's quarters in search of caffeine. Hot coffee had already been made, a table was set for eight, and other hikers started to mill about like hungry sharks circling their prey. The caretaker cooked pancakes on the griddle by the light of his headlamp and we were some of the first hikers to eat the first round of food.

We ate quickly, knowing we wanted to start walking and being cognizant of taking too much time at the table. The amount of hungry hikers sitting on the front porch increased by the minute, so we opened up our seats to the next two in line and shot out on the trail with surprisingly fresh legs.

As if we needed any more motivation than a vacation just five days away, our end destination for the day was the town of Cheshire, which meant town food. We had also planned on eating food at both the Cookie Lady's home and in the town of Dalton, two stops along the way to Cheshire.

With the exception of a hill early in the day, it was a very easy day of hiking. Eleven miles into our day, we reached the Washington Mountain Road. Just .1 miles down the road was the residence of the famed Cookie Lady, who was noted in the guidebook as a trail angel who offered services to hikers like shuttles to town, water, and camping. Most importantly, she also offered freshly baked cookies. While it felt completely normal to plan this stop, it was actually quite awkward once we arrived. It felt strange to walk up the porch steps, knock on a stranger's door, obviously in search of cookies, and honestly ask, "So, do you have any cookies?"

The Cookie Lady was happy to bring out a basket of cookies and seemed genuinely interested in our hike. We sat on her porch for forty-five minutes, petting their dog, eating her cookies, and chatting about the hike. The longer we sat there, the more antsy I felt about having enough time to cover the remaining nineteen miles, but again, Matt had character, and therefore I had it vicariously, so we sat on the porch and enjoyed the breezy shade with cookies and conversation.

We left the Cookie Lady with less than ten miles to walk to the town of Dalton, and just before 3:00 p.m., we walked right through the town. It was one of several towns where the trail took us on sidewalks, through traffic lights, and in search of white blazes on telephone poles. Before leaving town, we stopped for a late lunch in a sub shop and both consumed a hiker-normal amount of food, our hunger having increased with the past several days of high mileage. At the end of the meal, as we sat in a booth across from each other, I saw a sudden wave of exhaustion hit Matt. His eyes started to close, he laid his head down on the table, and he spoke of extreme fatigue. We thought he'd hit a food coma and agreed to start walking so he could wake up. Had we paid more attention to the dramatic shift in his energy levels, we may not have continued walking to Cheshire.

24 OPTIMIST HITS THE FLOOR

The nine mile hike from Dalton to Cheshire should have been easy. It was a nice, gradual ascent up a mountain and a nice, gradual descent down the other side and into town. In fact, it was easy for me, but it might have been the hardest miles yet for Matt.

We left the sub shop as soon as Matt hit his food coma, at least that's what we thought had happened. The entire uphill out of Dalton, including the walk on the sidewalk, was difficult for Matt, and he had to take multiple breaks to get his strength back. We reasoned that a bout of food poisoning was coming on since the effects hit him immediately after finishing his sandwich. But, stomach aches never came and he never threw up, so we eventually reasoned that it was a *unique* bout of food poisoning. I didn't know what to do or how to console him, other than to take several breaks and to walk at a crawling pace. I had never been the stronger hiker and it was a strange new role that I didn't yet know how to play.

The last half hour of hiking was on a downhill into town and I could see the road as we reached the bottom of the hill. Matt asked to take a break and I was stunned to see how bad he looked. His eyes drooped, he could barely hold his head up, and he said to me as he stood there in a daze, "I don't know if I can keep walking. We might have to camp right here."

What? With just over a mile to go, when we could practically see the town and we only had a road-walk left? I knew he felt weak but I hadn't realized it was that extreme, and I was shocked that he might not be able to hike another thirty minutes. However, I didn't object and I agreed to do whatever it took for him to make it through the miles, and more importantly, to make it to town if he needed medicine.

We sat on the side of the trail for ten minutes, after which he agreed to continue at a very slow pace. I led the way and we soon arrived in Cheshire, Massachusetts. There was a church in town that allowed hikers to use spare rectory rooms and bathrooms, and we made our way through town to find it. I practically pulled Optimist along behind me, as by that point he had a headache, body aches, and the chills. The fear of food poisoning shifted to that of a twenty-four hour flu bug and we both assumed it would only last for a day or less.

After finding the church, I made up our bed on the cold, tiled, rectory floor with an egg shell foam pad, our sleeping pads, and Matt's sleeping bag. He immediately curled up in his bag and fell asleep…for the next twenty hours.

I spent that entire evening alone, worrying about Matt. I ate pizza and a salad from a local restaurant, but my love for town food didn't feel the same as I ate dinner alone. He didn't eat any dinner or drink any water, and woke up a few times to babble in a daze and then head back to dream land. He spoke of exhaustion and flu-like symptoms, so we both let him do what he wanted, which was to simply sleep.

As I tell this, I'm somewhat surprised that our only remedy was to let him sleep. I didn't call a doctor, we didn't buy any medicine, and I didn't even research his symptoms on the internet. We were still of the belief that it was food poisoning or the flu because he felt sick immediately after eating. It was really quite stupid of us, considering our age and experience on the trail. It was another, "What were we thinking?" moment.

Matt slept through the night and got up the next day to pee, after he'd been lying on the floor for twelve hours. In normal hiking life, we could barely go more than two hours without peeing, especially through the night, so it was scary to think of how dehydrated he was. Still, he went back to sleep again until the afternoon.

By late afternoon, it looked like we were staying for another evening at the church, and it was my least favorite option. I had just found my motivation from the Beach Body Push and we'd hiked five huge days so far, with just four days left of hiking until vacation. I wasn't mad at Matt, but rather, I was frustrated at the entire situation and I wished there was something I could do to improve his health. The decision to hike was out of my control, ironically so because my control over that decision was what held us back for so long.

At 3:00 p.m., Matt woke up with more energy, popped a few Ibuprofens, ate some food, and talked about our plans for the day. He didn't want to stay in Cheshire any more than I did, but he feared getting back on the trail in such a weak state of health. It was a legitimate, real fear. We waited to see if the pain pills helped, and by 5:00 p.m., he felt revived. He was ready to hike, even if it was just to the first shelter out of town.

It was five steep miles to the Mark Noepel Shelter and our progress looked grim from the beginning. It was hot outside, especially in the late afternoon sun, the pain pills were wearing off, and the climb zapped all the energy stores Matt had reserved. We took the miles slowly, refusing to go backwards, and arrived by 8:00 p.m. Without delay, Matt set up his bed in the loft of the shelter and went to sleep.

The shelter was bustling with thru-hikers, section hikers, and weekenders. We weren't expecting such a crowd and it was hard to be social when we were so worried about Matt's health. We switched roles again that night while Matt said, "Hello and goodnight," just after we arrived, and I was left to be social. While being social went against the grain of my personality, I knew it took the pressure off Matt so he could rest up for the next day of hiking. Though the setbacks Matt was having differed greatly from the ones I had, I also realized what it was like to hike with someone that had difficulty covering the miles when all I had was motivation to keep hiking. I didn't like playing the role that Matt had played with me for so long and wondered how he ever stayed with me and kept it up. The irony was hard to swallow.

I was anxious to see how Matt would feel the next morning and he woke up feeling surprisingly good. By that point, the whole shelter was worried. The news of his health had traveled fast and it was hard to hide our concern. Everyone offered up solutions and wished us well as we headed up the trail that morning. Matt took more pain pills while I took most of his pack weight to make the day easier on him, and his health improved greatly as compared to the day before.

The morning's first climb rewarded us with stunning views from atop Mt. Greylock and we took a snack break in the warm sun. Matt looked much-improved and our theory that it was a short-lived sickness seemed correct. He didn't feel fully recharged, but he felt good enough for a full day of hiking and was ready to put in the effort to reinstall the Beach Body Push.

By the afternoon, we crossed into Vermont and began the 105.2 mile section of the AT that coincided with the Long Trail, a 273 mile trail through the Vermont Green Mountains. It was a beautiful afternoon with a comforting breeze, and the leaves let just enough sun pierce through the branches for a friendly heat. From then on, the trail had some technical patches of rocks and roots, but it was fairly easy in elevation and our pace picked up in speed.

Just as clouds rolled in behind us, with thunder in the distance, we made it to the Congdon Shelter, just off the side of the trail. Matt was re-energized and he seemed like his normal self, even after a twenty-four mile day. He talked with the others in the shelter while he sat and ate his dinner. Already set-up in the shelter were two men, a father and son. The father was a dentist and the son was an infectious disease doctor, and as we talked to the doctor, we re-considered Matt's mysterious condition.

The threat of Lyme disease had crossed our minds and other people's minds as we described Matt's symptoms of fever, body aches, chills and exhaustion. Yet, Matt never found the "red ring" on his skin, a dead-giveaway of a tick bite, or even an actual tick, to confirm the possibility of Lyme disease. We talked about it with the doctor in the shelter, but he too doubted that it was Lyme disease without the sign of a bite or a tick.

An intense storm rolled in as we talked with them that evening and we were grateful we'd made it to a shelter. We had considered cowboy camping along the trail because the skies looked so clear, but the fast-moving storm supported our decision to reach the shelter. The storm ripped through the area and even destroyed another hiker's tent. We went to sleep just as mystified with Matt's illness as the evening before but both glad he'd been able to put in a full day of miles.

Vacation was so close we could smell it in the air when we awoke the next morning. The cold fog that had rolled in the evening before still refused to lift the next morning, but the misty morning didn't dampen our spirits. Matt also felt normal again. Our mileage options were either twenty-three or thirty-four miles, and we knew we'd be pushing our luck if we tried to do such a big day, especially with Stratton Mountain awaiting us thirty miles into the day. We aimed to hit the shelter at twenty-three miles and took our time in getting there.

Over the course of the day, we walked through more mud than we could remember. Even the rain in Pennsylvania hadn't produced that much mud. We'd heard that June was too early to be hiking through Vermont and I hadn't completely understood why until we nearly lost our shoes in the suction-cup sections of muddy trail. Another hiker around us called the state Vermud and the name fit perfectly. I wondered when the trails ever dried out if the date was already closing in on mid-June and the mud was still several inches deep.

That evening, after miles of more mud with few points of interest to speak of, we made it to the Story Spring Shelter. It was a sad, dingy little shelter just off the side of the trail, next to a well-flowing spring. The gloomy, misty fog made the shelter feel old and depressing within the dense forest, as did the tarp over the front of it to keep out the bugs and the rain. The tarp created a dark, dank atmosphere inside, but we were too tired to care and there was no question whether we were staying the evening or not. It was already closing in on dusk and the next shelter was eleven miles away.

Most importantly, we went to sleep knowing that the next day's mission would change from Beach Body Push to Time for Vacation, and we looked forward to it immensely.

25 THE END OF AN ERA

One of our greatest feats on the PCT, for which we were honestly proud, was that we never took a single day off, also known as a zero. We hiked every day of our one hundred and nine days on the trail. We hadn't meant to start out that way. Before starting the PCT, I had heard many stories of Matt's legendary days off during his 2000 AT hike. I began the PCT with the mindset that no one would come between me and zeros. I planned on spending entire days just soaking my feet, eating copious amounts of food, and sleeping in a bed. It wasn't until three weeks into the PCT hike, when we hadn't yet taken a zero, that we contemplated avoiding zeros altogether. My motivation to walk was lower after experiencing the comforts of town, so I assumed it would be that much harder to get back on the trail after a zero. It made sense for us to stay on the trail each day if it meant a stronger probability of finishing, as long as injuries or sickness weren't a factor.

We began the AT with a similar mindset, never outwardly saying we would avoid zeros, but also never taking them. Having planned the family vacation well before we planned the thru-hike, we were left with a tricky decision. Should we break the streak of never taking a day off or not go on an annual vacation that brought people together from four different states? It all came down to the fact that I didn't want to know the entire family was together, on the beach, while I was suffering over wet, sloppy miles on the AT. I also knew that I'd passed the point of no return by entering Vermont. I had no doubt that I would still have the motivation to finish, even with a week off.

On the morning of our sixty-ninth day on the trail, we woke up knowing that by that evening, we needed to find a way to get from Vermont to South Carolina, most likely in a rental car. Unfortunately, we hadn't booked anything yet, never knowing what exit point to choose. The day we hiked just five miles because of Matt's mystery illness could have never been foreseen, so we were glad we never committed to anything. However, our current section of trail was lined with small towns with few rental car options. Rather than worry, we started walking that day with the hope that all the pieces would fall into place.

It was a wet, cool morning, with heavy fog as we made our way past streams and through dense forests. By mid-morning, we had climbed Stratton Mountain, a pleasant climb in comparison to so many others on wet, cold days. We braved the high winds and climbed the shaky lookout tower for our morning snack break, and started calling rental car companies in Manchester Center, Vermont, the only upcoming town. Nothing was available and little was available in the surrounding towns. The plan wasn't looking so good.

After Stratton, our cell phone lost its signal for the rest of the day and with Manchester Center our only viable option to get off the trail, we decided to postpone plans until arrival into town. It was twenty-one miles from our starting point and we weren't sure how fast we'd cover the miles. The mud made for difficult footing, as did the continuous presence of rocks, yet the elevation was calmly rolling after Stratton.

Breaks were kept to a minimum all day in order to save time for the evening's logistical challenges that awaited us. With just a few miles to go, after we'd been on cruise control all day, the clouds rolled in and we heard thunder in the distance. Just at that moment, as the skies darkened to dusk in the middle of the afternoon, we came upon a shelter junction. The shelter was .1 miles off-trail.

"What do you think?" I asked Matt. "Should we stop or keep going?"

"Let's keep going," we decided in unison, choosing to walk with the hope of getting to town before the storm hit.

We should have known by then that if the skies were that dark, and if the wind had picked up that much, that we weren't going to outrun the storm. Instead, we ran straight into it.

Shortly after the shelter, I knew we'd made a bad decision when lightning struck close to the trail, at the very same moment that thunder boomed over top of us. We were mostly hiking in the trees, but there were small patches of open spaces that were completely exposed to the lightning. The trail had short, steep ascents and descents, but we ran at any chance the trail allowed.

Soon the rain started and the hail followed shortly thereafter. It came in waves of intensity and we timed our sprints across the open spaces with the lightning, though I doubt it would have helped had lightning actually touched down. Matt had difficulty keeping up, not because of exhaustion but because he was wearing glasses. He had run out of contact solution and had worn his glasses for the last few days, only to have them fog up in the rain and the hard effort of running on the trail.

We played the cat and mouse game for the last two miles. I ran ahead through the exposed sections and waited for him on the other side before setting off at a run again. It was the war-zone feeling from Virginia all over again, where fear pushed us forward. Within the last half mile, the rain halted unexpectedly and the skies lightened up. The trees continued to drip on us from overhead, but we breathed easier once out of the threat of lightning. I was certain the trail wanted to send us off on vacation with something to remember it by.

As we approached the road my stomach was in knots with a new fear. I had never hitchhiked in my life and it was our only way into town. It was drilled into me from the beginning of my life that hitchhiking was a bad decision, no matter the situation. Matt and I had made it through the PCT and the AT, up to that point, without ever sticking out our thumbs to strangers. Sure, we had accepted rides, but they were always unsolicited, and even then, low in frequency.

I also refused to walk the extra five and a half miles into town on a busy road where cars flew past me on wet pavement. Vacation was just a hitchhike away, so once we crossed the road to the side directed towards town, Matt and I both stood there and reluctantly stuck out our thumbs. We didn't have to wait long, because the third car that passed us, a white pickup truck, pulled over and made room for us in the front seat among stacks of empty cups, envelopes, and food wrappers.

"You don't mind that we're soaking wet, do you?" Matt asked before climbing into the truck. "We can get in the back if you need us to."

I could see by the current state of the front seat that the driver wouldn't care, but it was polite of him to ask, because the storm hadn't left a dry patch of clothing on us.

"Nah, come on in," the driver said.

It was a quick and easy ride to town, and the driver said he'd often given hikers a ride on his way to and from his work on construction projects. He offered a few suggestions on rental cars and dropped us off at the local outdoor store to see if they had any information. We thanked the driver and said our goodbyes as we left the truck, and even though the first time had gone well, I still didn't like hitchhiking.

After the outdoor store directed us to the appropriate bus stop, we hurried to make it there, afraid of missing the next bus out of town. Our plan was to get to a bigger town. While waiting for the bus, Matt called rental car companies and all conversations ended quickly with the news that no cars were available. We scratched the plans to leave town because there was nothing better within our reach and we sat under the overhang in front of the local Rite Aid, contemplating what to do next while the skies sprinkled rain around us. Matt searched the internet on our phone while I shuffled through my pack for dry clothes.

"Do you guys need anything?" we both heard a woman's faint voice ask from several feet away.

We first looked at each other as if asking each other if the question was directed at us. Then Matt looked up from the phone while I hesitantly turned around. Three parking spots stood between us and a silver minivan, and in the van was a woman in her thirties, with blonde, chin-length hair. She faced us with her head sticking slightly out of the window.

"Are you guys ok? Do you need somewhere to get dry, or a shower or something?" she asked.

All of those things sounded wonderful, but we weren't entirely sure how to respond, especially since our main focus was on getting to South Carolina.

"Well... yeah!" Matt said.

We walked up to the driver-side window and saw a petite black lab sitting in the front passenger seat, as well as a toddler sitting in his car seat in the second row. We explained that we were trying to get a rental car out of town to go on vacation from the trail, but weren't having luck. We learned that the woman's name was Cara, and after hearing our explanation, she offered to take us back to her home so we could shower, do laundry, and use their internet to figure out a plan. She later told us that after she saw Matt's brand of glasses, she made the judgment call to let us into her home based on the fact that it was an expensive brand. I still smile when I think of that and can only thank our former employer's vision plan for paying for them.

All that mattered to us was that we had trail magic that couldn't have come at a better time, and that we made one giant step closer to vacation. To add to the shock value of a mom taking strangers to her home with her young child, after we arrived at their home and exited the car, we saw something else we hadn't noticed on the way over.

Cara was also six months pregnant.

My jaw nearly dropped once I realized how much trust she had put in us and I hoped she didn't regret helping us. I imagine the reality of her actions sunk in as we entered their home, but we got to work so quickly on putting our lives in order that any fear she may had should have faded quickly.

Once at their home, we started a load of laundry, showered, snacked on fruit salad and sandwiches, and scoured the internet for a plan. Cara sat alongside us with her laptop and helped us brainstorm on the best way for us to get to South Carolina as quickly and as cheaply as possible.

To tell this story now makes it all the more magical, because I can't imagine it happening in the real world. People don't regularly offer help to strangers, especially not car rides or access to their homes. I'm not even sure *I* would encourage that, and I've been the recipient of those rewards. The community both on and around long-distance trails, especially the AT, really was (and still is) uniquely amazing. People put their total trust in us, and us in them. Even more than trust, people spent money and time, two precious commodities, to make our hike that much more enjoyable and logistically easier. It was shocking, to say the least, to sit in Cara's kitchen with our clothes tumbling in the drier, when we'd been running through a thunderstorm just two hours earlier. We couldn't have made the story up if we tried.

The most awkward moment occurred when her husband, Greg, came home from work. She had already told him that she had picked up stray hikers, but it was both comical and scary when he walked into the kitchen and saw us, two strangers sitting at his kitchen table, eating his bread and using his wifi. We nervously made introductions and shook hands, trying to act like it was totally normal that we were there. The awkwardness didn't last for long; Greg had dinner on his mind and we had logistics on ours. Shortly after meeting Greg, Cara told us, "If you guys want to go into town to eat dinner, you're welcome to use my car. The keys are in the ignition."

We were speechless. She was driving a nearly new Honda Odyssey, which certainly wasn't cheap, and she'd still only known us for a few hours.

"Really?" we asked.

I wasn't sure I wanted either of us to be responsible for driving it, but she offered it again.

"Yeah, it's not a problem. Go to town – there's a good burrito shop and a pizza place."

We accepted the offer and headed into town for a dinner of burritos. Before returning, we filled up their gas tank and bought a large pizza and two quarts of ice cream to take back to the house. To top it off, the NBA Finals were on TV and Greg was a big sports fan. It didn't take long for us to line up shoulder-to-shoulder across the couch, each with a paper plate of pizza on our lap. During the commercial breaks, Greg surfed the internet on his iPad.

"You guys are walking all the way to Maine?" Greg asked us.

He turned his iPad around so we could see that he was looking at information on the AT.

"Well, yeah," Matt said. "Do you guys know much about the AT?"

"Not really," Greg said. "I knew it was around here, but we haven't been on it yet and I didn't realize it was so long!"

It was the ultimate kicker of the evening. Cara and Greg hadn't known much about the AT, nor had they known that it was relatively normal for people along the trail to open up their homes to hikers. Yet, they found themselves for the first time as trail angels, not because they considered themselves trail angels, but because they were simply good people who saw a chance to help other people. It's still a surprise when I think back on it.

Before going to bed, we had come up with a plan. Cara was headed towards Albany, New York, the next day for a doctor's appointment and offered to drop us off at the airport, where we'd found the best rental car. The trip was ninety minutes to the airport, but she insisted it wasn't an issue, and that it was practically on the way. We accepted the plan, booked a car, and went to sleep, exhausted from the whirlwind of the day. It was hard to believe that we had been on the trail at all that day with all that happened once we left it.

The next morning, we arrived at the Albany airport, slung our packs in the trunk of the car, and were finally on the road. It was a Friday morning, around 10:00 a.m., and we had a thirteen-hour drive ahead of us. We couldn't have been happier.

We'd been longing for a road trip since the Blue Ridge Parkway and Skyline Drive in Virginia, and delighted in the chance to sit for an entire thirteen-hour period of time that was normally spent hiking. We turned up the radio, sang above the songs, one of them in particular the Whitney Houston song from *The Bodyguard*, called friends and family, and enjoyed every minute of our first official thru-hike zero together.

Aside from a quick stop in Greenwood Lake, New York, to pick up the gear we had left behind in our efforts to save the hike, we drove straight to Myrtle Beach, arriving at 1:00 a.m. We fell asleep immediately, both tired yet intensely satisfied with our decision to go on vacation. An entire week stretched out ahead of us, with zero miles to hike, endless miles of beach to enjoy, and a car to take us anywhere we wanted.

Over the course of the next week, we enjoyed every minute of each day off from the trail. We spent our time eating meals with family, playing tennis, running on the beach, napping in the heat of the afternoon, and dipping in the pool. There was a unique feeling to our time off that week. Normally thru-hikers took zeros in towns close to the trail, so they never left the trail community. We had not only left the community, but we seemingly drove to another planet, or so it felt.

I won't knock the city of Myrtle Beach. There are redeeming qualities to it, and if given the chance to live there, I gladly would. But it's no AT town. It's a vacation town for families who go to the beach to relax, eat in restaurants, play putt-putt golf, and go shopping. There isn't much of a sense of nature, but rather, heavy traffic on a high-usage main road and lines of billboards, restaurants and stores. It's a true slice of America, and whether we like it or not, it represents a much bigger slice than that of thru-hikers.

We were the odd men out.

In a town like Myrtle Beach, we were so mentally and physically removed from the trail that we jokingly questioned if the trail even existed anymore. It certainly didn't seem to exist in the minds of any of the people we met, because no one knew what the AT was or why we had agreed to walk such a thing without getting paid for it. We had pulled ourselves off the trail like a plug out of the wall; it happened quickly and we had to adapt to a different life. We had spent so much time and energy on the trail for the last two months that it was as if our world simply disappeared from existence.

It made me feel very small and insignificant.

So what if I walked from Georgia to Maine? If no one knew the significance of it, was it all that significant? Could people really fathom the distance of 2000 miles when they barely walked more than the hundred meter distance from their condo to the beach? If they could grasp the enormity of the miles we covered, I looked pretty stupid for taking months to cover a distance that a simple day's drive could handle.

It also made my thoughts about quitting seem ridiculous.

We'd only been on the trail for just over two months and had less than a month left. It was a drop in time and I had spent hours crying over the decision to quit, a decision that should have never been brought to the table. Our time on the trail was a speck on the world map and I treated it like I was deciding the fate of the entire country. I felt embarrassed for being such a drama queen over a seemingly meaningless event. I wished I had never made such a fuss and wanted nothing more than to put it behind me and finish what I started, which is why it made it worse when my in-laws innocently teased me about quitting.

"Are you sure you're going to finish the trail, Julie?" they asked me, never knowing the effect their words had on me or how serious I felt about the topic of quitting. "Think you'll be able to make it after a week off?"

I know they didn't mean to hurt me and that they were joking, but I hated every moment that they questioned my desire or ability to finish the trail. Matt's brother had hiked half the AT in a constant state of rain, and even he teased me. Though he meant it in jest, it still hurt to have someone who could completely understand the desire to quit still tease me for thinking about it. I was frustrated with Matt's family for the first two days of vacation, and then I had a split-second epiphany that brought me clarity and comfort.

We were all sitting on the beach, lined up in chairs or sitting on towels, and the topic of my desire to quit came up again. In my mind, I had already built my case as to why I wanted to quit and I was ready to present it to the jury. My list included the rain, the rocks, the bugs…every challenge that a thru-hike presented.

But then, as I looked at each person down the line, I mentally tallied the challenges in each of their lives. The list included stressful jobs, young children, financial worries…etc. They too could present their cases as to why life was hard, but that didn't mean they dwelled on them or let those reasons justify quitting. While I could explain the physical and mental hardships of the trail and how they were different from real life, each of them could come back with their own stories of overcoming hardships. There were aspects of their lives that I would never experience first-hand, nor did I want to, and I certainly didn't want them to tell me how hard their lives were because of those things. Ironically, that was exactly what I had been doing all along in talking about life on the trail, telling people how hard my life was and why I should get a free pass to quit and take the easy road.

That day, I pulled myself out of the pissing contest to see who got up the earliest, who exerted themselves the most, or who deserved the vacation the most. In that contest, no one ends up a winner, everyone sounds like a whiner. Most importantly, no one ends up with a better understanding of each other's lives. In that moment of clarity, I knew there was no doubt I'd finish the trail and that I'd shut up about the challenges that we all experienced through life in some way.

In that week on the beach, we also received updates about Curmudgeon from Curmudgeon's online journal and from Curmudgeon himself, over the phone. We thought of him often while we were out on the trail, knowing he'd pass over the same rocky, muddy ground as us. As we sat in our air-conditioned condo, reading his online journal and picturing him somewhere out on the AT, it's accurate to say we felt completely detached from the trail life.

Curmudgeon had spent the evening of June 9 in Duncannon, Pennsylvania, the same evening we spent in a stranger's home in Manchester Center, Vermont. We were just over five hundred miles ahead of him.

Since we'd last heard from him, he'd ridden the same roller coaster of weather conditions, energy levels, and general enjoyment of the trail. While we were picking our way through the Pennsylvania boulder fields in the rain, he was gutting out the rain in Virginia. There was one evening just a couple days removed from Damascus where he got stuck tenting in a storm of heavy rain and sleet, only to awaken to a quarter inch of snow on the ground and a chill in the air that his legs hadn't known for a month. He went from shorts one day, to pants the next, to shorts later that day, continually amazed, just like we were, at the quick-changing weather. Also, the rain inevitably took its toll on his feet. At the end of each day, his only desire was to lie in his tent and tend to his feet, which resembled the two-day old bathtub feet that Jeff became accustomed to.

Though Curmudgeon had hit several low moments of extreme hunger, he was luckier than us at the halfway point. He made it to the Pine Grove Furnace State Park general store when it was open and easily consumed a half gallon of double chocolate fudge cookie dough ice cream. It was 10:30 a.m. when he took the half-gallon challenge, but it made no difference and he easily completed the task.

"I called Sharon right away," he said, "I knew she'd be proud!"

As for his wife Sharon, she talked to him regularly over the phone when he had reception and battery life. She had taken to writing notes during their conversations and took over the posts on his online journal so he didn't have to take the time or the effort to regurgitate the stories again. The trail had been nearly as hard for her as it was for him; she worried about his well-being every single day. She later told us that she purposely didn't read our online journal because she didn't want to know what Curmudgeon was about to go through.

While we were at the beach, Curmudgeon was in the thick of Pennsylvania and we knew the rocks were only going to get worse from then on. Even if the weather had improved since we walked through the state, we doubted that better weather could make the rocks of Pennsylvania much more bearable. He later told us that it was undoubtedly his least favorite state because of all the rocks and boulders.

Perhaps most impressive was the fact that overall, Curmudgeon was doing quite well, especially considering the weather conditions and the stress on his fifty-nine-year-old body. He averaged about twenty miles a day and he had no real injuries to speak of at that point, other than the normal aches and pains. In order to drop pack weight, he sent home his stove and cooking gear, and relied on cold food like trail mix, tuna, beef jerky, Little Debbie snacks, and Pop-Tarts.

Curmudgeon was living out his dream, and it was intensely satisfying to read his journal and to hear him talk about what he'd been through and how he found a way to keep going. I was glad I hadn't quit the trail, because I didn't think I could face him later when it was all finished. Of all people, he knew how hard it was and he was still finding the will to cover the miles that I had previously complained about. When I asked Curmudgeon about the challenges he faced during those rainy sections in Virginia, he summed it up better than I could have hoped to do myself:

"I thought about quitting many times but then I would think about how disappointed I would be if I did quit. I had too much time, effort and expense invested to quit. This might be my only opportunity to attempt a thru-hike. There were times that I was soaked from consecutive days of rain. My pack, gear and clothing were wet and I had blisters on my feet and chafing in areas too sensitive to mention. Then the rain would stop and the sun would come out. I would reach the top of a mountain and lay out my gear to dry and take in the magnificent views. My whole attitude would change. The good days by far outnumbered the bad ones."

Curmudgeon's story was an inspiration to me and one of the many examples of the powerful effects the AT community had on my thru-hike.

26 SHARING THE LONG TRAIL

By the end of the week in Myrtle Beach, our batteries were recharged and we were antsy to get back on the trail. My body was ready to get moving again and my mind was happy to oblige. Matt's mysterious illness of extreme fatigue surfaced again with two days left of vacation, but with a little extra rest and a few doses of ibuprofen, he was back to normal. We suspected it was Lyme disease, but with just a few weeks to go and with the quick improvement in his health with just a few pain pills, we decided to wait until it was all over to confirm. A huge bottle of ibuprofen, however, found a space in his pack before we left.

We were in high spirits as we drove back to New York. Our ride back to the trail was already waiting for us at the Albany airport, as we had planned ahead for the ride. As a result, the transition from Myrtle Beach to the trail in Vermont went as smoothly as possible. The moment we exited the car, put on our packs, loosened our hip belts from a week straight of excessive consumption, and said goodbye to our ride, it started sprinkling.

"It's welcoming us back!" I said to Matt.

Despite the fact that the rain held out until our first steps back on the trail, we were tickled with excitement to be walking again. We were in the final push to Mt. Katahdin, which sat just over 500 miles up the trail. I knew I was in it all the way, even if the skies rained on us for the remaining miles, though I hoped with all hope that they didn't.

It was an easy two miles from the parking lot to the first shelter, the Bromley Shelter, and we called it home for the evening, in no hurry to start too quickly after a week off. Our legs were fresh, I had new trail-running shoes, a new puffy, warm jacket, and we both had new sleeping bags. Also, most of our cuts and blisters had healed, just in time to face a wet, muddy trail. It looked the same as when we left it, maybe even muddier.

The next morning, we awoke to a misty trail with a low-lying, heavy fog. The week-long vacation made the weather more forgivable and we hiked on without much acknowledgement of the precipitation around us. Morning mist turned to afternoon sun and we quickly dried out, taking our time across the muddy trail. The long sections of suction-cup mud wore on us, so we decided to take it easy and finish the day by mid-afternoon at the Greenwall Shelter, twenty-two miles into the day. By then, we felt confident that we could finish and didn't feel rushed to put in big miles. We also didn't have an official plan for after the trail, as plans for the CDT had been sidelined, so we had plenty of time to finish the AT. We had both agreed that 2200 miles in one summer was enough for our legs and our sanity.

As we approached the shelter, which was .2 miles off the trail, we saw a full shelter. My heart sank when I saw a family of four and their dog, already laid out across the shelter floor. We still relied on the shelters each evening, having left our tent with Matt's parents to take back to Ohio. It was the first time we would have to hike on.

The father saw the disappointment on our faces and rushed to make room for us. After thanking them, we sat down on the shelter opening and took a moment's break to meet the family before eating dinner.

The family had an interesting story. The father and mother were out with their two teenage daughters who were out to hike the Long Trail. That was their last night together before the parents got off the trail and left their daughters to finish up the trail together. Matt and I were impressed not only because the two young daughters were mature enough to handle such a challenge, but because their parents were so calm in sending them off on such an adventure. Our mothers still worried every day that we were on the trail, and we were almost double the age of the sisters.

It was refreshing to spend the evening with a family and with two young hikers who were excited about the trail and eager to talk to us about thru-hiking. As we all went to sleep, the temperatures stayed warm and muggy, but we were so tired from our first full day back that we had no trouble falling asleep.

At around 10:30 p.m., I was woken up by Scout, the family's dog. He was tied up inside the shelter and growling towards the darkness. I squinted into the deep darkness beyond the shelter and heard a rustling in the bushes and the snapping of twigs.

"Matt, I think there's a bear in the bushes," I whispered to Matt. The adrenaline rushed through me as I stared into the darkness.

Two dogs suddenly popped out of the bushes and ran up to the shelter, each wearing collars with blinking red lights and antennas. I half-expected them to talk to us through translators, just like in the movie *Up*, but soon found out from the dad that they were hunting dogs. I didn't know what disturbed me more, the strange dogs with antennas or the fact that someone was out there hunting when I could have been night hiking or taking a pee in the middle of the night and been mistaken for a bear.

We shooed the dogs away, hoping their owner would call them or radio them in, but no one showed up and the dogs hung around. They were friendly dogs and they looked lost and frightened. Fifteen minutes later, after watching the dogs sniff around the shelter, we heard the rustling of bushes and snapping of twigs yet again, only to see a third hunting dog run up to the shelter.

"Geez, how many more are there?" I joked. By then, all of us were awake and watching the dogs pace in front of the shelter.

"Ok, this is a little much," Matt said. "Let's see if there's a phone number on their collars, because I don't think their owner is anywhere near here."

We called the number listed on one of dog's collars and spoke to the owner, who revealed that the dogs had been missing since 4:00 p.m. that day after chasing a bear into the woods. The owner was relieved to hear where they were and we promised to tie them to a tree so we could hike them out the next morning. As Matt closed the conversation, he asked, "One more thing. What are their names?"

"Oh, Buckshot's the male and leader of the group. Bandit's shy and won't go near you. Molly will follow you anywhere," describing the dogs to perfection. Molly had already cuddled up next to the dad, who slept on the ground outside the shelter, Bandit was near the bushes, out of anyone's reach, and Buckshot was pacing the area. Bandit, Buckshot, and Molly; it still makes me chuckle to say their names. I slept comfortably for the rest of the night, knowing that a bear wouldn't come anywhere near a shelter surrounded by four dogs, three of which were trained specifically to hunt bear.

The next morning was one of the most beautiful starts to a day that we'd seen in weeks on the trail. The sun gained strength early on and burned off the fog by the time we were just a few miles into the day. We hiked with the two sisters for much of the day and learned more about the trips their family had already taken, like kayaking and sailing, two adventures that Matt was increasingly interested in trying. The hiking was fairly easy, with a few steep ascents and descents, and we even had a break alongside a road where someone had left a cooler of snacks and sodas for passing hikers. I felt re-energized as we sat in the sun and enjoyed a can of Mountain Dew. The time after our vacation was like a fresh start all over again.

We all took one more snack break together at the Governor Clement

Shelter before beginning the four mile, 2000 foot climb to Killington. It was during the heat of the afternoon and though we were hesitant to get started, we took off at a slow pace and kept it steady up the long, arduous climb. I had been energetic at the start, but soon the heat and tricky footing took its toll. We were both drained by the late afternoon when we stopped for a break at the Cooper Lodge Shelter. The shelter was empty, it had beautiful views from its location near the top of Killington, and the warm sun was shining through the open windows of the shelter. There was even enough of a breeze to keep the shelter relatively bug-free.

We had only planned on taking a short break there, but the shelter was inviting and so was the company of the sisters who had already decided to stay there for the night. It was an uncharacteristic move on our part, but we stopped early for a second day in a row and were happy to be in the company of others.

We also stopped partially because Killington held a special memory for Matt. In 2000, he hiked the entire state of Vermont in his tighty-whities. All of his clothes had been soaked from rain near the beginning of Vermont and he got terrible chaffing on his thighs and chest from hiking in wet, cotton clothing. His underwear was the only dry article of clothing in his pack and he loved hiking in them so much after the first time he tried it, that he just kept doing it, even after his clothes had dried out. Matt loved the attention that other people gave him, though he did admit, "It felt a little strange to pass families with little kids." Once he reached New Hampshire, the chill in the air was enough to force him back into regular clothes, but he still swears that those tighty-whities saved his skin.

Killington was an important part of Matt's underwear hike through Vermont because he has a picture from 2000 with him atop Killington, dressed in nothing but hiking boots and dirty underwear, no longer white, but still plenty tight. His arms were raised in exaltation, his eyes squinted in the sun, and his mouth was wide open in a sort of spirit yell. The photo captured him in a moment of pure happiness with both himself and his surroundings. If the photo had a caption, it would say, "I have found what I want to do, and I am loving every minute of it."

I've seen that picture so many times that I can still envision his pasty white skin glaring against the green mountains and blue skies in the background.

Once we had settled into the shelter and taken a break from the climb, Matt wanted to go to the top of Killington to re-enact the photo. It was .2 miles to the top and I didn't want to walk another step that day. I wanted to lounge in the shelter. A few minutes later, another hiker showed up and agreed to go with Matt to the top. Once at the top, the hiker took Matt's picture as he stood there with every arm, leg, and facial expression in the same place. He wore nothing but running shoes and black running shorts and was nearly as pale as the first picture.

The re-enactment photo is again one of my favorite pictures, but it also reminds me of my downfalls. I regret not going to the top with him. It was something important to him and I should have realized it at the time. I thought he was going to the top out of obligation to repeat the picture, but he was going because he was excited and proud that he was at the same place for a second time in his lifetime, in another position to take such a memorable photo. His memory of that place was special to him, as was the chance to relive the memory atop the mountain, and I wasn't there to share it with him.

Chances are, we will never be there again and we certainly won't ever be in the same life positions as we were that day, on a beautiful afternoon in late June, in our early thirties, with few responsibilities except for those to each other. I missed out on a moment and I can never get it back.

The next morning, we woke up motivated to walk. Two days in a row of finishing early in the late afternoon had left us feeling fresh and we were ready to step up the mileage. Though the day started out cool and foggy atop Killington, by eight miles into the day, we dropped the 2000 feet that we had gained the day before and the sun came out and warmed the air. We also officially parted ways with the Long Trail. While the trails were still plenty muddy, the last two days of sun had helped dry them out and we kept a steady pace all day.

The state of New Hampshire was approaching quickly and we hoped to reach it by the end of the following day. It seemed crazy that the state of Vermont was almost complete. It had been the first state that made us feel like we had made real progress north and we were already leaving it for a state even further north.

As I remembered the days in Vermont before and after vacation, my most prominent memory was one thing: mud. It was called Vermud for accurate reasons but I still hadn't expected the trail to be as wet or muddy as it turned out to be. I also couldn't knock the state, given the amazing trail magic we received and the relative amount of sun that we saw during most days. That seventy-third day on the trail (not counting days off), our efforts to cover ground all day paid off as we walked into the Winturri Shelter with plenty of daylight left, with another twenty-seven miles in the books.

Julie Urbanski

27 OUR CUP OVERRUNNETH

While the fear of running out of food is ever-present in a thru-hiker's mind, there is another fear that is slight, but which grows proportionately over the course of the hike. It is the fear of running out of trail magic, as if each piece of trail magic counts towards one's grand total allotment for the trail. Eventually, that limit will be reached and karma will essentially run out. The feeling that, "it's too good to be true," seems like it should only happen so many times over the course of a thru-hike.

We had already experienced the epitome of that feeling in Manchester Center, Vermont, with our ridiculously epic trail magic before vacation. Not only did it feel like there was a limit to the trail magic we should have received, but it also felt like Manchester Center had already maxed out that limit. It was like Christmas as a kid. My parents let us choose between one big present, which took up all the Christmas funds, or many small presents. Either way, there was a limit.

That being said, it explains why the next bit of trail magic that we received was that much more unbelievable. Our cup of trail magic had already been filled in Vermont and therefore spilled over in New Hampshire.

On the morning of our seventy-third day, we awoke to a foggy, cold, wet shelter. Our sleeping bags were damp from the fog that had drifted into the open mouth of the shelter, and I grudgingly packed up a damp sleeping bag, knowing it would never dry out in the bottom of my pack, scrunched into a football-sized stuff sack. The fog was thick as we started our morning miles and though it eventually cleared, mist continued to fall around us in challenging terrain. Our short, choppy strides kept us from slipping on the mud and the elevation climbed and descended even more than the official

Roller Coaster section in West Virginia. It was my first hint that with the northern states came more difficult hiking, only without the official warning sign. There couldn't be a roller coaster section because that was the usual terrain for the entire state. I was both excited and fearful to reach New Hampshire later that day because I wondered if the rumors of the state's difficult miles were actually true.

The plan for the day was to hike the twenty-six miles to Hanover, New Hampshire, pick up groceries and a meal, and then move on to the first shelter, just a mile and a half out of town. By around 2:00 p.m., we reached West Hartford, Vermont, just as the mist turned to rain. The guidebook said there was a store down the road and we headed to it for cover. We poked our heads into the store to get out of the rain for a brief moment, and once inside, we were surprised to see the vast array of freshly made food. The potato salad and sub sandwiches caught our attention first.

With plenty of time to hike the ten remaining miles into Hanover, we sat down for a break and ate a late lunch indoors, a welcomed alternative to eating cold food on the side of a wet trail. Just as we started eating, two cyclists pulled up outside and quickly introduced themselves to us after entering the store. Their names were Doc and Truckin, two thru-hikers from the class of 2009. Without hesitation, Truckin wrote her phone number on a napkin and said to call her if we needed anything in Hanover, where she lived as a traveling nurse. As she handed us the napkin, she said in a slight Southern drawl, "If you need somewhere to stay, you're welcome to stay at my place. You can do laundry too and we'll take you to a grocery store if you need to resupply."

It only took one brief moment for Matt and me to glance at each other and then accept the offer. With the weather outside continuing to rain, I was happy to stay indoors with two thru-hikers who knew exactly what we loved the most about town: showers, laundry, and food. Most importantly, we knew there was an Indian restaurant in town named The Jewel of India. Before they left, we confirmed our approximate arrival time and suggested the restaurant for dinner.

"Did that really just happen?" I asked Matt after Doc and Truckin walked outside. It was such a quick exchange with them that we hardly knew what hit us.

Suddenly our slow steps that we'd taken on the muddy trail earlier in the day turned into bounding strides. Our mantra to get us through those last ten miles was, "The Jewel of India." We repeated it at least every ten minutes. Fortunately, the terrain eased up considerably after lunch and we walked on a road the last few miles of the day. The mist continued but I hardly noticed it. I knew we were headed towards a warm shower and a night indoors, and for at least a fleeting moment, I felt like we'd beaten the rain.

Once in town, we called Truckin, and after she picked us up in the pouring rain, the evening quickly rolled on. Most of our conversations were consumed by trail talk and an explosion of memories from all parties. It was late by the time we went to sleep, with the flow of conversation so natural that it was difficult to find an end point to cut it off. What impressed me the most was that complete strangers could get together and enjoy each other's company after meeting for less than five minutes, merely because we had the one common bond of hiking the AT. It was trail magic at its finest and another moment when I fell in love with the community along the AT. It inspired me that a simple footpath spanning fourteen states could create such a culture of camaraderie and generosity.

When I called my mom that evening to tell her about our newest bout of trail magic, she said, "That's amazing you can trust people like that to just stay in their home!" I felt lucky that I could experience such a unique side of humanity.

The next morning, the magic continued with a full continental breakfast cooked by Doc. It was an early morning for Doc and Truckin to head to work, and for us to head back to the trail. After filling up on coffee and food, Truckin took us back to the trail.

Just as we pulled into town, the low-lying clouds unleashed a heavy downpour and we whimpered in the car like dogs refusing to go outside in the rain. We were hesitant to get soaked within the first five minutes of walking and hoped to wait out the rain in town. Truckin had to go to work, so instead of heading directly to the trail, she dropped us off at the local coffee shop.

Two hours later, after updating our blog and calling home over large mugs of mochas and palm-sized cookies, we headed out into a cloudy day. It had stopped raining and the trail was calling. As we made our way over a muddy, rocky trail, with a few short steep climbs, we could smell the Indian spices coming out of our sweaty pores. I wasn't sure if I felt sick or satisfied as I smelled myself going uphill.

Since we started later than expected, we stopped just eleven miles into the day at the Moose Mountain Shelter, just after the climb up Moose Mountain. Though the shelter had a great viewpoint from the side of the mountain, we had to settle for a view that looked out into a thick, white blanket of fog. Particles of water swirled into the shelter, right onto our gear. It was only a matter of time before everything was damp.

A small corner of the shelter was out of reach from the fog and we huddled closely into it in an effort to keep our sleeping bags dry. An hour after arriving, we heard footsteps of an approaching hiker from behind the shelter. He rounded the corner of the shelter and to our surprise, it was Coney, another thru-hiker we'd heard a lot about. He too was from

Cincinnati, Ohio, and aptly named Coney because of his love for Skyline Chili. It is a popular Cincinnati restaurant known for its chili, made Cincinnati-style, with chili atop spaghetti noodles, topped with mounds of finely shredded cheese and served alongside an appetizer of oyster crackers. His parents even sent him cans of chili to the trail.

Coney looked cold, wet and miserable. We may have looked just as bad, but we were still on the high of the trail magic from the night before. His chin-length, dark brown hair dripped water onto his equally wet rain gear, his calves were speckled with mud, and his annoyed expression left us questioning whether to speak to him and risk pissing him off, or just let him be. It was apparent that he too had had enough of the wet, muddy trail and of the never-ending rain, but he warmed up to us quickly with his witty, entertaining personality. We had an immediate connection and reminisced about our mutual hometown of Cincinnati, vented a little bit about the AT, and shared our stories of trail magic.

As I went to sleep, I was satisfied to be in the second-to-last state, but I also feared the upcoming terrain that I'd heard so much about. At the beginning of the hike, I had pictured myself in fantastic shape by New Hampshire, but as I lay there in my sleeping bag, I felt a little soft. I felt like I was at the base of a huge mountain, looking up at its steep ascent, and looking down at my gooey belly, wondering where I'd gone wrong with such good intentions. It was not my ideal start to New Hampshire.

I told myself before I fell asleep, "One day at a time, Julie. One day at a time."

28 THE RUMORS COME TRUE

Ever since the state of New Jersey, which seemed like a distant memory by the time we made it to New Hampshire, I carried with me a memory that made a lasting impression.

The memory was a conversation we had with another hiker in the pavilion atop Sunrise Mountain, just outside of Branchville, New Jersey. We were resting on the pavilion's cool, stone floor. It was hot and muggy, and the breeze blowing through the pavilion offered respite from the mosquitoes. A hiker sitting at the far end of the pavilion heard we were thru-hikers and immediately offered up his opinion on the northern part of the trail.

"The last twenty percent is eighty percent of the effort," he declared.

"Oh, have you thru-hiked before?" Matt asked, excited to talk to a former thru-hiker.

"No, I've just heard that about New Hampshire and Maine, but I've hiked some of New Hampshire," the man said.

We were often skeptical of other people's advice because we were confident in our ability to push through even the hardest terrain and still cover relatively big miles. Neither of us argued that the last two states wouldn't be easy, but neither of us was ready to agree. I had yet to walk through it and wanted to decide for myself, and Matt didn't remember the end being extremely difficult. It also felt useless and even defeating to worry about the upcoming difficulty of the trail when we were in the thick of dealing with the challenges of New Jersey.

While I wasn't ready to believe the hiker's claim, the warning about the eighty/twenty rule of the trail stuck with me. That being said, it was no surprise that after waking up in the Moose Mountain Shelter in New

Hampshire, the only thought I had was, "The last twenty percent is eighty percent of the effort."

Even at the beginning of New Hampshire, I started to believe the adage, and each ensuing day afterwards further solidified my belief. In addition to the eighty/twenty rule, I contributed my own saying: "You ain't seen nothing yet."

We awoke to pouring rain outside our shelter on our seventy-sixth day. All our gear was damp from the full night of fog drifting into the shelter and I lay there thinking about how clean and dry our gear had been just a day before in Hanover. Using the privy was even more of a blow to my ego. It didn't have any walls, so the rain soaked me as it blew sideways, drenching my clothes. I couldn't hurry the privy process if I tried, so I started the day with wet clothing and damp gear.

Coney seemed just as bummed as we were to start the day with rain and fog, and all of our spirits were low. Nothing about the muddy terrain had changed since Vermont and we trudged along all day, leap-frogging with Coney.

We experienced our first real climb in New Hampshire on Smarts Mountain, a true bitch of a climb. The trail gained 2100 feet over four miles, but with a fairly flat mile and a half in the middle of the climb, the 2100 feet was actually gained over the remaining two and a half miles. My ideal climb was a maximum gain of 500 feet per mile, and that climb equated to 840 feet of gain per mile. I struggled, to say the least. Near the top, we scrambled up slick, steep slabs of rock, and white blazes painted on the faces of the rocks led the way. I was shocked at both the difficulty of the climb and the change in terrain at the top, and I had a feeling this was just the beginning.

I was also freezing by the time we made it to the Fire Warden's Cabin at the top, an enclosed shelter that offered a break from the elements. Even though the date was closing in on July, it was still snowing at the top. While the cabin blocked out the wind and snow, it was still cold inside, and since we no longer had a stove, we couldn't cook a warm meal to warm up. Sitting there in our wet clothing, our body temperatures were too low to stay much longer. I quickly choked down a packet of cold, instant mashed potatoes before we started the descent from the mountain.

Near the bottom of the descent, we finally felt our core warmth come back to us and all the precipitation stopped. After the climb were several sections of bog boards, which were long boards of wood to walk on in order to avoid the knee-deep bogs surrounding the trail. Many of the boards were six to twelve inches wide, and often just as slippery as the rocks from the constant presence of mud and rain on their smooth surfaces. We walked over many of them that day, avoiding much of the swampy mud surrounding the trail.

On the way up our next big climb for the day, Mt. Cube, I approached a section of bog boards. Just as I put my right foot down on the board, I felt the board give way under my foot and my right leg went knee-deep into the mud. I involuntarily stepped my left foot down to push myself up, but that only caused my left foot to sink in the mud. Now I was in thigh-deep mud. I couldn't use my hiking poles to push me out because those too would just get sucked into the mud. As I struggled with the bog surrounding me, Matt stood there in shock. It all happened so fast that neither of us really knew what to do. Matt described it as, "One second you were right there in front of me, and the next second, you were gone!"

After the initial shock of both legs being stuck in the mud, I panicked with the fear of being trapped in the bog and was close to hysteria as I pleaded to Matt, "Get me out of here!"

He pulled me out, but not without the difficulty of my left shoe getting stuck between two other boards deep in the mud. It was a horrifying experience and I was only able to laugh it off after I'd been pulled to stable ground. I was also hesitant to lead after that.

The trauma of the experience faded quickly and we were already able to find humor in the trick board as we made our way to the other side of the bog. Once through the bog, we contemplated waiting for Coney in order to warn him about the board. We even thought about hiding in the bushes to see Coney come through and fall prey to the same bog board, but we decided against both options. He had stayed in the shelter atop Smarts Mountain longer than us and we didn't know how long we'd be waiting for him. We also knew he was having a rough day and we didn't want to be a part of something that could worsen the day. When he caught up with us a couple miles up the trail, we looked down at his mud-covered calves and knees and said, "I see you found that bog board, eh?" I later found out that Zippers also stepped on it, only her hands went into the mud as she tried to catch herself from falling.

The next climb up Mt. Cube was even more difficult than Smarts Mountain. It was nineteen miles into the day, so our energy levels had been depleted, and each slippery step on the slabs of rock atop the mountain tightened my nerves with the increased stress. I started to fear the downhill more than the uphill because of the slick footing and crept slowly along the trail, keeping my center of gravity close the ground.

By the time we made it to the Ore Hill Shelter later that evening, the skies had cleared and the temperatures had increased. We fell asleep immediately after lying down and I feared what awaited us for our next day in New Hampshire: Mt. Moosilauke.

Well before the trail started, when we received our guidebook in the mail, I perused the book in order to gauge the difficulty and amount of climbs that I'd face over the course of the trail. It was a tortuous thing to do to myself, but I wanted to know what kind of elevation changes to expect. The one climb that stood out to me was Mt. Moosilauke, and there we were, finally reaching the day when we would face the climb after so much anticipation. The trail gained about 3500 feet of elevation over the course of four miles. It looked scary on paper and it was one of the few climbs that Matt remembered being difficult for him back in 2000. If he remembered a difficult climb, I knew that I was sure to struggle.

Not to our surprise, the morning was misty and cool, and the wet, rocky trail made for slow miles. Nine miles into our day, the climb to Mt. Moosilauke started. We kept a steady pace up the entire mountain, some parts incredibly technical in footing, some parts rocky, and some parts smooth. Near the top of the climb, we reached the steepest section, which then leveled out to a gentle trail before we reached the very top. While the climb was difficult, the expectations of the level of difficulty were so high that by the time we reached the top, we were tired but not spent. I felt like I'd conquered the mountain and wanted to ask it, "Is that all you've got?"

The top of the mountain was covered in a dense fog that blanketed us with tiny water droplets. We could barely make out the figures of other people at the top and we hunkered down into a man-made bowl of rocks to get out of the cold wind. As we sat within the rock walls, we ate a snack and put on extra layers of clothing in order to avoid the oncoming chill from sweating on the uphill and sitting for a break at the top. The same fog greeted Matt and Animal on their hike, only it was much colder for them in mid-September. In fact, it was so cold that Animal put on a pair of ski goggles. His mom had added them to his last resupply box when she heard how cold it had been getting. While she had good intentions, it was a ridiculous piece of gear to carry. But, it made for an entertaining moment when Animal strutted across the top of Mt. Moosilauke, half his face covered with a pair of tinted ski goggles.

One thing Matt hadn't remembered, or at least forgot to tell me about, was that Moosilauke wasn't known for its ascent. It was the downhill that I should have feared. While I basked in my moment of glory atop the mountain, I was totally unprepared for what awaited us on the other side. Much of the descent was on steep, slick sections of rock, with metal handles and wooden steps nailed into the rock. While I trusted them to hold my weight, I also knew how far I could fall with one misstep or one loose piece of wood. The footing was so nonexistent in some spots that we held on to tree branches for safety as we let our feet slide down the wet rock faces, swapping out an old branch for a new one as we made our way down.

As we slowly descended the mountain, our pace two times as slow as our climb, I said to Matt, "How did you forget about this part?" His memory was so overshadowed by the ski goggles that he forgot that the hard part was the *second* half of Mt. Moosilauke. Once we reached the bottom of the climb at Kinsman Notch, my nerves were so shaken that we had to sit for a short break just so my mental and physical energy could come back to me.

After leaving Kinsman Notch, we pushed on for the rest of the day into early evening, eager to get in as many miles as possible. We knew the harder terrain and elevation changes would inevitably decrease our mileage, but we wanted to fight reality for as long as we could. It was a blow to the ego to admit that we weren't capable of hiking big miles on such mountainous, technical trails, and Matt and I were as stubborn as they came. After twenty-four miles, we called it a day at the Eliza Brook Shelter. As I looked ahead in the guidebook that night, I was afraid our lessons in mountain climbing had just begun.

Julie Urbanski

29 SURVIVING THE WHITES

One of my favorite sections on the Pacific Crest Trail was the John Muir Trail, a 211 mile trail in Central California that mostly overlaps with the PCT. It was beautiful, it was remote, and most of all, it was terribly difficult. Before we started the John Muir Trail, people warned us that our mileage would be cut in half in that section due to the number of grueling climbs and descents over mountain passes, each with several thousands of feet of elevation change. Of course, being the stubborn hikers that we were, we didn't believe them and did everything in our power to sustain our twenty-five mile daily average.

We finished the John Muir Trail portion with a small amount of pride and an extreme amount of fatigue. While we kept up our average, it about killed us to push so hard each day and we each lost the bulk of our twenty-five pound weight losses in that one stretch. At Tuolumne Meadows, the end of the shared section of trail, I was ready to quit both the trail and my relationship with Matt because I was so tired after reaching my limits of both physical and mental strength. We both continued the trail, but the John Muir Trail taught us that we should have taken *some* advice from others and gone a little slower in order to avoid jeopardizing the hike and our relationship.

For these reasons, the PCT was fresh in our minds as we made our way through the White Mountain National Forest. Everyone told us our mileage would decrease significantly in the Whites with the difficult terrain and elevation fluctuations. I wasn't too concerned, remembering our ability to defy the odds on the PCT, until I heard Matt tell me that he and Animal had a day in the Whites when they could only eek out nine miles. Nine miles…that was single digit territory, somewhere I hadn't been since I called it quits in Greenwood Lake, New York, after just eight miles into the day.

"But don't worry," Matt assured me, "I think it was because we did a lot of side trails that day."

I wasn't convinced. He and Animal were nineteen and twenty years old, with energy and ignorance on their side, and they hiked nine miles one day and barely managed low teens on other days. I was ten years older than them and I felt like I had spent my energy and ignorance on the PCT. I had hiked enough miles by that point to know how much I wanted to suffer and to know that I would be asking too much of my twenty-nine-year-old mind and body to push myself to the same extremes as those on the PCT.

Matt and I had another taste of the Whites when we climbed Franconia Ridge in the late afternoon of our seventy-eighth day, just over 1800 miles into the trail. We watched the skies all day, fearing a thunderstorm would hinder our progress over the two-mile stretch above tree line on the ridge, but once at the top, we tossed aside our fears. Neither fog nor rain had followed us to the ridge and the views were unmatched. It had been an arduous climb, but the memory of the efforts faded as soon as we reached the top's panoramic views.

I hadn't realized how deprived I'd been of good views from the mountaintops. For a lot of the trail up until that point, I had pegged myself as a non-scenery person, but that was because I hadn't *seen* any for so long. Picture-perfect scenery was so prevalent on a daily basis on the PCT that I had taken it for granted. My appreciation for the mountains and the views they could offer was renewed on Franconia Ridge. I knew then that the Whites would crush me physically, but that I could mentally handle them because of the rewards we were given with such breathtaking views. Throughout the entire trail, I had been searching for the balance between resentment for the difficulty and gratitude for the beauty. I found it in the Whites.

I wasn't the only one who felt this way about scenery along the trail and about the Whites. While Curmudgeon struggled with the technical difficulties, he also deemed the Whites to be his favorite section, saying they gave him a new appreciation for the mountains that he hadn't found while living in Ohio. Zippers also loved the satisfaction that came with putting in a hard climbing effort and being rewarded with astounding views.

That evening, we were drained of energy as we shuffled into the Garfield Ridge Shelter, nineteen miles into our day. It was a little early to stop, but the next shelter up the trail was .7 miles off the trail, and there was no convincing either of us to hike the extra side-trail mileage, especially not in a section as difficult as the Whites. Our mileage was still controlled by our lack of a tent, and we arrived to a crowded shelter of thru-hikers, sectioners, and weekenders. The unique crowd at the shelter, including the caretaker, made for an entertaining night. As the conversation jumped from topic to topic, the fog rolled in and tucked us in for the evening like a thick, white comforter.

With such a low mileage day behind us, Matt and I were eager to start hiking the next morning. We picked up another hiker, Flying Squirrel, who wanted to join us as we made our way through the Whites. The weather often shifted quickly and the terrain was challenging even for the best hikers, so Flying Squirrel saw the opportunity to join us rather than hike alone through the Whites. We were glad for the company as well. As much as we hated to admit it, Matt and I often ran out of things to talk about, so we usually hiked together in silence. The injection of a new person sparked a conversation fire, so we welcomed Flying Squirrel's presence.

Other than a flat, six-mile section near Ethan Pond, which seemed uncharacteristically easy for the Whites, we struggled to keep a steady pace. Because we had started early, our odds of getting in good mileage were fairly high despite the slower miles. Fortunately, the weather was on our side and gave us sunny skies with a small breeze that was enough to keep us comfortably warm. On the other hand, once we passed the Ethan Pond Campsite shelter around 2:00 p.m., the next shelter was forty-two miles away.

We hadn't done that kind of mileage on our best days in Virginia and we didn't want to pay for a hut (lodging run by the Appalachian Mountain Club) in the event that the two nightly work-for-stay thru-hiker spots were taken. Our solution was to cowboy camp that evening atop Mt. Jackson. Just before our intended campsite at Mt. Jackson, we climbed the Webster Cliffs, which felt reminiscent of my first time at a climbing gym. Though I had no upper body muscles to speak of, I used what I had to pull myself straight up and over the rocks, and again I wondered, as I often did on those straining sections, "How do old people do this?" I was baffled at the difficulty we faced each day in the Whites, with each ensuing climb and descent offering a new challenge in either the terrain or the location of rocks along the trail.

As we went to sleep atop Mt. Jackson that evening, the sunset blazed around us as we lay in our sleeping bags and our phones showed a zero percent chance of rain. It was the best scenario we could have asked for, front-row seats to a fantastically clear sunset in a section void of a shelter for forty-two miles.

The next day was significant from the start because it was our eightieth day on the trail. We were just a touch over 1840 miles into the trail, with 340 miles left to walk. Based on the elevation chart in the guidebook, we knew we had a long, tough day ahead of us. Because we weren't sure what sort of mileage we could do, we started early with the hope that time would be on our side, given the large amount of daylight that we had. We planned on putting in a sustained effort over the course of the day, keeping our foot on the gas pedal at a speed that allowed for maximum fuel efficiency.

We were still with Flying Squirrel and we all took our first morning break outside the Mizpah Spring Hut. As we sat on the benches outside, clear skies allowed for a warm sun and I was thankful our weather in the Whites had held out so far. I was also hopeful that the weather would continue. I knew how volatile the weather could be and I didn't want to repeat the near-hypothermic conditions of the Smokies.

As we sat outside the hut, I looked around at the families staying at the hut, on vacation from work and school, and for the first time, I wasn't jealous of them. I didn't envy their short hiking trips, their enclosed huts, or their cooked meals. I knew the price they paid for that kind of experience, both in actual cost and in the sacrifice of their time spent at work in order to pay for that kind of vacation. The huts weren't luxurious, but they also weren't cheap. At that point, after camping for free every night with an underlying goal of spending as little money as possible, I felt it would not have been worth my time at a job to pay for a bunk at the hut, and I was glad to be on the other side of the hiking spectrum. I could understand the families' perspectives and the enjoyment they got out of taking such a trip and staying in the huts, but that kind of life wasn't for me, not at that time. I had a simple, compact life, with the freedom to walk at my own discretion and on my own watch, without the attachment to a job to pay for that freedom. I realized that from the perspective of those families out for a few days, maybe I had the enviable life.

Less than five miles later, after relatively easy hiking, considering we were in the Whites, we arrived at the Lakes of the Clouds Hut. It sat at the bottom of Mt. Washington, the second highest peak on the AT. It was sunny when we arrived and we could see the top of Mt. Washington from the grand window in the hut's dining room. The mountain is constantly covered in clouds, so it was a rare moment to see clear skies. But, as we sat in the hut, the clouds rolled in and our hopes of a clear Mt. Washington literally faded before our eyes, along with the view of the mountain.

Though it looked terribly steep in the guidebook, the hike up to Mt. Washington was easier than we expected as we made our way up large, rock steps. The higher we climbed, the more people we saw on the trail and the thicker the clouds. By the time we made it to the parking lot at the top, we couldn't see the buildings until we could almost touch them. Matt had already warned me that people could also drive up to Mt. Washington, so I wasn't surprised to see a large crowd of cars, cameras, and children at the top.

We stood in line to take our picture with the sign marking the top of the mountain, and it felt a little anti-climactic to wait my turn to celebrate the accomplishment of making it to the top. It didn't bother me that other people could drive there, but my efforts to walk to the top did feel slighted as I took my picture with the sign just like everyone else. I wanted to make our moment more special by holding up a sign that said, "I just walked here from Georgia!"

Coming down from Mt. Washington was incredibly different from the hike up. While there was a significant downhill just after leaving the parking lot at the top, the trail became a roller coaster of rock-heavy terrain, careful footing, and slow miles. Luckily, the fog at the top didn't reach far past a few hundred feet down in elevation and we could finally see ahead of us again as we made our way over the challenging terrain.

As we covered the six miles from Mt. Washington to the Madison Spring Hut, the clock ticked on and the miles progressed slowly. The morning had been so promising because of our fast pace over the relatively easy trail, and I had hoped for a high mileage day. However, our normal pace of three miles per hour barely hit two miles per hour that afternoon. Adding to the list of difficulties, we were also swarmed by bugs. I thought they were some kind of mutant variety of intensely strong gnats that were especially attracted to my skin. After swatting them off my neck and hairline, I would inspect my hand for dead bodies and see my own blood instead. I said out loud as we hopped from one large boulder to another on the way to the hut, "If these are gnats, then black flies must be awful!"

Matt laughed as he assured me, "Those *are* black flies!"

"Oh! Well that explains why they're so bad!" For some reason, I had expected them to look more like actual flies.

We felt relieved as we arrived at the Madison Spring Hut and promptly plopped down on the benches inside the hut. I could barely hold my head up as I ate potato chips with a spoon out of a gallon-sized Ziploc bag. I was literally shoveling in the food in order to keep up with the calorie deficit created from such hard hiking. Awaiting us after the break was Mt. Madison.

The .4 mile climb to the top of Mt. Madison was a steep, boulder-ridden ascent of over five hundred feet. I pushed hard on the uphill, only to realize too late that I should have saved my energy for the three-mile, 3100-foot downhill. It didn't seem possible at the time to have a descent worse than that of Mt. Moosilauke, but Mt. Madison proved me wrong. The descent was exposed, windy, and precarious because of impending thunderstorm clouds. It was also full of false summits. The trail wasn't actual dirt trail, but rather endless ledges of boulder fields, worse than anything in Pennsylvania. My hiking poles wedged themselves into rock crevices and my knees took the brunt of the impact from jarring steps up and down the huge rocks. We could see several hundred feet ahead of us, where the trail dropped off and disappeared, and I thought each time, "Surely the trail gets into the trees after that point up ahead, onto a normal trail after that." Nope; it was one false summit after another. We were still able to hike thirty-mile days among the rocks of Pennsylvania. That day on Mt. Madison made me question just how rocky Pennsylvania really was.

Coming down from Mt. Madison, I was so tired and I felt so dehydrated after walking in the moisture-wicking wind that I wanted to cry, but I couldn't. I didn't want to break down in front of Flying Squirrel, but I also wasn't sure how to stay positive for such a sustained period of time over the challenging trail. All three of us had separated from each other by at least a hundred feet and I was left alone to deal with my mental demons through the rocks, going to depths I hadn't seen in a while. I managed to avoid any major breakdowns and focused solely on my steps, which slowly helped me reach a more manageable trail.

Once we hit regular trail, with unrestricted strides and less tricky terrain, we easily made our way to the visitor center at Pinkham Notch. We sat down on the benches outside and discussed where to sleep for the evening. It was approaching 7:00 p.m. and we needed a solution. The next shelter was still thirteen miles away and the prices at the lodge at Pinkham Notch were too steep for our budget. To put it simply, we desperately needed trail magic.

We asked and the trail delivered. As we came up with our plan for the evening, a man that we'd seen hiking near the Madison Hut also arrived at the visitor center.

"Do you guys need a ride into town?" he asked us.

His truck was parked at the visitor center and he was on his way out of town, towards Gorham, where there were plenty of cheap hotels. We seized the opportunity for a ride into town and a half hour later, we had a hotel room booked and were already seated in a pizza restaurant.

It was a completely unexpected end to the day. Looking back, it was unbelievable that the day started with a sunrise atop Mt. Jackson, held three different hut stops, two difficult climbs, and one demoralizing descent, only to end twenty-two miles later in town. The Whites had humbled us that day, but a hot shower and a clean bed made the day a little less painful.

The next morning, we stocked up on food at the gas station next to our hotel, breakfasted on donuts and coffee, and hitched a ride back to the trail. It was mid-morning by the time we started walking again, and all of us were lethargic at the start. My knees were throbbing from the descent down Mt. Madison and I doubted the day would be any easier with the Wildcat Mountains in our near future. Their name alone scared me and the guidebook's elevation chart solidified my fear.

We started off slowly and walked even slower as the day wore on. The effort from the day before, along with the excitement of being in town and staying up too late with phone calls, internet, and TV, had caught up with all of us. I passed the day silently, too tired to say or feel much. The one saving grace was the weather. We had clear, blue skies with breathtaking views through the trees and along the ridges, and I welcomed the hot sun. It felt good to sweat again. I even stopped looking at the guidebook once we made our way through the Wildcats. It was *all* hard at that point, whether it looked that way in the guidebook or not, and I didn't care what was coming up next. I was going to hike it whether I knew it would be hard or not, so I stopped getting worked up about upcoming elevation changes.

As we approached the late afternoon, we rounded a bend and seemed to enter a different climate zone. The wind shifted and blew straight into us, and precipitation fell lightly around us. I was surprised that turning a corner could produce such a sudden shift in weather patterns, and then I reminded myself, "Oh, that's right; I'm still in the Whites."

Thirteen miles into the day, I was burnt out and I felt numb from the past few days of hiking. I was walking the tightrope of a physical and mental breakdown, and while I could sense how close I was to going down that path of negativity, I knew the danger in going there and I made the choice to stay positive. I also knew that we should stop early to rest. It was only 4:00 p.m., but we finished our day at the Imp Campsite shelter, the first shelter we'd seen in the last forty-two miles. While we had the time to hike another six miles to the next shelter, I considered myself lucky for even getting that far on such continuously hard terrain. Neither Matt nor Flying Squirrel needed to be convinced to stop early as well.

We had the shelter to ourselves, aside from the caretaker who had just hiked in that day and who was excited to see thru-hikers join him for the evening. It sprinkled outside while I lay in my sleeping bag in the shelter's loft and watched the rain through the opening of the shelter, the abyss of the woods laid out in front of me.

As it neared 7:00 p.m., another hiker walked up to the shelter opening. We didn't know it then, but he would soon change the course of the rest of our hike and even our lives.

His name was Rumblestrip and he was from Ohio.

Julie Urbanski

30 WE'RE FROM OHIO!

I didn't think much of Rumblestrip when I first saw him. Heck, I didn't even think he was a thru-hiker.

The moment he walked into the shelter, I took him to be an inexperienced hiker who was out for a short trip. He wore a metal, external-frame backpack, an oversized cotton t-shirt with a green camouflage design, and khaki-colored cargo shorts, that at the time, I couldn't tell were zip-off pants. On his feet were Teva-like sandals strapped over thick, mid-calf socks, and his hair was a tangled mess of shoulder-length brown locks. He looked like a kid out on his own in the woods for the first time, which I soon learned wasn't too far from the truth.

"Any idea how far it is to the next shelter?" he asked slowly, with what I thought was a strong Southern accent.

As he asked the question, he thumbed through the identical thru-hiker's guidebook that we had, and Matt asked, "I see you have the thru-hiker's book. Are you out for a long section?"

He must have been so offended.

"No, I'm thru-hiking," he answered matter-of-factly.

"Oh, well what's your name?" Matt asked.

"Rumblestrip," he answered, nearly rolling the r as he said his name.

"Where are you from Rumblestrip, because you must be from the South with that kind of an accent," Matt asked, the curiosity killing him.

"No, I'm from Ohio," Rumblestrip answered, each syllable of Ohio drawn out and pronounced as Oh-Hi-Oh.

"We're from Ohio!" Matt and I both exclaimed, more shocked to hear he was from Ohio than to hear he was also a thru-hiker. We'd never heard *that* kind of accent in Ohio, even on the Ohio River in Cincinnati, where some of the Kentucky twang tended to cross the bridges.

Rumblestrip explained he was from Bainbridge, Ohio, near Chillicothe, which I guessed was about an hour and a half northeast of Cincinnati. I had a hunch he was somehow involved with the strong Amish community that lived there.

Just by looking at Rumblestrip, I could tell there was something special about him and that he had a story to tell, but we wouldn't get to hear it that evening.

"Well, I'm out of food, so I'm going to push on to the next shelter so I can hit town early tomorrow morning. I'll see you later," he said as he walked away.

He was there for all of five minutes and it was already past 7:00 p.m., yet he still had six miles left to hike. My impression of Rumblestrip was false from the start and he suddenly seemed much tougher than I had originally thought.

The next morning started with a steep incline of over eight hundred feet up to Mt. Moriah, and I said to Matt multiple times, "How the hell did Rumblestrip do this last night?"

He had started his day behind us and had managed to finish the day ahead of us, and even though we hiked fewer miles, I still found Mt. Moriah to be unbearably hard. I was glad we hadn't pushed on the evening before after seeing how difficult the morning was on well-rested legs and fresh minds. The descent was again just as difficult as the ascent, in terms of footing and slickness of rocks, and we lost 1300 feet in just 1.1 miles. The only saving grace of the morning was that we would soon be in Maine. The border was less than twenty five miles away. I liked the thought of being in the last state on the trail.

We were soon rewarded with a soft, woodchip-like trail along the East Rattle River, and it was heavenly to finally look up without the fear of falling. I let the slight downhill carry me all the way to the road crossing into Gorham, New Hampshire, the second opportunity to reach the town. At the road crossing, we said goodbye to Flying Squirrel. We had been the company that Flying Squirrel needed through the Whites, but Flying Squirrel was in need of a break, a resupply, and a package from home at the post office. After we said our goodbyes and well-wishes, we resumed the trail as a couple once again. It was enjoyable to have Flying Squirrel's company, but after several days in a row of thinking as a group of three people, Matt and I were ready to resume our normal rhythm of hiking with each other.

The conversation flowed well that afternoon and Matt and I passed most of the afternoon without ever noticing the terrain or the elevation changes. The footing was slightly easier, enough to make a noticeable difference in our pace, and we made it just in time to the Gentian Pond Shelter before it started pouring outside. Just five tiny miles stood between us and the border of Maine, and I looked forward to the next day.

That evening, after no one else had showed up, and it looked like we would have the shelter to ourselves, Matt brought up the inevitable topic of sex. It was the first shelter we had to ourselves and Matt was going to be sure to take advantage of it. I was tired, dirty, and in no mood as I sat there on a hard, wooden floor in an old shelter. Since giving up the privacy of our tent, that part of our relationship had greatly diminished and Matt refused to pass up our own personal shelter.

A relaxing evening turned into an argument and just as we were starting to raise our voices to each other, we barely heard another hiker walk up to the entrance.

It was Rumblestrip.

"Well, there's goes my chance for sex," Matt thought, while I thought, "Great, now we don't have to argue anymore."

Rumblestrip's entrance was the end of our argument and the beginning of our friendship together, and Rumblestrip decided these things without ever knowing it.

I was glad to see Rumblestrip not only because his entrance quickly changed our topic of discussion, but also because I wanted to hear his story. He looked young and inexperienced, yet strong and determined, and the thick accent from Ohio undoubtedly needed further explanation.

It wasn't long before Matt dove into a round of questions about Rumblestrip's life story and history with the trail, and every one of Rumblestrip's answers was as fascinating as the next.

I was correct that he was young. He was in fact just eighteen years old, having just graduated from parochial school in his Mennonite community in Ohio. He didn't even have the fuzz of facial hair yet and he had been on the trail since mid-March. The calendar was just coming up on July.

Rumblestrip was at a transition point in life where people his age in the community were usually making the choice between staying in the community or leaving it for a different life. There wasn't a hard and fast deadline for him to choose and the hike seemed like the perfect fit for him that summer.

"How in the world did you ever find out about the AT?" Matt asked.

I'm sure it was a common question for Rumblestrip. I pictured his life as a Mennonite as living on a farm with no electricity, no car, no running water, and definitely no internet to read trail journals online or much less know about such a trail. He assured us his life wasn't *that* cut off from the rest of the world, though they did live very differently compared to most. He also explained that his accent was unique to his community. The more I heard him talk, the less Southern the accent sounded, though I still didn't know where to place it, which made sense, since it belonged to a pocket of people I'd never conversed with.

We felt silly as we admitted our stereotypical views of his culture to him and as we asked him to clear up what was truth and what was myth, he was glad to answer any questions we had.

"I'd rather you ask me than just assume something wrong about us, like most people do," he said.

I couldn't believe we were talking to an eighteen-year old-kid with such wisdom and patience. He'd probably been misunderstood most of his life and he still didn't mind answering question after question as they poured out of our mouths.

Rumblestrip's dad, who shared a passion for hiking and the outdoors, had read Eric Ryback's book on hiking, one of the prominent figures known in the early years of thru-hiking. Rumblestrip loved the book and he and his brother hiked a small section of the AT in the Smokies in the summer of 2010. While on that trip, they met AT thru-hikers on their own journeys north, and after talking with them, Rumblestrip confirmed that thru-hiking was something he wanted to try. He spent the next year saving up money by selling his family-farm's produce at the local market and by working with another brother on construction projects.

His parents agreed to help him pay for food, so long as he bought his own gear and paid for all other expenses along the way. We could tell he went to the local outfitter and spent the least amount of money on gear as possible. He didn't have extremely fancy gear, much less a brand name on him, but he'd obviously made it that far and had no intentions of quitting that I could tell. I loved the fact that he was an old-school, never-depend-on-the-gear-to-do-the-walking kind of hiker. He also didn't seem to notice or even care how different he was from the norm.

He made it to the start of the trail in mid-March after a long day's ride on a Greyhound bus from Ohio to Gainesville, and then took a shuttle to the AT Approach Trail. The first sense of fear hit him on those first few steps on the Approach Trail, where he walked by himself and faced the entire trail laid out before him. The adventure and the miles finally felt real, just as they did for us once we reached Springer Mountain, and he had a long way to go. He had left behind his family, his home, his farm, and the familiar rhythm of summer in Ohio, all to embark on a uniquely challenging feat that was completely out of his element. It was also his first real experience of being on his own, of making his own decisions, and of making new friends along the way that shared his passion for the outdoors. I would have loved to have been there for the start of his thru-hike.

He received the name Rumblestrip within the first few days on the trail while seated among a circle of people talking about old pet names. Rumblestrip said he grew up with a guinea pig named Rumblestrip, name as such because he likened the sounds it made to that of a tire rolling over a rumble strip on the side of the road.

The only thing that really surprised Rumblestrip on his first few days of the hike was the sheer amount of other people on the trail. He expected to have the trail all to himself, along with a few thru-hikers, and was just as surprised as we were to be surrounded by crowds of people in the shelters and even on the trail. He increased his mileage early on just to distance himself from the clumps of people and eventually made friends with a group of hikers that called themselves, "The Wolfpack."

Once he had the continuity of hiking with other people, he really started enjoying the trail because of the strong bonds he created after just a few days. What was all the sweeter about his love of the Wolfpack was that it was doubtful that he'd ever seen the movie, *The Hangover*, to know that his friends were playing off the movie. For him, it was a creative title for a group of hikers and for us, it made us smile to know that there were still parts of the country untouched by popular media.

It was abnormal to be around someone who was from the same country as us, and even from the same state of Ohio, but whose exposure to pop-culture was so minimal that he'd never even heard of *Forrest Gump*, much less *The Hangover*. Our jokes were often lost on him with a reference to some part of a movie or a show, only to be followed by, "I'm guessing you've never seen this..."

We guessed he was one of the few in his community who had ever done such a thing, so we continued to question him that evening and over the next few days, about his life both on and off the trail.

When Matt asked him, "Well, what's everyone else your age doing with their life?" Rumblestrip's answer was filled with such passion and conviction that we knew we had struck a chord.

"They're all out drinking and smoking, and watching movies full of violence and sex. And that is *not* how I want to waste my life. I want to spend my time doing something useful with myself, not just sitting inside getting drunk."

"They have access to that?" Matt asked.

"Oh sure, they're not supposed to, but they still can," Rumblestrip answered angrily.

He was a soft-spoken person, but we knew when we'd touched a nerve that he felt strongly about. After a short time, we realized he was the "speak only if spoken to" type of person. He was comfortable in both silence and conversation, and only brought up a topic if it held importance. It relieved the pressure of a continuous conversation and we enjoyed being in his company, even if no one said a word.

We felt lucky and happy to be a part of his life adventure. I wondered how long we would have the privilege of sharing Rumblestrip's company after we had uncovered so many details about him that first night in the shelter together.

31 I CHOSE THE WRONG PATH

On the morning of our eighty-third day, we crossed the New Hampshire border into the state of Maine, our fourteenth and final state on the trail. Just over 280 miles stood between me and Mt. Katahdin, the northern terminus. The finish. Atop the mountain would be a sign announcing the end of the trail, a sign that I'd seen in so many AT thru-hiker's photos. While I could already picture my finisher's pose, I still had a long way to walk.

I could barely see the border sign as we passed into Maine in a dense morning fog. Rain sprinkled from above and dripped from the trees, and I found myself less motivated than I was just a moment before on the other side of the border. I thought that crossing into Maine would inject a new energy into me. Instead, I felt the same as I did just moments before in New Hampshire. I was tired from the Whites and I knew we still had incredibly difficult sections awaiting us in Maine. It was one of the first real moments that I looked forward to the finish and I calculated that we had nearly two weeks left of hiking. Merely a drop in time in normal life, two weeks of hiker-time sounded like a long time, especially if the cold rain continued. While I was confident I would finish, I doubted it would be smooth sailing until the end.

I was in a pensive mood as I walked alone, with Matt ahead of me and out of sight and Rumblestrip well ahead of us both. I recognized early on that morning that I was in a grumpy mood. Some days just weren't as fun as others and some days I simply woke up on the wrong side of the floorboards. This was one of those days. It would be a great disservice to you if I pretended that these days didn't exist.

What did I do with the crappy mood I was in? I used my abundance of time to think, something which could be both helpful and detrimental because of the mood I was in. At first my thoughts were detrimental. I thought about the miles left to walk, the pack I had to carry, and the volatile weather I had to face. I was negative, I was whiney, and I wanted to cry. None of this is fun to hear about, but it is true. Once I let myself have a temporary pity party, I moved beyond my immediate surroundings. I thought about my life and the choices I had made that not only led me there, but which would also lead me down my future path. The expectations I had set forth for myself at the beginning of the trail, the expectations which had taken a backseat to the daily particulars of the hike, began to resurface.

I wasn't sure if I had really changed since the beginning. Physically, I was at the same weight as when I started, much to my chagrin, as I'd been hoping to finish the trail thinner and to celebrate without the hindrance of calorie counting. Mentally, even though I no longer felt negativity pulsing through me, I couldn't fully grasp what had changed about me. Maybe my expectations of the changes that would occur within me were too high, or maybe I thought they would have been a little more recognizable.

Because I let myself think about the finish, I also thought about life after the trail. What did I truly want to do with my life? I had a unique freedom from work and yet, I wasn't sure I was taking full advantage of that freedom. We started the trail with the hopes that by the end of it, we would know what we wanted to do next. Instead, it was as if the net we had cast out had only grown bigger, collecting more and more ideas for future adventures. We seemed further from a decision now that we could see in so many directions. A bigger net wasn't necessarily a bad thing, nor was a long list of adventures, but the grump in me wanted the comfort zone of a definite plan.

As I walked through the misty rain, I contemplated the possibility of thru-hiking another trail. There was still the CDT, the last jewel in my triple crown. I knew Matt would want to hike it one day, most likely sooner than later because of our current lack of big responsibilities, such as children. I rolled the CDT over in my mind and became overwhelmed by the prospect of suffering through more wet, cold miles. The adult in me knew that my lack of preparation on the AT had led to unnecessary suffering that could be avoided on the CDT, and that they were two entirely different trails, but the child in me entered the downward spiral of "if only" moments.

I thought about my collection of decisions that had led me to that moment of walking in Maine and wondered where I'd be had I not made some of them. I looked back on the decisions as if the repercussions were somehow avoidable by re-considering them and wishing I had made a different choice. If only I had majored in Spanish, I would have a different career. If only I had never hiked the PCT, I would not have felt the need to hike another trail. If only I had not quit my job, I would be back in a dry office, sipping office coffee and eating peanut butter toast for breakfast. I went so far as to question my decision to be with Matt. He was a large part of the reason I ever thru-hiked in the first place. Thru-hiking was one of his life-passions and that was not going to change, so should I change my relationship with him? Every fiber in me knew it wasn't possible to undo a decision or to change the next ten that followed the path of the first decision, yet I still entertained the idea of changing them.

Once I caught up to Matt, I told him what I had been thinking about. I admitted all the decisions I wished I could have changed and reasoned why I thought my present happiness had been affected by the choices I had made over the last several years. His silence was enough to tell me that he didn't agree with me and that he thought very differently about past decisions. After a few minutes of walking across bog boards, struggling to keep our balance on the muddy, slick wood, he followed up with questions.

"Why do you keep harping on decisions that you can't reverse? How come you can't see that you get nowhere by spending so much time regretting the past? Why not focus on what you're saying and doing right now to make this shitty situation better?"

I didn't have an answer; silence was my only response. I didn't know what I had been expecting him to say, but I knew that wasn't it. I let a gap increase between Matt and me so we wouldn't have to talk to each other, and I thought about what he said.

The answer clicked when I later heard a close friend say the exact words that I had been thinking all along.

"I chose the wrong path," my friend said. "I should have never gone to school at…because then I would have never gotten a job doing this…and then I wouldn't be living here." My friend entered the same mental black hole that I was all too familiar with.

Hearing another person say that he chose the wrong path and listening to that person go through the "if only" list showed me exactly what I sounded like that morning in Maine. As I heard my friend say it, I thought, "That's completely useless to think that way. Nothing you say or wish can change your current situation, so why don't you just move forward and try to make the present moment better?"

Another thought that came to my mind was, "Is that what I sound like?"

I had thought the same phrase so many times over, never stopping to think about the effects it had on me and others, or about the fruitlessness of the thought.

That moment of clarity also led me to wonder if I had been wrong from the beginning in how I approached the trail. I had expected the AT to change me, to lead me to my true self, a self that was fulfilled, passionate and living in the present moment. I really did expect to find my shiny new self under all the layers of rust that I was chipping off over the last eighty days. Instead, I was left wondering who I was and what I wanted to do with my life. I hadn't come any closer to finding myself and I was confused and frustrated as I walked those first miles in Maine.

Ironically, after taking into account these questions, these thoughts, and these contemplations, the one saving grace was that I was still in Maine. At first, the remaining miles seemed like a harsh reality to face with almost two weeks of hiking ahead of me. On the other hand, I had two more weeks to work through these questions before I returned to normal society. Not all was lost. I still had a chance. Like the other eighty-two days before, I took the only option that was a constant. I kept walking.

Part of the reason I had been grumpy that morning was also because I knew what was coming up that afternoon. I knew the day would require a special breed of good behavior and the child in me fought it. I didn't want to acknowledge that I would have to be undeniably positive through a short, one-mile section. That one mile was seemingly harmless in length but treacherously long in time and effort because of its obstacle course-like terrain. The Mahoosuc Notch was rumored to take up to three hours to get through because of all the climbing over boulders, inching through crevices, and scooting down slabs of rock.

The weather cleared by the time we reached the notch and the sun was shining as we entered its gauntlet. I felt like I was on the set of *American Gladiators*. Before we started the notch, Matt and I both promised each other that we were going to have fun with the pure ridiculousness of it all. And that is exactly what we did for the entire two hours that it took to cover one mile. I cast aside the Stopwatch in me that strove for efficiency and chalked up the entire experience as, "I set out to hike the AT, and if this is where the AT takes me, then so be it."

We weren't in a hurry, we knew we were stopping at the next shelter after a short, fifteen-mile day, and we took pictures and videos along the way in order to record the notch in all its glory. As we made our way through, we squeezed through a point where two rocks met, and Matt recalled the moment in 2000, when he broke his external frame backpack in that very same spot. He had leaned into the choke point of the two rocks, assuming his pack would eventually follow, and was surprised when the cloth on his pack ripped off the metal frame, causing him to stumble towards the ground. Duct tape held his pack together the rest of the trail.

Shortly after the notch, we were ready to call it a night at the Speck Pond Shelter. The first day in Maine had done some damage on our minds and bodies, and the shelter was full of other hikers, including Rusty and Bigfoot, two names we'd seen in the journals over the last few days.

That evening, the rain flooded the trail once again as we slept in a crowded shelter, with inches between each hiker. On my left side was Matt and on my right was Bigfoot, too close in my opinion. I woke up at 2:00 a.m. just six inches from his face, his mouth open in a full-on snore with stale breath blowing my way. It was still odd for me to sleep in such close quarters with strangers, especially old men who snored loudly and forcefully into my face. I was glad to be tired and fell asleep quickly after turning on my other side to face Matt.

Julie Urbanski

32 OUR SUPPORT CREW

Sometimes there are days when you want to break the mold. Do something different. Eat pasta salad for breakfast or pancakes for dinner, hit the snooze button on the weekend alarm or get up early on a Saturday and go for a run in the silent morning. Anything to break the monotony of an old routine. You realize that both yourself and others have found it too easy to call your next move and you want to keep them guessing.

Matt and I were no exception to this desire as we continued through Maine. We could in fact be defined as fast hikers, only because we covered more ground in one day than most, but we didn't love the pressure that came with that label. It was expected that we'd push through even the worst of weather or the sloppiest of terrain because we were tough and liked to reach our physical and mental limits via more miles. Some days that just wasn't true.

I questioned my level of toughness and oftentimes dreamed of ten to fifteen-mile days with hours of lounging in a shelter. Yet, I knew I was capable of doing so much more, my mind and body fine-tuned machines that just needed a trail to really test them. The wrestling match between my emotions and my abilities often favored my abilities, but one particular day in Maine, Matt and I broke the routine and followed our emotions.

The weather dealt us terrible cards at the beginning of Maine. We had the company of Rusty and Rumblestrip on our eighty-fourth night in the Hall Mountain Lean-to, quite possibly one of the crappiest shelters on the trail, with a foot-wide hole in one side of the floorboards. The next morning, we awoke to pouring rain once again and I considered the prospect of it raining for the rest of the entire trip. Yes, I'd still finish, but damn, that would be a gloomy way to walk through Maine. It was a long morning of slow hiking, with slippery footing on both the mucky trail and wet rocks.

With all the rough, wet footing, our feet took the brunt of the impact, and we took every advantage to free our feet from our shoes and massage the aching bones and footpads. Matt's shoes were on their last miles. The heel on his right shoe was hanging on like a loose tooth that needed one good pull to break the connection. My mesh shoes were also getting torn up. Holes opened up at several of the pressure points with my feet, which allowed soil and pebbles to drift around in my shoes until I took the time to empty them.

After a treacherous walk across the slick rock atop Bemis Mountain, with barely a patch of grass to grip my hiking poles into, we took a break from the new wave of rain clouds in the Bemis Mountain Lean-to. Thirteen miles was all we'd covered so far for the day and it was 1:00 p.m., a record-slow pace for us. On a daily basis on the PCT, we easily had twenty miles in by 2:00 p.m. because of the smooth, relatively obstacle-free terrain. Each ensuing day on the AT reminded me that the memories of the PCT were long gone, and the more I tried to fit my past hike into the current frame of the AT, the uglier the picture became.

The Bemis Mountain Lean-to was empty and as soon as we rested for a few minutes, the cold began to creep into our wet clothes and bodies. We changed into dry clothes, snuggled up in our sleeping bags, and decided to take a nap as the rain drummed on the corrugated roof above us. A decision had not yet been made as to whether we were staying for good, but I had a feeling it would be mighty hard to convince myself to put on my wet clothes again and keep walking in the rain.

Rumblestrip soon showed up and looked a little disappointed that we appeared to have stopped for the day, but it didn't take him long to join us in putting on dry clothes and hanging out in his sleeping bag. It was then a party of three.

As we sat there with Rumblestrip, we learned a little more about him and his thoughts on the trail. I was most interested in knowing how he played the mental wrestling match of quitting and staying on the trail, especially given the weather over the last few days.

He recounted the first and only day he seriously thought about quitting. It had been early on, around the Nantahala Outdoor Center. He had taken a zero in town with the Wolfpack and reluctantly hiked out alone the next day, leaving the Wolfpack to spend more time off the trail. As he walked the long, eight mile climb out of the NOC by himself, he thought about quitting. He missed his family more at that moment than any other and found himself asking, "Why?" Why was he hiking? Why had he left his family for that kind of a life? Why did he want to walk from Georgia to Maine?

Rather than go back to town, he picked a point later down the trail and told himself he'd decide then if he was going to quit. By the time he made it there, the homesickness had worn off and he'd entered the Smokies. He was out of his funk and had good memories from the time he'd spent with his brother just a year before in that same area. While he never doubted his capabilities of finishing the hike, that was the closest he came to mentally giving up and he attributed much of that low moment to starting back up after a day off in town.

Later on in the hike, Rumblestrip met a few more thru-hikers that he enjoyed the company of even better than the Wolfpack. He spent a lot of time with Coney, who we'd just met days before, and Savage, another hiker that we'd never met. Before meeting them, he hiked a lot of miles alone and never really thought about making good friends along the trail. They were the first friends that made him realize just how good, good friends could be, and how much he needed them in his life. Rumblestrip admitted to having few friends back home besides his brothers and he found that one of his favorite parts of thru-hiking was the friends he made in the process.

At that point, I could tell Rumblestrip missed Coney and Savage. We were his new friends, but we couldn't replace the old ones that he probably felt most himself around. They had gotten separated after a couple of different town stops, and now that Coney and Savage were behind him, he had no idea whether they were within one mile or twenty. Being behind other hikers had its benefits of knowing where everyone else was rather than just guessing at their whereabouts. Instead, Rumblestrip was up front without a clue if he'd ever see his friends again. He wrote messages to them in the journals in the shelters, one particularly heart-breaking message, "Savage, where art thou?"

As we sat in the shelter that rainy afternoon, listening to Rumblestrip's perspectives, other hikers rolled in one-by-one, each one grateful for the break from the rain. That afternoon, Rusty stumbled into the shelter, soaking wet and ready to join us for the evening. He was a teacher in his late twenties with blond hair and glasses that fogged up constantly in the rain. It was a good distance from Maine to his home in the Midwest, and he was out to add another piece of his section thru-hike to the books. Even in bad weather, he was light-hearted and positive, and I enjoyed the humor he brought to the group. There was soon no doubt that all of us were in for the evening.

Next walked in an older man that none of us had ever met. He appeared to be in his sixties and he tossed his poles in the shelter, slung off his pack, and sat down on the edge of the shelter, resting from the challenging terrain we had all just covered. His name was Caribou, a lawyer from Maine. He had just hiked in that morning from the road to Andover, nine miles back, and was out for a few days. Caribou had hiked much of the trail in sections and despite his age compared to the rest of us, he had a sprightly spark in him. We recognized right away that he was witty and deeply knowledgeable about the trail. I liked him immediately and I couldn't believe the cast of good characters that surrounded us as the rain continued to soak into the squishy ground outside.

Two other hikers showed up later that day and the conversation never stopped with so many people in the shelter and so many stories to share. I particularly loved hearing Caribou talk. He demanded attention in the way he phrased things so well. I couldn't imagine having missed him had we decided to hike on. Caribou also turned into the resident Santa Claus in the shelter.

"Anyone want a ham sandwich?" he asked as he pulled out a gallon-sized Ziploc containing three sandwiches wrapped in plastic.

"I always bring extra for other hikers," he explained as he tossed them across the floorboards to two accepting hikers.

"I've also got an extra Mountain House meal if anyone wants one."

It was non-vegetarian, or otherwise we would have jumped on the opportunity. Again, he gave it up to the first taker.

"You wouldn't happen to have an extra headlamp, would you?" Matt asked jokingly. He'd accidentally left his back in Myrtle Beach and we'd been sharing mine ever since.

"I do!" Caribou said. "It's just a little one from Home Depot. They came in a two-pack, so I've already got one. Here you go." He tossed it to Matt from across the shelter.

Later on, after Caribou had cooked his Mountain House meal for dinner, he had leftovers. He even shared those with Rumblestrip, who was eager to partake in a warm meal since he didn't carry a stove.

Since we were on a roll with Caribou, Matt asked him, "You wouldn't happen to know if the next town of Rangeley has any good outdoor stores, would you? We're looking to buy a tent but we can't tell from the guidebook if the stores will have what we want."

We'd been missing the privacy of our tent and we thought about buying one for the last two hundred miles of the trail. The forced mileage between shelters had also been bothering us; we missed hiking without a destination for the day.

"Well, what kind of tent are you looking for?" Caribou asked.

"We were hoping to get a lightweight tent, like a tarp tent, but I doubt any store will carry something like that," Matt answered.

"Hmm," Caribou said, "I don't think there's a whole lot that you can get in the towns coming up."

After that, he threw out all sorts of ideas, like picking us up off the trail in a couple of days to take us to a bigger town. We had posed a difficult question and he really wanted to help us find a solution.

"Actually," he started in, "I have a two-person tarp tent that I don't even use. It weighs less than two pounds. It's just sitting in my garage among lots of other gear that I don't use. I'll mail it to you when I get home."

"Um…ok!" we both said. We didn't know how to respond, but after all he'd done so far, we knew he was serious.

"How about I send it to Caratunk? Will that work?"

We were planning on being in Caratunk in a few days and it would work out perfectly for us to pick up a new tent there. We agreed and gave him our contact information. Though we were accustomed to unique trail magic, Caribou's generosity still shocked us. It just didn't seem real. We have since used that tent on another thru-hike, with plans of hiking many more miles with it.

Hiking through endless days of rain finally improved after the next day's wet morning morphed into a sunny afternoon. Our motivation had been recharged from the long afternoon in the shelter with other hikers and we looked forward to town that day. Elevation changes also eased up considerably and by early afternoon, Matt and I were already seventeen miles into our day at the road into Rangeley, Maine. The sun was shining and we soaked up the heat that rose off the blacktop as we stood there waiting for a hitch. A white van soon pulled over to give us a ride.

As the van slowed to drop us off in the parking lot of the supermarket, we saw Rumblestrip's pack propped up against the outside of the building. He'd been ahead of us all day and had the same plan as we did of groceries first, town-food second.

After resupply and laundry chores, we all visited an ice cream shop and sat on the plush, green lawn behind the shop as we savored our cones. The town was surprisingly bustling for it being such a small, remote town. I looked down at my watch for an explanation.

"Hey, it's July 4th! Happy Independence Day!" I said to Matt and Rumblestrip.

We toasted our freedom with our cones and I was happy to share that moment with both Matt and Rumblestrip. As we sat there, I thought about electing ice cream as my favorite food and it occurred to me that Rumblestrip's diet of ramen noodles and Oreos must have been vastly different from that at home, on a farm. I asked him, "Rumblestrip, what's your favorite food out here."

Without his normal pause to stop and think, he immediately answered, "Oh, Snickers, for sure. I have to limit myself to two a day."

I questioned how he would get his fix once he went home and then I smiled as I wondered what the community would do if they found out he was smuggling in Snickers bars.

Once back on the trail, we spent another evening in the company of Rumblestrip at the Piazza Rock Lean-to with a nineteen-mile day behind us. The next day's mileage options were either seventeen or thirty-five miles. The days of thirty-plus miles were long gone, along with the easy trails of Virginia, and we elected for another short day. It was a clear, beautiful morning that seemed to change the scenery with the sudden outpouring of sun and warmth. Saddleback Mountain awaited us first, and with dry conditions, the soles of our rubbery shoes gripped the rocky, slanted ascent. Because of the open, exposed faces of the rocks, I felt beads of sweat trickle down the side of my face. It felt good to sweat again.

By late afternoon, we arrived at the Spaulding Mountain Lean-to. We were still in the company of Rumblestrip, who seemed to have enjoyed us enough to stick around for the last few days. He had a one-person tent and didn't need to follow the shelters' mileage, so I knew he could take off and hike without us at any moment. Rusty even showed up later that evening. He'd spent the prior evening in Rangeley and hiked all day to catch up to us. We had counted him out of the loop since he stopped in town, so we were both shocked and excited to see him.

Now that I can look back on that time in Maine, I see that the company of others is what helped us get through Maine, particularly that of Rusty and Rumblestrip. They were fun, they were positive, and they had magnetic personalities. Because of them, I felt compelled to be better. I was on my best behavior around them. I didn't want them to think I was a boring pessimist who only detracted from the trail experience. Rather, I wanted to be fun to be around. I liked their company and wanted them to keep coming back. Their presence had a trickle-down effect on both my attitude and my relationship with Matt, both of which were greatly enhanced.

Following the streak of forced mileage, we awoke again to another decision between nineteen and twenty-nine miles, and yet again, opted for the shorter day. The crisp morning air was even more fantastic than the day before and the hiking was magically easier with sunny weather.

The afternoon held a long, six-mile descent of three thousand feet. By the end of it, I hated to admit it, but I was tired of walking downhill. My quads were gummy by the time we made it to the road crossing that led to Stratton, and rather than break at the road, we hiked a little further up the trail, where we took a long afternoon break in the sun.

As we sat there, I felt the eerie shift in wind and Matt and I rushed to pack up. Within a few minutes we were back on the trail, walking at an accelerated pace. Three miles stood between us and the next shelter and we weren't sure if the skies would hold out. The sun was still shining but the wind was undoubtedly bringing something directly towards us.

Matt was ahead of me on a gradual uphill climb while I lagged on rocky steps. With about a mile to go, I heard the first rumble of thunder and I knew time was running out. I could still see Matt and I started hauling as fast as I could, pushing hard off my poles to propel me uphill. He later said he knew I had picked it up when he heard the clinking rhythm of my poles increase in frequency.

I eventually passed him on the uphill and as we came to the crest of the hill, with less than a mile to go and a slight downhill ahead of us, the first bolt of lightning came within range. We ran for it. We'd been perfectly dry and we weren't taking any chances with being so close to a shelter. My poles allowed me to practically ski over the technical trail and that time, Matt struggled to keep up.

Out of breath and exuberant with our timing, we arrived at an empty Horn Pond Lean-to and celebrated our feat of beating the rain. Within minutes of our arrival, the skies opened up and the rain made up for the last two days of sunshine with a storm of intensity we hadn't seen since Virginia. First the rain came down heavily, then it blew sideways, and then pebble-sized hail fell and bounced off the ground. Each ensuing level was more drastic than the previous one, and all I could think was, "Thank goodness we made it!"

I didn't have to wonder long about Rumblestrip and Rusty, because they soon followed, not as lucky as we had been in beating the storm. Rumblestrip arrived first, his thin, light blue pack cover blown halfway off his external metal frame. The pack was like a lightning rod strapped to his back and he looked scared. We told him that we were surprised that he was behind us when he normally hiked faster than us, so he sat down to tell us why he was behind. He was still angry at himself as he told the story.

"So I passed this couple on the downhill to the road crossing into Stratton. Then I decided to take a short break along the footbridge on the other side of the road. It was such a nice spot and it felt so good to put my feet in the water. Then, just as I'm about to get up and go, the couple passes me back. I didn't want to start hiking and pass them right back, so I just waited another half hour before starting up again. Then I heard the thunder and before I knew it I was in the middle of the storm and getting pelted by hail, all because I didn't want to pass that couple again."

I could relate with aversion to leap-frogging. I hated passing and re-passing people, for no particularly logical reason. A few minutes later, Rusty arrived, his glasses fogged up, his hair a blond mop of tangles, and his breath just as labored as ours had been when we arrived. He too had a story as to why he was so late in coming to the shelter.

"Well, I made it to the road to Stratton and a woman offered me a ride into town. I was so proud of myself; I managed to get in, eat a burger, and get back out on the trail, in just forty-five minutes. Forty-five minutes! That was it! Then I heard the thunder, and then the lightning, and it was all over.

I should have never had that burger. I knew it was too good to be true!"

While we sat cozy and dry on one side of the shelter, they hung up their wet belongings on the other side. Just minutes stood between the times we arrived to the shelter, but those minutes had made all the difference. Our luck held out long enough to avoid the rain and to have another evening in the company of Rumblestrip and Rusty. Even the rain outside the shelter couldn't bring me down that night, as I was feeling the sentiment of being a northbound thru-hiker near the end of the journey. Squash's recent journal entries summed it up best. "Damn it feels good to be a NOBO."

33 CATCHING THE A TEAM

At pre-dawn, I heard a crunching sound just a few feet away. I looked out into the bushes and trees in front of the shelter, but the light was still too dim to see anything. Whatever creature was milling around in the bushes, snapping tree limbs and eating vegetation, it looked large, and I thought there might be two of them. I feared it was a bear, dreaded that it could be a cub and its mother. I laid my head back down with my eyes fixed on the darkness, fearing a bear encounter at any moment.

"Julie," Matt whispered to me, "I think there are two moose out there. I can just barely make them out. It looks like a mom and a baby moose."

My first thought went to the baby. I didn't know how moose felt about their young being close to other creatures, but if moose were as protective as bears, I was even more nervous for the moment when the moose saw us.

"They're right in front of the shelter. Look!" Matt whispered.

I looked out and in the dim, foggy light I could just barely make out the two moose. They were working slowly over the vegetation, grabbing huge clusters of leaves into their mouths and chomping down on them, one forceful bite at a time. With each placement of their hooves, several twigs snapped under their weight. Just in front of them read a sign, "Do Not Enter. Re-vegetation in Progress."

By then, Rusty and Rumblestrip were awake, still lying in their sleeping bags and watching the moose show unfold in front of the shelter. Each one of us barely breathed, for fear it would scare them away.

The moose slowly approached the side of the shelter that Rusty was on and took their time in picking and choosing their breakfast along each side of the shelter. We all laid our heads down once they were out of view and I assumed they would follow a path away from the shelter. Instead, they walked around the back of the shelter and rounded the other side where I was lying. Matt's curiosity got the best of him. He crept up next to me, where he could hear the two moose just on the other side of the shelter wall, and he poked his head out around the corner to see the moose.

As he poked his head out, he came face to face with the mother moose, their heads within three feet of each other. The baby moose continued eating behind the mom, but the mom stood there stiffly, looking at Matt. Matt was too frightened to move. He waited for the moose to make the next move.

The mother moose must have assumed Matt to be harmless, because she swung her head down and continued roaming through the bushes for more food. They sauntered slowly once again through the bushes in front of the shelter and were soon out of sight.

Whew! It felt like I had held my breath for an entire half hour. Even though it was barely dawn, none of us could fall back asleep after that kind of a moose encounter. We repeated the story at least five times among the four of us before it got old, and even then we still hadn't calmed down from the rush of adrenaline. I was awake, alert, and ready to get moving.

Once we gathered ourselves, Matt and I looked at the day's mileage. If all went well and we were able to get in good miles, which looked possible based on the guidebook's elevation chart, we wanted to hike twenty-seven miles to a shelter that was just four miles before the Kennebec River. The river had a mandatory ferry service that had to be used to cross the river, but it only ran from 9:00 a.m.-11:00 a.m., and we didn't want to take our chances in missing it the next day.

We also had a hunch that we might see Zippers and Stretch again. They'd become the self-proclaimed "A Team" in their recent journal entries. Lately they'd been hiking with a group of hikers, including Squash, Fosters, Youngin, and Girl with 4 Dogs. Based on the journals, they'd not only been covering good miles together, but they'd also been spending time in town together, like a Fourth of July bash in Stratton that involved a lot of food and a lot of beer. Most of all, they seemed like they were having a hell of a good time hiking with a group. We'd been slowly catching them over the last two weeks, ever since we returned from vacation, and because of the tight ferry schedule, we had a feeling we would catch them. Either way, just the thought of seeing them again was enough motivation for me as we walked that day.

Awaiting us early that morning were the Bigelow peaks. The rain had stopped and the morning fog quickly burned off to reveal a gorgeous summer day in Maine. While the climbs were tough, I barely broke a sweat with the crisp morning air to cool me. The climbs were also manageable because the upcoming afternoon looked pancake flat. It was our first chance in a long time to stretch out our legs over fairly smooth terrain. By

4:00 p.m., we made it to the West Carry Pond Lean-to. We still had ten miles to walk and while we felt our energy sputtering a little, we agreed to push on and hike into the evening, if necessary.

Before continuing, Matt took the opportunity to bathe in the pond just in front of the shelter. It had been a hot afternoon and we had walked through pockets of heat and mosquitoes in the dense forests. Matt wanted to start the next miles as cool and as clean as possible. I, on the other hand, did not bathe. To Matt's disgust, and rightly so, I shunned bathing in even the hottest of conditions because of the possibility of being cold. The water was frigid, but with a few shivers and squeals, Matt plunged into the water in just his running shorts and rinsed off nine days of dirt and sweat. As he fluttered around in the cold water, I watched from the edge and took pictures. He entered a moment of pure exhilaration and I saw a childlike happiness in him that I hadn't seen in a while.

We glided over the last ten miles and as we approached the back of the Pierce Pond Lean-to, we could hear a few voices and I was sure I heard a dog bark. As we rounded the side wall of the shelter to reveal it's opening, there they were, the A Team.

"Optimist and Stopwatch!" Zippers yelled. "We thought we might see you guys today!"

It was a tight shelter in the six-person capacity space with Youngin, Zippers, Stretch, Girl with 4 Dogs, and two of her dogs, but they managed to squeeze us in. We spent the rest of the evening reminiscing about all that had occurred since the last time we saw them in New York, when I had thought about quitting.

We had a lot of catching up to do.

When we left them back in Greenwood Lake, New York, they had taken a day off at Stretch's mom's home in Albany. It was a balmy ninety-five degrees as they sat on the front porch of her house, and for the first time, the idea of quitting crossed Stretch's mind. New York was a tough state for a lot of people, and they were no exception. Stretch's desire to finish what he started was what kept him on the trail.

Vermont had also not been friendly to them with weather, as the rain of Pennsylvania returned after the buggy heat in New York. Rain and fog defined most of their days in Vermont, not to mention the mud beneath their feet. We could completely relate to them and knew the efforts they must have made to stay positive. There was even a particularly low day of motivation, when Stretch took his first four steps of the day, only to say to Zippers, "I can't wait for today to be over already."

While in Vermont in mid-June, they took another zero at Stretch's dad's house, a relief from the weather and a chance to look forward to the end. They set a summit date for Mt. Katahdin as July 16 and bought the champagne that would be hiked to the top to celebrate. For Zippers, who doubted their relationship's stability, it was with mixed feelings that she planned for the end. At the time, all she could think of when she thought about champagne on Katahdin was, "Right now I'm just focused on finishing Vermont!"

By the time we caught up to them in Maine, Zippers had mixed feelings about finishing the trail. She had the same ironic emotions as I did as she crossed the Maine border. She felt like crossing the border should have kept her enthusiasm up through the end, when in fact she was faced with the reality that Maine was still a long state to walk through. As we had done recently, Stretch and Zippers put the rainy days behind them and were making the best of their last days on the trail by hiking with a group. In telling them about our last few days with Rusty and Rumblestrip, I saw that we shared a similar pattern.

The next morning we crossed the Kennebec River in a small canoe, our only aquatic miles, after which we made our way to Caratunk. Matt recounted his story of crossing the river with Animal in 2000, when a ferry wasn't strictly enforced. They crossed the icy river just as September was passing into October and Matt fell in several times, pack and all, while slipping on the smooth rocks beneath the surface. Matt even lost a flip-flop in the process, his Navy-issued sandal bobbing downstream to be lost forever as he struggled to keep his balance above the water. Animal filmed the entire crossing with a handheld VHS camcorder. He didn't care how heavy it was and was determined to film their trail experiences. They both still talk about watching that sad, lone flip-flop float away on the surface of the Kennebec River, never to be seen again.

Once we arrived at the Caratunk Post Office, it was nothing short of Christmas, complete with five care packages from family and friends, including a tarp tent from Caribou. We were free from the shelters and anticipated the ability to sleep in our private space once again.

I was no longer scared of Maine's terrain as we hiked an easy twenty-three miles that day to the Moxie Bald Mountain Lean-to. Zippers and Stretch were already there when we arrived and we were giddy with excitement in putting up the new tent for the first time. We both loved our new home.

The plan for the next day was to resupply in Monson, the last town stop on the entire trail before reaching Baxter State Park, the home of Mt. Katahdin. The hiking looked so flat and monotonous in the book that I stopped looking, and shortly into the morning, we caught up with Zippers, Stretch, Youngin and Girl with 4 Dogs. Stretch and Youngin hiked a good distance ahead while the rest of us, including Matt, chatted for the rest of the afternoon. Stretch normally hiked ahead of Zippers and then took breaks while he waited for her to catch up. I sensed that it bothered Zippers that she never actually hiked much with Stretch.

The more we got to know Zippers, the more we learned about her relationship with Stretch. Even though they held it together and stayed positive around other hikers, Matt and I knew first-hand how straining a thru-hike could be for a relationship, and I had a feeling there was much more bubbling beneath the surface. Zippers and Stretch had been hiking together for nearly four months, and while they experienced the normal ups and downs that thru-hiking brought to the relationship, their future together looked doubtful. They weren't talking about future plans as "we" anymore.

Zippers could even pinpoint the exact day that she knew that their relationship would end, and it was no surprise to me to hear it was atop Mt. Madison, the section in the Whites characterized by endless fields of boulders. The section is forever etched in my mind as one of the longest, most tortuous parts of the AT.

Zippers and Stretch had arrived a little too early to the Madison Spring Hut, which sat at the base of the climb and descent of Mt. Madison. They'd had luck with staying in huts by taking advantage of the work-for-stay program and had put in a hard effort to make it to the Madison Spring Hut to secure their spot. Unfortunately, the decision for them to stay wasn't in their hands. The workers at the hut denied them work-for-stay positions, saying it was too early for them to stop, and that there was time for them to hike on. It was one of the aspects of the huts that Matt and I disliked, that our fate was in the hands of the hut workers and that an hour or two difference could mean stopping for the day or hiking on. It was also the reason we kept to the shelters and cowboy camped instead.

They were both pissed that they were told to move on from the hut and didn't look forward to the next three miles until the Osgood Tent Site. With the climb taking them over huge boulders, Zippers fell behind Stretch's faster pace. Zippers arrived at the poorly marked top of Mt. Madison, a barren, windswept pile of rocks, and she had a hard time finding where the trail continued next.

At the top, Stretch wasn't in sight, Zippers was alone, she had no idea where to go next, and she doubted that Stretch was concerned about her whereabouts. The reality of their relationship hit her at that moment and tears welled up as it sunk in. She knew the relationship was over.

Overwhelmed with the acknowledgement of their relationship's failure, Zippers sat down and cried. She felt sorry for herself for the first time ever on the trail and couldn't tell if she was upset because the relationship was ending, or because she truly hadn't thought of a backup plan. The relationship *was* the plan, and her tears turned to anger at herself. She was mad that she hadn't thought of a Plan B and she was mad she was sitting there crying, feeling sorry for herself. I could relate to every phase of feelings that she went through. It is the ultimate humbling experience to be atop a mountain, alone, with just your own self to face. Self-honesty is unavoidable.

Zippers also knew that eventually, Stretch would also be angry with her for taking so long, so she did the only thing that was still certain in her life. She kept walking. The ever-present miles were uniquely comforting to her at that moment. She knew she could still count on the miles. It was a part of long-distance hiking that she came to love, the certainty that there were always miles left to be walked, no matter what else fell apart. The realization that she could at least count on the miles was, in her words, a cathartic experience, and that is probably the best way to describe the ever-present miles that a thru-hiker faces, even if everything else seems unstable.

As we walked those flat, easy miles to Monson together, I could see that Zippers was torn between two sentiments. While she was struggling with a case of "get me the hell out of the woods," as she called it, anxious to enjoy creature comforts again, she also knew the next steps afterwards were uncertain. Stretch would be starting graduate school in the fall, but it was likely she wouldn't be going with him. Part of her also wanted to appreciate every fleeting minute on the trail. I too felt the need to make the best of the remaining days, days that I would never be able to live again.

The rest of the warm, sunny day rolled on as we covered all kinds of topics together, from weight loss, to periods, to 401ks. Later on, the topic inevitably turned to my inability to find happiness on the trail. I told a few stories of my worst days and how Matt still stayed with me even in my sourest of moods and strongest of outbursts. I hated admitting those moments that I was least proud of, but I wanted to paint an honest picture of how I felt about thru-hiking. Then Zippers said something that has stayed with me ever since, and that hurt to hear, only because it was the truth.

"Matt, you must have so much patience," she said.

She said it jokingly, but there was honesty in her tone and it hurt. I knew my negative mentality often strained our relationship and I knew Matt was a saint for dealing with me. I just didn't want it to be so apparent to others. I thought others had been fooled into thinking we had a perfectly balanced relationship of give and take, and I was bothered that others could see its flaws and my shortcomings. I resented the truth that Zippers so succinctly stated, and for a brief moment I was angry at her for being so openly honest. The anger quickly faded when I let my own self-honesty sink in.

We easily made it into Monson after a quick hitch from the road crossing. Rumblestrip, who had arrived in town much earlier because he hiked on later the night before, looked thrilled to see us when we reunited in front of a hostel. We were happy to see him too. He represented a simple, yet deep friendship that had become a uniquely fulfilling part of our thru-hike. All of us reconvened for a late lunch in Monson before Rumblestrip, Matt, and I hitched a ride back to the trail. The rest of the crew had planned on stopping there for the evening, but we looked forward to getting in more miles.

I was sad to leave Zippers. I could tell she was upset and was even half-tempted to offer our companionship to her for the rest of the hike. I decided against it, not wanting to cause any more waves for an already rocky boat. We said our goodbyes and I knew then that I'd never see them again, at least not on the AT.

With leaving the last AT town, there was only one more destination to turn our attention towards: Mt. Katahdin.

Julie Urbanski

34 MAINE ISN'T FINISHED YET

While leaving Zippers behind in Monson was hard, it would have been even harder to let Rumblestrip walk out of town alone. Just a hundred and fifteen miles were all that was left to walk and there was an unspoken understanding between Rumblestrip and us that we'd stay together until the finish. We had told him that he could join us on our drive back to Ohio if he was still with us at Katahdin, since his family's farm in Ohio was practically on the way home for us. We planned on renting a car to drive home and he had neither a driver's license nor the desire for a day-long Greyhound bus ride, so we assured him we'd help him with logistics.

That afternoon, we walked a short, rolling three miles to the first shelter, the Leeman Brook Lean-to, and we were ready to call it a day after twenty-one miles and a town stop. We had a beautiful campsite next to the side of the shelter and because the mosquitoes were out once again, we were glad to retreat to a tent.

We had just entered the 100-Mile Wilderness, a section with essentially no resupply points from Monson until Abol Bridge and a road into Millinocket. On a trail like the AT, where the opportunity to reach town seems ever-present, it's a big deal to have such a stretch without resupplies. Matt remembered practically running through the 100-Mile Wilderness his first time through, so I had confidence we could do the same. I was also glad to be a northbounder with trail-tested legs rather than a southbounder just starting out and faced with such a section.

Apparently the woods were listening to my confidence and decided that Maine still had plenty of gnarly terrain and difficult elevation changes ahead of me. The next day was surprisingly challenging. The elevation chart looked bumpy at best, with one significant climb of 2000 feet, but otherwise, it should have been easy to get in the twenty-three miles we had planned. Instead, at 7:30 p.m. that night, we found ourselves over a mile and a half away from the shelter, with dead legs and low motivation.

Matt and I were ready to camp at the first flat spot we could find rather than push on to the shelter, and we did exactly that once we passed a stream with a large patch of soft ground just beyond it, big enough to fit our tent and Rumblestrip's. All three of us were tired and went to sleep quickly. I went to bed wondering if Matt's memory was somehow skewed with this section of the trail and I hoped for a better tomorrow.

The next morning's hike was technical terrain that kept us rolling up and down and the afternoon held a climb up White Cap Mountain. The temperature was near perfect as we walked the drawn-out, eleven mile climb of three thousand feet. The first half was a gentle incline that was noticeable, but not taxing. The second half consisted of four major peaks, each with a climb followed by a descent. It felt like the elevation took us two steps up and one step down, all the way until White Cap Mountain. I was worn out as I sat atop White Cap Mountain in hopes of a view of Mt. Katahdin.

With just seventy-two miles to go, the guidebook noted that there were views of Katahdin from the north side of White Cap. All of us, including Rumblestrip, strained our eyes for a view, but we couldn't see anything beyond the hazy valley below. Another day-hiker atop the mountain pointed us in the direction of Katahdin, but the skies just weren't clear enough to see it. We would not get a view of it that day and Rumblestrip looked dejected as he sat there waiting for the haze to lift. Unfortunately, the black flies had come out to join us, so we gave up the search and headed down the mountain. It was our ninety-third day on the trail and we knew we were within just a few days of finishing.

Within a mile of our destination for the day, the East Branch Lean-to, the sun was overtaken by dark clouds. We made a run for it. Rumblestrip joined us, not taking any chances in repeating the hail storm from several days ago. Out of breath and pumping with adrenaline, we arrived to a half-full shelter and immediately claimed our spaces on the floorboards. The weather followed behind us and soon it was storming just beyond the open mouth of the shelter. It was a quick-moving storm and after the skies cleared, we took our chances and tented just outside the shelter. The tarp tent held up well in another aftershock of rain and we spent another night bug-free in the privacy of our little home.

The next day's elevation chart looked like someone had taken a ruler and drawn a straight line across the page. If we couldn't do some kind of mileage in that section, I was all out of hope for running through the 100-Mile Wilderness, which Matt still claimed he and Animal did. At that point,

I had been humbled by Maine and just wanted to survive the state.

Because of the low elevation of the day, most of it around five to six hundred feet, it was hot and stuffy in the deep woods. I felt suffocated by the trees and yearned for a cool breeze to keep the bugs off my face. Everything was buzzing around me, including mosquitoes, black flies, and horse flies. The big horse flies had a tendency to circle around my head, dive bomb my face and ears every few seconds, and keep up with me for miles. I made the best of it by swinging my bandana around my head like a lasso as I yelled out into the empty woods, "Yeeeehawwww!"

Three months of walking in the woods had changed my definition of entertainment.

Sixteen miles into the day, we were toasty hot and I couldn't shake the intense desire for a nap. Matt caved in with me and we set up our tent on the shore of the Jo-Mary Lake to be out of the bugs while we took a long break. Rumblestrip joined us and took a long swim in the lake. I fell asleep in a clammy sweat and my skin stuck to my sleeping pad like a strange form of Velcro.

It took all my willpower to start walking again. Three miles later, we all stopped for another break at the Potaywadjo Spring Lean-to, hoping it would wake us up. I stumbled into the shelter, feeling broken despite the terrain being pancake flat. I just couldn't win with Maine.

As we sat there, another hiker silently appeared from the trail on the north side of the shelter. He was headed south and stopped to join us for a break at the shelter. I wasn't sure what to make of him. Though he carried an ultralight pack and spoke knowledgeably about the trail, there was something different about him from other thru-hikers. I didn't have to wait long to find out that he was Freebird, a sort of trail legend.

Freebird has made long-distance hiking more than just a hobby. He's practically made it a lifestyle. He seemed to have an insatiable thirst for hiking not only different trails, but also the same trail, like the AT, just in different directions, different seasons, or different speeds. That year, he was slowly southbounding his umpteenth thru-hike of the AT. He had some serious mileage on his legs and I was happy we ran into him on such a low energy day, because he seemed to have more energy than all three of us combined.

Two hours later, with at least thirty trail stories recounted among us, we were still at the shelter with Freebird. We were his attentive audience, eager to hear his legendary trail stories that spanned decades, and he seemed just as enthralled in the conversation as us. He was a gifted story teller, complete with humor, suspense, surprise, and impressions of other hiker's voices and mannerisms. His eyes lit up with every new story, every tiny detail in his memory, and every quote from another hiker. It was as if we met twenty new hikers that day with all the people in Freebird's stories.

When we finally stood up to leave, I half-expected Freebird to walk backwards with us because he seemed to have hours of stories left in him. Instead, he kept walking south while we made use of the few hours of daylight that remained. Meeting him was another moment when I fell more in love with the AT and with long-distance hiking, because there were people like Freebird who loved the trail and who could show that love with such eloquent story-telling.

Four and a half miles later, after a smooth trail along the Nahmakanta Stream, we stayed at the Nahmakanta Stream Campsite. We went to sleep with the thought that the next day could be our second-to-last day on the AT. Logically, I recognized that I had put in the time and miles to get to that point, but part of my mind couldn't make sense of the proximity to the finish.

The next morning, our ninety-fifth on the trail, I flipped to the next guidebook page and realized that we had reached the final page of miles. Once we reached the end of it, we would be at Mt. Katahdin. The anxiety and disbelief that I felt at that moment sent chills down my spine.

The only elevation change to speak of early that morning was on Nesuntabunt Mountain. As we neared the summit, there she was in plain sight: Katahdin. Through a wide split in the trees, the mountain loomed curiously both in front of and above us. It also seemed so close for still being over thirty-six trail miles away. Rumblestrip was in a trance as he looked at it and I had to admit that seeing our destination from afar, yet still close up, was inspiring. I was proud that I had made it that far, overcoming the rain, the bugs, and my own self. I felt butterflies in my stomach as I thought of the tears I cried on my last day on the PCT, when the miles we'd been counting for three and a half months finally wound down to zero. I thought back over all we'd been through on the AT and felt that I'd lived a lifetime of emotions in just over three months. I also felt that as another thru-hike came to a close, I messed up a lot of its pieces, just like I had on the PCT, and I knew I still had so far to go as an individual. I could have done it better. Seeing Katahdin for the first time made me face that fact.

It was hard to believe a view of the mountain could affect my thoughts and my emotions that greatly, and it wasn't even the end just yet.

I remember little from that day, other than feeling like we were running through the last third of the 100-Mile Wilderness, and I finally believed Matt's memory. Around 4:00 p.m., we emerged onto a paved road, the other end of the 100-Mile Wilderness tunnel. After walking a short distance up the road to Abol Bridge, where there was a store and campsites, we took a long break in the dusty parking lot outside the store. We soaked in the hot afternoon sun as we reveled in the fact that we were at the base of Katahdin.

In order to have a shorter day to ascend Katahdin, we hiked another four miles into Baxter State Park. We feared punishment by a ranger for breaking the park rules of no camping in the park, but took our chances in order to be closer to Katahdin. Matt and I felt better in a green tent among the woods rather than Rumblestrip's bright orange one.

It was a balmy evening and the bugs were horrendous, even with 100% DEET on our skin. The mosquitoes kept the celebration conversation to a minimum between us and Rumblestrip. We said goodnight to each other and went to sleep for the last night on the AT.

Our last night...I was shocked to utter that phrase, and it wasn't because I was quitting that my time on the AT was coming to a close. I was actually going to finish the journey with Matt and Rumblestrip by my side. We went to sleep with just eleven miles left for the next day, with a plan of getting up at dawn before anyone could see our campsite. We also needed maximum time to descend Katahdin and hitch a ride to any possible town. The lack of a plan after the summit wore on my nerves, but it was out of our control until Katahdin was behind us.

Until then, all I could hear was a whisper in my head, and it said, "Katahdin."

Julie Urbanski

35 FLIP THE SWITCH

On the morning of July 14, our ninety-sixth day on the trail, I woke up to the same mileage pressure that I had felt the last ninety-five days. It couldn't be helped. No matter how much therapy I could go through to hash out my issues with the miles, the pressure would still be there. I accepted it and I now know that in any trail I start, until I finish it, I will have the miles on my mind until they are gone. Because of that pressure, I was eager to get started. I had a feeling we had a long day ahead of us.

Almost immediately into the hike, we met an ultramarathon runner who was finishing his seventy-two day run of the trail. We hadn't seen or heard of him until that moment and I thought, "Damn, we're getting caught and passed by someone on our last day!"

The competitive side of me still came out, even with less than ten miles to hike. We congratulated each other on our upcoming finishes and I watched the runner bound up the trail. "I'll be doing that soon," I thought. I couldn't wait to run again, free of a pack and light on my feet.

Within the first two hours, we reached the Katahdin Stream Campground and waited for Rumblestrip. It was the true starting point of the ascent up the mountain and we wanted to share that part of the hike with him. He arrived less than ten minutes after us and we all assessed our packs, throwing away any unnecessary weight for the remaining five miles. Single digit miles were all that remained and it felt very abnormal.

As we went through our packs, Matt asked Rumblestrip a question that had been on both of our minds since the day we first met him.

"So Rumblestrip," Matt started, "how much *does* your pack weigh?"

It was a metal external frame pack and though it looked light, we doubted it could be *that* light given its construction. The question lit a fire in

Rumblestrip that we weren't expecting.

"Why does everybody think, that just because I have a metal frame backpack, that it must weigh forty pounds!" He was half joking as he said it but I guessed we weren't the first to ask such a question. It was one of the rare moments that Rumblestrip's true, dry humor came out.

"I'm just joking with you," Matt said. "But seriously, how much does it weigh?"

We both picked up his pack and it was surprisingly light, not that I'd ever be convinced to carry such a pack. But, he was eighteen years old and had a zest for life and years of farming to strengthen him, so I doubted he had any issues carrying it. As we packed up for the remaining miles, a gentleman called us over to his campsite. I won't lie, I hoped trail magic was involved.

He was a group leader for young hikers, but he had stayed back with one of the girls who had broken her leg recently. A few minutes after talking with them about the AT, I started getting antsy about heading up the mountain. Then he showed us the gold mine.

It was a trailer, yes a trailer, full of food. Tortillas, cheese, veggies and dip, chips, soda, fresh fruit…it was all there in coolers, and it was all extra food from the group. All I had left were a few candy bars, so I filled up on one of everything before we started the climb.

The beginning of the hike was surprisingly easy for the first two miles. Streams of people went both ways on the trail and our pace was significantly slower because we waited for others to pass us on their way down, or had to wait our turn to pass others on their way up. Once the ascent really began, the trail turned into a rock climbing obstacle course. It was much, much harder and more technical than I expected.

As we labored up the trail, the wind picked up in the exposed sections. I gave up on my hiking poles and strapped them to the back of my pack. It was hard hiking for the middle miles. Groups of young kids were even climbing the rocks and the adults looked more scared than them. Some adults were sitting off the side of the trail with the look that said, "How the hell are we going to do this?"

Most of all, I tried to go with the flow and take it all in. "I may never be here again in my life, so I'd better appreciate it right now," I thought.

The top felt forever away with each new layer that we reached, but in the distance I saw a cluster of people. I assumed they were atop Katahdin but I didn't let myself get excited. "It ain't over until I see that sign," I said to Matt. He too saw the clump of people still quite far away and we continued walking. The last mile was much easier than the middle ones and our choppy strides over smaller rocks were much easier to maintain than rock climbing.

As we approached the top, I couldn't see the famous Katahdin sign. All

I saw was a crowd of about thirty people milling around. Then the people in front of me stepped aside like clouds parting to reveal the sun, and there it was, just three feet in front of me. Katahdin. The finish. The sign declaring the northern terminus of the Appalachian Trail.

I couldn't wipe the grin off my face.

I had pictured it so differently, just the three of us reaching the top with no one around to hear us whoop and cheer. Instead, we were surrounded by thirty strangers and I felt a little silly in celebrating too energetically. We waited our turn for pictures and as another hiker took our photo, we finally yelled out cheers of excitement. The ranger sitting off to the side asked, "Are you guys thru-hikers?"

"Yeah," Matt said through a big smile.

"Wow, you guys are early! Congratulations!"

Suddenly we were the stars of the show and people around us starting asking questions. We answered a few, but quickly stepped out of the limelight and sat along a rock wall, facing out into the views of the valley. It was sunny, with a few puffy clouds above us, and the wind was chilly on my sweaty back.

Rumblestrip sat facing the Katahdin sign with an uncontrollable smile and said to us, "I'm scared to look away from it, for fear it will disappear."

We toasted our last Snickers bars and Little Debbie Nutter Butter bars in celebration and basked in our finisher's glory. It was an early afternoon in mid-July, and we were finished with our AT thru-hike. It felt good to be done.

As we sat atop Katahdin, Matt couldn't help but think back to the first time he arrived at the top to touch that famous sign. He recounted the story to Rumblestrip and me as we ate our last candy bars. On October 9, 2000, he and Animal finished their thru-hike. The last possible day for them to climb Katahdin would have been October 15, and with the trail already covered in snow, they couldn't have cut it much closer. But they did it, despite all the naysayers at the start of their hike in mid-June, despite carrying a metal external frame pack, despite wearing cotton t-shirts and cargo shorts, despite visiting the emergency room for a moth in Matt's ear, and despite lacking any more room for error, he and Animal finished what they set out to do.

I loved hearing his finishing story from 2000 as we sat atop the same mountain, eleven years later and a lifetime of difference between the two hikes, with an eighteen-year-old Mennonite from Ohio whose world would be forever changed. I could not have asked for a better finish or for better company.

I felt pride, I felt joy, and I felt sadness. Our moment had passed and it was time to get down from Katahdin. If I ever wanted that one moment of complete freefall into exhilaration ever again, I'd have to complete another thru-hike. It came and went that quickly, just as the entire trail did as I looked back at the drop of time that passed in order to cover the distance. I knew the miles were complete, but that I wasn't finished thru-hiking. There would be another one someday, most likely the Continental Divide Trail. But we still had to get down from Katahdin before I let my mind think any more about the future.

We traded in white blazes for blue blazes as we followed a side trail down the mountain. Our chosen path down the mountain was the Knife Edge, my least favorite term in hiking because it implied steep drop-offs on both sides of the trail. It wasn't so much the steep sides that bothered me as it was the relentless piles of boulders that we had to maneuver over for several miles. The descent was arduous and exhausting, but I loved it. I knew we were finally done. I let the rest of my cares roll off me and I focused simply on the steps in front of me. They were just bonus miles and bonus calories burned for the celebratory pizza and ice cream. As I'd heard Zippers say, "I will miss half gallon ice cream days." There just aren't many times in life where I'll burn enough calories to keep up with my love for ice cream, so I knew I should enjoy the calorie burn while I still could.

Within an hour of finishing a near-four month journey, a journey that took all our concentration and efforts for every moment of each day, our brains quickly switched to logistics mode of an entirely different purpose, with the new mantra of, "Get us home!" We still didn't have a ride to town or even a ride out of the park, but we had friends in Portland, Maine, who had floor space if we could at least make it there. Portland became our goal for the evening.

It was late afternoon by the time we breathed a sigh of relief from the stressful downhill and we entered a parking lot full of cars. Each one of them was a potential ride out of the park, yet it was hard to approach people and say, "Um, can you give us a ride out of here?"

Few people were even at their cars, so we decided to just start walking the exit road from the park and put our thumbs out for each car that passed. Ironically, the first car to stop was a big white van. They opened up the side sliding door, and who was inside but eight Amish folks, identified as such by their unmistakable dress in bonnets, skirts, overalls, beards, and bowl haircuts. The shock on Rumblestrip's face was priceless.

It was a fairly awkward ride. We knew we smelled something awful as we sat wedged between them on the black-leather bench seats, and we knew Rumblestrip probably didn't want to reveal that his identity was much closer to them than they realized. Thankfully for them, it was a short ride to the park's exit, where they dropped us off and continued on their way to a campground within the park. We thanked them for stopping and stepped out onto the road, ready to walk to Millinocket if we needed to, a town about twenty miles away.

A mile down the road, another car stopped. It was a day hiker that I remembered seeing on the descent and he offered to give us a ride to Millinocket. Once in the car, we discussed our exit strategy and the need for a rental car. The closest place to get one was at the airport in Bangor, Maine, and we confirmed with our phone that we could pick one up. Our ride never admitted his end destination for the day, and we all got the feeling that was by no mistake. Yet, once we reached Millinocket, he said, "Well, I'm headed past Bangor anyway. I'll just drop you off at the airport if you can get a rental car there."

I immediately booked the rental car from our phone. Technology was remarkable. One moment I was sliding down a rock on my butt, miles from civilization, hoping I didn't fall off the side and die, and the next moment I was driving to the airport to pick up a car that I reserved with a phone.

From the airport, we drove to Portland, Maine, and arrived around 10:00 p.m. In hiker terms, that was way past our bedtime, and from all the day's excitement, our batteries were completely drained. By the time we went to sleep at midnight, we'd been up for nineteen hours and I almost cried tears of exhaustion rather than tears of joy.

We stretched out on a hardwood floor with our sleeping pads and sleeping bags, and fell asleep beside an open window where the cool summer breeze gave the illusion that we were still outside. At that moment, it felt like we'd been removed from the trail for at least a week with how quickly the scenery changed and how forcefully we thrust ourselves back into the real world.

After a short stop in DC the next day, we headed back to Ohio. Rumblestrip's family didn't have a phone, so they didn't know when he would be home. They knew his general whereabouts because they sent care packages to him along the way, but that was it. Once we crossed the Ohio state border, Rumblestrip put on his suspenders, a part of his identity that he'd paused while on the trail and which he carried in his pack the entire way.

It was a beautiful day and as we drove through parts of West Virginia, with all the hills and bends in the road, I thought back on the trail. I picked through each piece of it in my mind, seeing the parts I loved, seeing the parts where I went wrong, and in the end, wishing I had done it better. I couldn't fully process it all just yet but the drive home helped me start the process.

We dropped Rumblestrip off in front of his house and met his brother and father, who both looked shocked to see us pull into the driveway. They were about as talkative as Rumblestrip, so we didn't linger for long. We gave him a hug goodbye, not knowing if we'd ever see or hear from him again. At home, he had no electricity, no phone, and certainly no internet.

We could only communicate via snail mail or on the random chance that he reached us from the phone at the market where his family sold produce. It was hard to let him go after spending so much time with him, and yet exciting to wonder what his life would be like from then on. He was changed forever by the thru-hike, whether he or his family realized it at that moment or not.

When we got back in the car, we saw that he'd left his identity as a thru-hiker under the back seat. He'd thrown away his camouflage t-shirt and baseball cap. But, he'd kept the six-pack of Snickers bars that our friend had given him in DC. I knew he couldn't totally shed his thru-hiker self.

Later that day, we arrived at Matt's home in Findlay, Ohio. As we approached the front door, Matt said, "Oh, it smells like home already!"

We had finally made it to somewhere we didn't have to leave the next day. That was when the real celebrations began and when the digestion of the trail started. I hadn't been able to fully reflect on the experience with the stress of getting home, but after a full night's sleep of over thirteen hours in a bed, I could begin.

36 TAKE IT FROM THE TOP

After the Appalachian Trail was over, after I laundered my clothes six times to erase the stench, after I consumed my fair share of celebratory ice cream, and after I put our gear away in storage, I had to face the trail. I had to think about what it all meant and what I got out of such an experience.

I was lucky that I was in no rush to return to work and neither was Matt. We'd saved up enough money to continue being purposefully unemployed. All I had was time on my hands to reflect back on the AT and to see what thoughts floated to the top as I sifted through them, looking for meaning it in all.

Once in Ohio, we visited a lot of family and friends, both in Findlay and Cincinnati. Each person, after giving hugs and warm welcomes home, would casually ask us, "So how was the hike?"

It was a question that I was prepared to hear, yet not prepared to answer, and to this day, I still can't fully grasp what my answer should be. I usually want to say, "Well, how much time do you have?"

How does a person answer such an open-ended question that encompasses months of events and a lifetime of emotions? It was a hard task to do, to mentally recount nearly four months of memories and package them up in one beautiful box to hand over to people, with the label, "My AT experience."

In answering such a question, I find that people are bullet-point lovers. We are used to scanning texts for main points, reading one liner updates on social websites, hearing the gist of a story so that we at least know the bare minimum. We are not used to settling in for a fifteen minute run-down of an adventure, much less an hour slide show of all the pictures. I tried that the first time after the PCT and noticed the boredom settle in very quickly.

Yet, I couldn't blame people for only being interested in a quick summary of the adventure. If they wanted to know more details, they would ask, and therefore I would go into more depth. Still, I never was good at coming up with my one-liner to describe a journey like thru-hiking the AT. I gave the noncommittal, "It was great!" answer. Sometimes people would follow-up my answer with questions that touched on the big topics, like what I thought about the trail, what I got out of it, and how I felt about doing it again. Shortly after finishing, I knew I needed to form answers to those big questions.

The one shining star of the AT that led me to truly fall in love with the trail was the community. The trail is accessible at so many points, by so many big populations of people, that it was impossible to ignore the social aspect of the trail. While this was hard for me to get used to, with sharing space on the trail and in the shelters, it made for an incredibly unique experience. The quality and sheer quantity of people we met along the way, whether on the trail, in town, or even through online connections, were unmatched. Even further, the generosity of those people was astounding.

The shelters on the AT were a beating heart for the social life on the trail. They allowed the strong pulse of people to flow easily along the trail, temporarily moving in and out of the shelters. We could always count on the shelters to be there and could usually count on other people to be using them. There was a comfort in knowing that if we longed for the company of others, all we had to do was visit a shelter and we could be assured at least a roof over our heads and possibly good conversation. Because of a near void of shelters on the PCT, we just didn't have that sort of social aspect with camping in random, scantly-used, flat patches of ground off the side of the trail.

The other piece of the community that I noticed was the unconditional love for the trail, for its health, for its vitality, and for its longevity. There was a tangible feeling that groups of people were concerned with the trail's upkeep and existence, that they cared a lot about the terrain we covered. I felt privileged to take part in something that others willingly donated their time, effort, and money to support. While the sense of community was very strong on the PCT, it felt more prevalent throughout the entire AT.

The strength in the AT community is what also allowed us to gain some of our most unique perspectives along the way. We spent a lot of time talking with other hikers as we sat in the shelters. It was impossible to avoid strangers when we had to sleep just inches away from them in the shelter and we actually preferred to get to know them before cozying up for an evening. In that process, we got to know *a lot* of people. And for a few of them, we got to know them very well.

Curmudgeon, Zippers, Stretch, and Rumblestrip were some of those key people that we got to know well both on and off the trail, and whose different perspectives we appreciated because of the enlightenment they brought to our own hike. Being able to share in their experiences allowed me to step outside of my own self and see all the different types of people that completed a thru-hike.

I could not begin to know what it felt like for Curmudgeon to take that first step on the trail as a fifty-nine-year-old who hadn't spent more than a week away from his wife in their thirty-four year marriage, who had a granddaughter at home, and who chose to forgo four months of income from his personal business. Though my perspective was most similar to Zippers, I couldn't imagine what she felt to have such high expectations for her relationship, only to watch it slowly unravel as she succeeded in completing the thru-hike. Stretch was a twenty-four year old in between school careers, with a love for the outdoors instilled in him from a young age, something I could never claim, and with a stoic personality that I admired. I wore my emotions so outwardly on my face and body that others could immediately know my mood. Lastly, Rumblestrip was an eighteen-year-old Ohioan, having never spent much time outside of his Mennonite-defined world, but with a resolved wisdom of who he was and the kind of person he wanted to be.

It was overwhelming to take in the personalities, perspectives, and purposes of all these different people, and my hike truly was unforgettable because of the presence of such people.

We all choose to hike for different reasons, we choose to continue for different reasons, and we choose to sign up for another hike for different reasons. Yet, the trails are the same for everyone, and we all have to get from Point A to Point B. Past that, the trail doesn't care who you are or what your reasons are, and it's all up to you to cover the distance.

For Matt, who has taken to the woods to walk at three different times in his life, his reasons for hiking can't be summed up in a single meaning, one bullet point, or one purpose. Each time, his perspectives on life have been vastly different. All three times that he's hiked, the woods have been a therapeutic experience, giving him time to think and reflect. He's gained personal strength in a magnitude that normal life just can't compare with, and each time that he's hiked he's been reminded of his capabilities, his desires for his future self, and his confidence in achieving lofty goals. At the end of each thru-hike, he's walked away with new vigor and an excitement to start fresh in the world of endless opportunities for new endeavors.

Most importantly to Matt, the stripped-down, technology-free, simple life of walking in the woods, oftentimes leaves Matt with more clarity than he could ever gain from living in the real world. The reality adjustment that he gets from hiking, like a visit to the chiropractor, may hurt a little at first, but leaves him absolutely satisfied with the results.

If I were to give an honest answer to someone who asked me what I got out of the AT, it would be, "I finished it, but I still have so far to go."

While the PCT was a crash course in aspects of long-distance hiking, like water, food, and gear, I concentrated much less on those pieces on the AT because they were already ingrained in me. I could then focus much more on the development of me, which occurred throughout such an adventure. Not that we didn't struggle with some parts of the AT, but compared to our first days on the PCT, we were practically experts.

I'd love to say that I finished the hike having solved the meaning of life, but instead it left me with the knowledge that I still have so much more to learn about myself and others, and so much more that I can improve upon to make both my life and the lives of others that much better. I am not done growing and I am forever changing, two facts that are comforting because I hope I still have a long life ahead of me.

As I thought about my take-away from the AT, I recalled the day in Maine where I regretted past decisions that led me to that moment on the AT. I was angry at myself for having never found my passion. Thru-hiking did not seem to be it as I walked across muddy bog boards in a misty rain. I had tried several different jobs by then, hated every one of them on so many different levels, and felt like a failure for having never figured out what it was that I loved to do. That same day, after I looked back on the pattern of my life, I asked Matt, "Why don't I like anything I do?"

I've always been of the mindset that I have a calling in life and would start enjoying my life once and for all if I could just find that calling. I've been searching for years, taking quizzes in magazines, reading books about personal destinies, trying to remember if I liked puzzles or mud piles in grade school for some kind of hint, and still, I have never found that elusive, eureka moment where I lift up my ticket to life fulfillment and say, "Here it is! I'm supposed to be a dental hygienist!" I've always treated my calling like it was a hidden egg at an Easter egg hunt which would lead to enlightenment once I unearthed its existence and identity.

That day in Maine made me reconsider how I thought about my true self. I started to wonder if maybe searching for that self wasn't the best way to go about finding it, that maybe finding it wasn't even possible. I started to wonder if maybe I had to create it. This whole time, I've been waiting around for the world to show me what it is I like to do. Instead, maybe I need to create a way to fit into the world, to create my own purpose rather than wait for it to come to me. Maybe I need to figure out on my own what sparks a fire within me.

That's great that I realize that I need to create myself, but how do I go about doing that? For me, it is through adventures like the AT, adventures that offer unique experiences that mold who I am, that give me new skills and perspectives, and that introduce me to new people and new ways of living. I can't just hole up in my apartment and hope my aha moment will come without much effort on my part. Creating myself within this world demands much more effort than I've already put forth, but half the battle is realizing that it is up to me to create my calling, to define my purpose, and to go out and face the world no matter how much fear I have of failing in the process.

Even just a week after finishing the trail, the bad memories started to fade and my promise of "never again" slowly morphed into "next time."

Call me a glutton for punishment, but I can still see myself thru-hiking many more trails. Because I know that I could have enjoyed the AT more had I prepared better with different gear and food, had I come in with a different attitude about the difficulty, and had I dealt with challenging situations differently, I could have walked away with a much more positive experience.

The old adage, "what doesn't kill you makes you stronger," rings true for me in thru-hiking, to a limit. While I enjoyed the personal strength I gained from lifting myself out of low moments, I also didn't *always* want to be at the bottom of a well, treading water and scraping at the walls to survive. I could only take those low moments for so long before I snapped. I need to improve upon my ability to minimize those low moments. Thru-hiking does imply some suffering, but it doesn't have to lead to the level of hatred that I held towards the trail at times, mostly because of faults entirely of my own.

Going forward, I know what I want. I want to walk a trail and be in love with it at the same time that it causes me to reach the deepest of despair and the highest of happiness. I want to be so fully present in each moment, my life and perspectives enriched from living so vibrantly, that I end the trail and say, "I gained, I lost, and I loved, but I never had any regrets, and I'd do it again if given the chance."

Whether I like it or not, the label of a hiker has been placed on me, and somehow I keep finding myself with a long-distance hike on the back burner in my mind. I take my breaks from hiking, but the pull to go live outside for long stretches of time eventually comes around like a full moon, so bright that it keeps me awake at night with its intensity. I love the raw lifestyle, I love using my own body as my machine to cover distance, I love the self-honesty it demands when the pleasantries are over, and I love the bond that thru-hiking has built between Matt and me. I don't know of many couples who can say they've shared a small tent together for months at a time, that they've smelled the bodily stench of two weeks without a shower and still wanted to have sex, or that they've seen each other's mental state hit rock bottom. Matt has loved me through moments where

I've told him, "You really shouldn't love me, because even I don't love myself right now."

All that being said, taking in all the pros and cons of hiking, and knowing just how volatile the roller coaster of a thru-hike can be from the first step on the trail to the last blaze to follow, I would repeat it all without hesitation. The PCT, the AT, and most likely all my future hikes.

And it's all because of Nietzsche.

While we were hiking, Matt loaded up his iPod with college lecture series, his favorite being the one on philosophy, his college major. The most memorable was the lecture on the notion of eternal recurrence, a Nietzsche-driven idea. The story given in the lecture painted a picture of a life where sometime later in life, a demon visits you, only to give the news that you are destined to repeat every moment of your life. That includes every feeling, every decision, and every event of your current life. Your life will be repeated over and over again, which for some people, including myself, is a dreary prospect. I'd never want to repeat getting cut from the high school volleyball team, being rejected from a guy I had a crush on in college, or hearing my parents argue behind their thin door in the home of my childhood.

The question Nietzsche asks is what your response to the demon will be, and what that says about how you live your life. Will you curse the demon and be crushed by the prospect of eternal recurrence, or will you welcome him and treat his proposal like it's the best offer you've ever had? If you answer the demon, "No way! What a horrible idea!", what does that say about how you live your life? Are you really adding meaning to your life on a daily basis, no matter how much effort that might take? What importance do you place on every decision, every action, every thread of existence that crosses your path?

In hearing the lecture, I realized that the choices I make suddenly hold much more weight if they affect me an infinite number of times. I'll think twice if I have to live with the consequences of decisions that I may have not otherwise made with a clearer head or a better conscience. Finding meaning in all that surrounds me, from the rocks on the trail to the people that I meet, seems all the more important, especially because it is only me that assigns meaning to my life. My life truly is what I create it to be and I have a responsibility to myself. How I live my life is up to me and the results that stem from my choices are also mine to claim. It's a very powerful feeling to recognize my accountability for my own life and for my duty to find meaning in my life.

In going back to the lecture, Nietzsche's response to the demon's prospect of eternal recurrence was along the lines of "play it again." He viewed his life as piece of artwork that he was continually creating through his choices and life experiences, all of which he aimed to find meaning in, and said he'd be happy to live his life over and over again.

It was bold of Nietzsche to respond in such a way, but in thinking back on my own life, considering all the highs and lows that I've gone through, given that many of them have come from long-distance hiking, I too would look that demon straight in the eyes and without hesitation, I would take the opportunity to repeat it all, and say, "Take it from the top."

EPILOGUE: THE RESULTS ARE IN

Curmudgeon:

Once we arrived in Findlay, Ohio, the hometown of Curmudgeon, the updates on his hike started flowing in and we heard how the rest of his journey unfolded. We were shocked to hear some of the details as we sat in a coffee shop one day with his wife Sharon.

By that time, Curmudgeon had reached one of his lowest moments on the trail. It started when he noticed a red rash covering his chest, which he suspected to be a spider bite. He thought nothing more of it and continued hiking. A few weeks later, when he arrived in Bennington, Vermont, he had physically hit rock bottom. His headaches and neck aches were at their peak of his pain threshold, he hadn't been able to sleep some nights because of back pain, and he had Bell's palsy-like symptoms in his face. He had already planned to meet Sharon in Bennington for a few days off and was barely functioning by the time he got there. He was scared for himself and his hike.

In describing his physical state in Bennington, Sharon said, "I went to pick up Tim and I saw this hiker from across the parking lot. He looked old and feeble, but he was wearing the same clothes Tim always wore, a red shirt and black shorts. I thought to myself, 'Surely, that can't be Tim,' but as he got closer, I couldn't believe my eyes. It was Tim. I now know what my husband will look like when he is ninety-two years old."

They immediately went to the emergency room and a blood test confirmed that Curmudgeon had Lyme disease. His odds of finishing greatly diminished and for the first time in the hike, he feared his hike would end. The last thing he wanted to do was end his journey early because of Lyme disease, but the circumstances were leading up to that.

Sharon pressured him to come home with her; it was difficult for her to see him in so much discomfort. Curmudgeon gave it serious thought, but with so much time and effort already invested in the hike, every thread in his body wanted to finish the hike. They waited for a few days around Bennington to see how the antibiotics affected him, and the aches and pains subsided enough for him to continue. He started hiking once again and it took two more weeks before the Bell's palsy-like symptoms faded.

Once Curmudgeon made it to the base of Katahdin with just five miles to go, at the Katahdin Stream Campground in Baxter State Park, another surprise was in store. Sharon was there waiting for him.

All the emotions of the hike hit him the moment he saw her. He knew the end was real and that just five miles later, it would be over. He couldn't tell if he or Sharon was more excited for him to be finishing his journey, but he savored the fact that Sharon was there to see him at the finish.

Curmudgeon made it to Katahdin with several other thru-hikers and had glorious weather for the occasion. It was warm, the sky was clear, and he could taste the excitement in the air as other hikers congratulated each other and popped corks of champagne bottles. He looked back on his four month journey that was ending that ninth day of August, and though he knew it was a long time to be on the trail, it felt like just a few weeks had gone by.

His emotions were tangled in knots as he felt the opposing desire to go home for good and finally be with his wife again, and the strange inclination to simply turn around and hike back to Georgia. The air atop Katahdin has a magical way of mixing with a hiker's mind, and Curmudgeon was no exception.

Yet, the trail wasn't done with him yet.

On Curmudgeon's descent on the Knife Edge trail, he fell on particularly rough footing and tore his rotator cuff. It was a terrible blow to the finisher's high he'd been on and added to his already increasing list of injuries and expenses incurred on the trail.

Once he made it home, back to life as a construction project manager, a husband, father and grandfather, not only did he have to have surgery to fix his shoulder, but he also had to undergo a month's worth of intravenous antibiotics for the Lyme disease that flared up once again. The cost of the trail had in fact added up to far more than he expected, a surprising reality to face considering the trail was less physically difficult than he expected it to be. He completed the hike two months sooner than he expected.

Curmudgeon admitted that he would love to hike the Pacific Crest Trail at some point. Yet, his window of opportunity shrinks with each ensuing year in his life, and if anything, the AT opened up a world of new possibilities. The trail also showed him that the window will only stay open for so long. He turned sixty just after finishing the trail in August.

If there was anything that Curmudgeon took away from the hike, it was a renewed faith in his fellow man. He was astonished at the kindness of strangers on the trail and in the surrounding towns. People gave him food, transportation, shelter, and most of all, encouragement. And it was all for free, without a single line of small print, or even an impression that they wanted something in return.

Thank you, Curmudgeon, for sharing your journey with Matt and me, with all the other 2011 AT thru-hikers, and with all the family and friends at home and along the trail, rooting for your success. You are the kindest Curmudgeon we've ever met. You are an inspiration to many for living out a dream that so many others go to the grave simply talking about.

Zippers and Stretch:

The day before the summit up Katahdin, Zippers and Stretch had a short, ten-mile day to the Katahdin Stream Campground, where they met Stretch's parents, who'd brought coolers of food and all the celebratory fare for the next day. They were still hiking with Youngin and Girl with 4 Dogs, and spent most of the day reminiscing over the best moments from the last four months on the trail.

For Zippers that evening at the base of Katahdin, the fact that the next day was the end hadn't sunken in for her. She wrestled with opposing emotions all evening, best summed up in her journal entry from that night:

"Despite being anxious to return to the comforts of a house, I will miss our challenging, transient lifestyle – the satisfaction of making the miles every day, the simplicity of so few belongings, the beauty of being outside, the sounds of the birds singing, the rushing brook next to a campsite, the camaraderie of other thru-hikers and how quickly they become family, laying my head down next to the folks I've spent the day with, made and eaten dinner with and shared a dream with. The ease of a life guided by the white blaze for I truly do not know what is next. The Katahdin sign tomorrow signifies the end of a four month, ten year crazy half hearted whim journey and the beginning of my life as a doer – not that I know where to begin."

As a couple, they had seen the best and the worst of each other, had motivated each other, had pushed back while another pulled, and had dealt with their own emotions while thinking of the other person's. These are pieces of a relationship that most married couples may never experience, but because of the raw lifestyle of the trail, they had to face each other every single day, whether it was a good one or a bad one.

The next morning on July 16, they awoke to a fantastically beautiful day in Baxter State Park. They too purged their packs from unnecessary weight and all headed to the trailhead together, including Stretch's parents. Being a Saturday, the trail was packed with people going up and down the summit. At the first sight of the summit, Stretch took off at a run to reach it, and Zippers and Youngin followed. Stretch reached it first and let out a loud holler of joy, with Zippers next. It was pure joy and elation at that moment of reaching the top together, and Zippers will forever remember that vision of the three of them, standing at the finish sign, letting out screams of joy and taking in the enormity of the moment.

After Stretch's parents arrived, they basked in the finisher's glory for nearly two hours as they lunched on champagne and lobster rolls. It was an elaborate celebration with a full photo session with the Katahdin summit sign, and they hung on to the moment as long as possible. Blue, sunny skies were overhead with warm temperatures surrounding them, and they couldn't have asked for better weather.

Zippers' eyes filled with tears at one point, taking it all in as they lingered at the summit. It was a picture perfect day for everyone, with the weather, the food, and the celebrations.

At the same time of loving each moment atop Katahdin, she hated so much about that spectacular day. She hated that she knew the relationship was over, despite it never being verbalized. She hated that the life she'd grown to love was ending. She wished she were leaving the trail a little thinner, something I too had wished for. She also had to part with the people she'd spent the last few weeks with, Youngin and Girl with 4 Dogs. The one word she used to describe it was bittersweet, saying no other word could do it justice with the mix in emotions that she felt about the finish.

Eventually, they had to admit they were finished.

They said goodbye to Youngin and Girl with 4 Dogs; they were hiking down the Knife Edge while Zippers and Stretch were going back to the Katahdin Stream Campground. It would be a long time, if ever, that their paths crossed again.

Zippers wrote down every single day's occurrences along the way in a journal, except for that last day. It took her an entire month after the trail to face the reality that in writing that last journal entry, the hike really was over. The glory of finishing atop Katahdin became another memory in the books.

Everything changed for both of them after the trail. Stretch moved to Missoula within a few weeks of finishing and started a graduate school program, while Zippers moved to Livingston after landing a new job. Their lives held traces of the trail, but on a daily basis, they were completing tasks entirely different from before.

When I asked Zippers what she got out of the AT, besides the realization that underwear on a daily basis was seriously overrated, a piece of wisdom I too had picked up on the PCT, she summed it up perfectly:

"A fantastic story. A broken heart. The best legs of my life. Amazing friends. A true appreciation for the gifts that show up every day, whether we notice them or not. The ability to notice them. Admiration of friends and family. An immediate kindred connection with other thru-hikers, trail supporters, and big dreamers. Not just a sense of accomplishment, but a firm understanding. Knowledge that barriers are created and destroyed in my own mind. An appreciation for simplicity, fresh vegetables and cold beer. A developed palate for peanut butter and tortillas. A calm knowledge that I will hike the PCT one day. Serene gratitude that I am blessed with friends and family that support me in the pursuit of my dreams."

Thank you to Zippers and Stretch for sharing your thru-hike with Matt and me, and with so many other people along the way. You took risks with yourselves and your relationship in the thru-hike, and in the end, still strove forward and finished what you set out to do.

Rumblestrip:

Once we dropped Rumblestrip off at his farm, his family was quick to cut his long, scraggly hair. He was happy to be home and eat fresh, home-cooked meals again. Twenty-four jars of peanut butter over the course of the trail, along with two Snickers a day and countless packets of Oreos and ramen noodles, were enough processed food for a lifetime for him.

It was awhile before we ever heard from Rumblestrip, but he finally managed to reach us from the phone at the produce market. We had sent him copies of his photos atop Katahdin, along with some of our own photos from the trail so he could show them to family. He hadn't carried a camera, one of the regrets he had after the trail. Months after finishing, he told me that he still held with him the key moments of seeing Katahdin for the first time and of reaching that famous Katahdin sign, two moments when Matt and I were with him.

When I asked Rumblestrip what he liked most about thru-hiking, he said, "The scenery and the people."

"Really?" I asked. "I thought you really liked walking outside."

"Actually, I'm not particularly fond of walking; everyone just assumes that since I hiked the trail, I like to walk. It's the scenery and the friendships that I liked the most."

Friendship was an aspect of the trail that Rumblestrip hadn't expected to be a prominent keepsake from the trail. Prior to starting, he thought he'd spend most of the trail alone, but was pleasantly surprised to meet several key people that he fell into a good friendship with. Even months after finishing, he was still sad that he never said goodbye to Coney and Savage. It was a part of the trail that I too disliked, that we could never count on seeing other hikers, no matter what plans they had. People stayed in towns, stopped short one shelter for the day, or oftentimes simply felt like hiking when we didn't. I can still remember the exact moment on the Blue Ridge Parkway in Virginia, when I watched Whitney Houston walk up the trail as we sat for a lunch break. I said to Matt, "I bet we never see him again," and we didn't.

Thru-hiking the Appalachian Trail was just the start of Rumblestrip's adventures. He spent the next nine months after the trail saving money and planning more travels. We helped him figure out how to get a passport, a debit card, and airline tickets to Hungary, where he participated in organic farming for four months. In that time, he traveled to several other countries and even managed to join a traveling circus.

While Rumblestrip was in Hungary in May of 2012, we were in Prague, Czech Republic, on a two month adventure of our own, and we met up with him for the first time since the trail, almost a year later. He was still quiet and dry-witted, but even more questioning of the world around him and the world he grew up in, still walking the fine line between what he wanted to learn and what he already knew. The two worlds were constantly in contrast of one another.

He summed up his feelings beautifully when he told me that he'd had a song lyric in his head that he just couldn't shake because he felt it described him so well. Though the lyric wasn't exactly the right wording, I liked his version better and found it incredibly fitting:

"So young to travel so far, but still old enough to bear the scars."

Rumblestrip, you are one of the wisest people we've ever known and it was a pleasure to have taken part in your first adventure away from home. We know that you will continue to create a fascinating life.

Optimist and Stopwatch:

Two things remain that should be noted as well about Matt and me. After hearing Curmudgeon's story about Lyme disease and as a precautionary step, we both got tested for the disease. While I came out clean, Matt received a call the very next day from the doctor, "Yep, you've got Lyme disease. I'll call in a prescription today."

We were glad to have finally solved his mystery exhaustion illness, but it was still unsettling to think that Matt had contracted the disease. He never saw a tick embedded anywhere on his skin, nor did he ever see the telling red rash of a tick bite. Matt was at least the sixth hiker we'd heard of that got Lyme disease and I'm sure there were many more.

Secondly, in early February of 2012, at 6:00 a.m. on a chilly morning in Huntsville, Texas, Matt and I again found ourselves starting the Rocky Raccoon 100 Mile Trail Race. We wanted redemption. We got it, sort of. The first two hours of the race were run in a heavy downpour, complete with lightning and thunder. It rained 1.9 inches over the course of the race, which was 1.7 inches more than any of the previous races in the last fifteen years. We just couldn't win. To cap it off, Matt had food poisoning the night before the race.

While I really, and I mean really, wanted to quit the race after eighty miles, I heeded the advice of Matt and took a nap in our tent...for an hour and a half. It was a bit excessive. After the nap, I changed my clothes, slapped myself awake, busted out my power songs on my iPod, and finished the race as the sixth female in 22 hours and 34 minutes. That race and the feelings and emotions I went through in just under twenty-four hours, could easily be a book in itself.

Matt had a very difficult time with the food poisoning, but he refused to quit. Every twenty miles, he rested in the tent that we had set up at the finish line and simply took his time. 27 hours and 56 minutes later, he crossed the finish line after seeing the sunrise for the second time in one race. It was an incredible letdown to have run so slowly, considering he was in shape to vie for a space in the top ten finishers, but he swallowed his pride and accepted the results. He finished and he had to be ok that it was not entirely what he pictured the race to be. As another redemption to his redemption at Rocky, he ran the Leadville 100 Mile Trail Race in August of 2012, proudly finishing in 23 hours and 55 minutes. He still thinks he could have done better. The Optimist in him will never quit.

Julie Urbanski

ACKNOWLEDGEMENTS

It is one thing to believe in yourself. It is another to have others who believe in you as well. I'm grateful that I have many people in my life who not only believe in me, but who also love and support me in all my endeavors, no matter how unlikely I am to succeed in them.

Thank you first to my best friend, my husband, my Optimist, my Matt. You have given me a best friendship that I never imagined would be possible, not to mention a whole lot of love that I rarely give to myself. Thank you for your patience, your input, and your excitement for life; otherwise, I just might be a hermit.

Thank you to my mom, my dad, and my sister for giving me a stubbornness that at times, is just stupidity, but which has driven me forward in my lowest of moments. To the rest of my family and friends, thank you for being so good to me and for giving me love and friendship, two things for which I may not always be deserving, but which enhance my life beyond measure.

Lastly, a huge thank you to Curmudgeon, Zippers, Stretch, and Rumblestrip, for sharing your stories, your thoughts, your journals, and your time. A lot of this book wouldn't have been possible without your input and our thru-hike would have been greatly diminished had we not spent time with you. A special thank you to Zippers for full access to your journal and therefore your most intimate thoughts and feelings.

A special thanks to the Appalachian Trail Conservancy for making the Appalachian Trail possible for us all. And to all the 2011 AT thru-hikers, each one of you is a badass for completing such a journey.

RESOURCES

Throughout the book, I mention the guidebook that Matt and I used and that one book was an invaluable resource for our trip. Thanks to David "Awol" Miller for *The A.T. Guide*, Jerelyn Press, 2011.

Specific figures regarding the number of hikers on the trail each year are taken from the Appalachian Trail Conservancy's website at www.appalachiantrail.org.

ABOUT THE AUTHOR

Originally from Cincinnati, Ohio, Julie has traveled through much of the U.S., whether on foot, via bicycle, or in a car. She has hiked the Pacific Crest Trail, the Appalachian Trail, and the Colorado Trail (2007, 2011, 2012), and bicycled down the Pacific Coast from Portland, Oregon, to the border of Mexico. In addition to living in Ohio, Maryland, West Virginia, California, and Washington, she and her husband have lived abroad in Spain, Ethiopia, Mexico, Guatemala, and Italy, and hope to have many more worldly experiences.

Julie is an avid runner, always chasing a faster time or a longer distance, having completed one 100 miler, one 50 miler, a 50K, and 19 marathons, including the Boston marathon. Her husband Matt is the force behind her and the impetus that lands her in unique, challenging, and otherwise dreary situations that always seem to end on a positive note of self-realization, mental strength, and the desire to do it all over again. Julie and her husband currently live in Seattle, Washington. To read more about their past, current, and upcoming adventures, visit their website at urbyville.com.

Her other work includes *The Trail Life: How I Loved it, Hated it, and Learned from it*, a book about her first long-distance hiking experience on the Pacific Crest National Scenic Trail in 2007.

Made in the USA
San Bernardino, CA
04 June 2014